CW00553919

# AGHO␣␣␣␣

## At the Left Hand of God

Robert E. Svoboda

RUPA

Published by
Rupa Publications India Pvt. Ltd 1986
7/16, Ansari Road, Daryaganj
New Delhi 110002

*Sales centres:*
Allahabad Bengaluru Chennai
Hyderabad Jaipur Kathmandu
Kolkata Mumbai

Copyright © Robert E. Svoboda 1986

First published in the United States of America by
Brotherhood of Life Inc. 1986.
This edition published by arrangement with the original publisher.

All rights reserved.
No part of this publication may be reproduced, transmitted,
or stored in a retrieval system, in any form or by any means,
electronic, mechanical, photocopying, recording or otherwise,
without the prior permission of the publisher.

ISBN: 978-81-716-7342-1

Thirty-first impression 2016

35 34 33 32 31

The moral right of the author has been asserted.

This edition is for sale in the Indian subcontinent only.

Printed at  Printed at Shree Maitrey Printech Pvt. Ltd., Noida

This book is sold subject to the condition that it shall not, by way of trade or
otherwise, be lent, resold, hired out, or otherwise circulated,
without the publisher's prior consent, in any form of
binding or cover other than that in which it is published.

## VIMALANANDA'S DEDICATION
## FOR THIS BOOK

*Dedicated to One who is the source of life*
*The Dynamic Cosmic Energy which pervades the entire*
  *universe perennially*
*The fountainhead of supreme joy, divinity, and magnanimity:*

### My Mother Tara

# TABLE OF CONTENTS

# PREFACE

My teacher, the Aghori Vimalananda, spent many years perfecting his knowledge of Tantra and its advanced discipline Aghora. He distilled his experiences and presented me with the essence. My comprehension of Tantra is due entirely to his instruction and is redolent of the influence of his personality.

*Tantra* is the science of personality. Just as *Ayurveda* was promulgated by the ancient sages of India as a truly holistic way to maintain the physical body, and just as *Ashtanga Yoga* is meant to optimize one's spiritual nature, Tantra is a mental science, a meta-psychology, a method for exploring the mind and developing the range of one's perceptions.

It is said that the state of undifferentiated unity is the only absolute reality, and that the cosmos possesses only a relative reality because it is not permanent and unchanging. The universe possesses all possible qualities and attributes, and each being within the universe possesses a limited number of qualities and attributes. Personality is the self-identification of the ego with a set of attributes. All beings possess egos and therefore all beings have personalities. The cosmos Herself possesses the ultimate personality, the supreme expression of the totality of manifested existence: the *Adishakti*, or *Adya*.

To state that humans, animals, trees and flowers possess their own individualities and idiosyncrasies is less apt to induce controversy than to assert that even beings which are disembodied or which are embodied, but are less individualized than we, also possess personality. The issue of disease is a good example. Diseases are beings with parasitical intentions. Some have collective bodies, like worms, bacteria or viruses, just as bees and ants show signs of collective consciousness. Other diseases, bereft of their own bodies, arise within organ systems of some animal or plant due to metabolic malfunctions.

When the intruding personality differs significantly in sophistication of organization from its host, physical disease is likely for then the attacker's ego will be insufficiently developed to assume control of all essential physiological functions. Conversely when the spirit of a dead human enters the body of a living human it will feel right at home and the disease will display predominantly mental symptoms such as altered values and habit patterns.

Whatever the intruder, cure is the expelling of the alien and the return of the normal personality. An individual's immunity exists on the physical levels in white blood cells and in anti bodies, and on the mental level in the degree of personality integration; the cause of immunity is the ego's power of self-identifying with body and mind. The word "ego" is used here not in a Freudian sense but as an indicator for the force of individual identity in the organism. The stronger the self-identification the greater the immunity to attack from another personality which might usurp some area of the ego's domination. Every cell is ceaselessly remembered by the ego as being part of its organism. When the organism dies the cells are free, in the absence of the ego's grip, to go their separate ways. If a cell rebels against the ego's domination and seeks to proliferate itself into a new personality, the result is a cancer. Be the predator external or internal, disease is its onslaught on one's personality.

According to Tantra everyone is ill who is doomed to live with a limited personality. Only those who go beyond time, space and causation to become immortal can be said to be truly in harmony with the cosmos and therefore truly healthy, since health is derived both from internal balance and from harmony with the environment. Hence one significant area of Tantric research has always been methods for prolonging one's life. In one sense the added years are significant mainly because they indicate the degree of successful achievement of the rituals.

Ayurveda is also concerned with longevity, but its approach is to strengthen the individual's innate personality. Yoga, recognizing the essential impermanence of the human personality seeks to efface it entirely to permit one to return directly to the unlimited Absolute. Tantra aims to replace the limited personality with an unlimited, permanent one.

An individual may fail to become eternal but may in the course of Tantric practice accumulate sufficient energy (Shakti) to obtain some extra-ordinary power, called a *Siddhi*. Wisely used, Siddhis can accelerate one's spiritual evolution. Commercialized, Siddhis bind one down more firmly to the wheel of cause and effect.

One simple sort of Siddhi involves the collection of some particular herb at the astrologically appropriate moment with the appropriate ritual. After further preparation such plants can bestow superphysical powers on their users. The plant species selected is one known to have an affinity for the sort of power desired. The ritual draws that power into the plant at the moment when it is available in the cosmos to be tapped. The herb's own personality is then overshadowed by the personality of the force drawn into it.

Metals and gems are also used in Tantric alchemy. Indian alchemists like their Western counterparts searched for the Philosopher's Stone, the way to turn base metal into gold. While exoterically this base metal referred to iron, bronze, brass and copper, the esoteric reference was to the transmutation of the base metal of the individual's limited consciousness into the gold of enlightenment, a state of unlimited consciousness. An alternative meaning suggests the transmutation of the base metal of the body into the gold of immortality via the touchstone of *Amrita*, the elixir of life.

It is said that herbal-based preparations can prolong one's life for 400 to 500 years, but that through the use of mercury there is no end to how long one can live. Mercury is regarded as the ultimate metal because it is the sole element which can be brought to life. Repeated herbal applications and treatments with fire bring the mercury to life. It is then treated like a child its appetite is awakened and it is fed. At an appropriate point it is sacrificed. The personality thus created is thereupon liberated to display its attributes; and with its assistance one can create gold, fly in the air, or live eternally—or rather the new personality can take over one's body and live eternally through it. Mercury which is less efficiently prepared cannot bestow immortality but can cure disease and increase longevity. Insoluble preparations of mercury and sulfur are widely used in Ayurvedic medicine; such compounds are by-products of alchemical experimentation.

Immortality is a desirable goal in the context of the Indian belief in reincarnation. If one has a long list of karmic connections to be lived through it is infinitely more convenient to live through them all in one lifetime rather than be forced to endure rebirth again and again. Herbs and minerals are only two methods for achieving immortality, however. Another method is practiced by *Aghoris*, Tantrics who have superseded all ritual limitations. When they find themselves near death (any good Yogi will know of his impending death six months in advance as his *Prana* or life-force begins to flow out of his body), Aghoris deliberately leave their bodies and enter the bodies of corpses, taking them over and making them live for as long as they please, until they decide to change bodies again.

Most dead personalities cannot move about so freely on their own, and some Tantrics worship in graveyards and charnel-grounds simply to catch hold of human spirits to force them to perform work. This is also a sort of Siddhi. The sort of work possible depends upon the power of the captured personality. This method produces quick results but it is dangerous, for a minor error in ritual may result in insanity, death, or worse.

Other ethereal beings who never took human form can also be bound by Tantra and their tremendous power harnessed. The most puissant are the deities, personifications of various cos-

mic forces. The ultimate Siddhi is control of Adya, the personification of the entire cosmos.

Essential to the production of any Siddhi are *Mantra, Yantra,*
and *Tantra.* In the journey toward Siddhi, Mantra is the energy which moves your vehicle (the Yantra) according to the road
map (Tantra). In an industrial analogy the finished product (Siddhi) emerges when the raw material (Mantra) is fed into the
milling machines (Yantra) according to a fixed process (Tantra).

A Mantra is a collection of sounds. When pronounced their
vibrations provide energy to the Yantra. Sound appears on the
electromagnetic spectrum as one variety of energy which can
be manipulated by the Tantric. There are three main types of
Mantra:

    a) Descriptive—usually in Sanskrit, these Mantras describe
        either the process undergone, the desired goal, or both.
    b) Meaningless—aggregations of sounds which have no
        known meaning in any human language.
    c) Bijas—individual nasalized syllables.

*Bija* means seed, and these "seed-sounds" produce fruit according to the *Bijavrksha Nyaya,* or the Law of Seed and Tree. The
frequent repetition of these Bijas eventually results in a sort of
standing wave, permanently energizing either an external Yantra or some area of the aspirant's brain, resulting in the continuous production of a specific effect, one which is coherent
with the personality invoked. Four types of *Vani* or speech exist
for the pronunciation of Mantra:

    a) *Vaikhari*—vocal speech
    b) *Madhyama*—nasalized speech
    c) *Pashyanti*—purely mental repetition
    d) *Para*—telepathic speech, in which only the intention
        but not the sound is conveyed.

The more subtle the speech, the deeper its effect on both the
individual and the surrounding environment. Just as a laser produces coherent light, a human brain can produce coherent energy when a single frequency (Bija) is selected and is amplified
appropriately with Yantra and Tantra.

The Yantra is the crucible in which the herb, mineral, animal, or human is prepared through the Mantra's energy. The

Yantra contains the energy, reflecting it back upon itself until it can accumulate to that point when as in a laser it, of its own accord, projects itself. The projection assumes the form of the deity appurtaining to the Bija repeated. When Mantras other than Bijas are employed the energy will continue to accumulate until it is used or is otherwise discharged. Here the Yantra acts something like a capacitor. Yantras are frequently diagrams drawn on birchbark, crystals or copper plates, or they can be drawn with powder or sand. Images may be used as Yantras, but the best Yantra is said to be the human body.

Tantras are the three main varieties according to the aspirant's capabilities: external, internal and mixed. The *Pashu* or animalistic type of aspirant is by nature greatly attached to the enjoyment of external sense objects and so should perform external worship to control these urges to outwardness. The *Divya* or divine type tends to be introverted and need not bother with external ritual. These aspirants require *Antaryaga*, internal sacrificial rites.

The *Vira* or heroic type can perform both external and internal worship competently with thorough attention to detail. Everyday life becomes a sacrificial rite for a *Vira* with each act an act of worship hidden at all times from the casual observer. For a *Vira* the entire world is a graveyard, filled with the dead. A true Tantric regards every human being (including himself) as already dead since the fact of birth makes death inevitable. For a Tantric, and even more so for an Aghori, the entire world is his playground and his temple.

Still, rituals which make use of literal corpses and skulls are available for those who wish to get quick results. Such practices are part of the *Vama Marga*, or Left-Hand Path, which is the violent counterpart of the *Dakshina Marga*, or Right-Hand Path. The Dakshina Marga is meant for those who seek steady progress with reduced danger of setbacks. The Vama Marga is described as "Shighra, Ugra and Tivra," or "fast, terrible and intense." On this path the chances for catastrophe are great unless a powerful guru's protection is provided. The sexual rituals which have made Tantra notorious are part of Vama Marga.

The ritual in which sex appears, which is known as *Panch-*

*amakara*, is actually of three types depending again upon the class of the celebrant, and in only one type does actual sexual intercourse occur. That version is meant only for Tamasic people, *Tamas* being mental inertia or dullness. The intensity of the five (*Pancha* means five) articles of worship—meat, fish, parched grain, wine and sex—overwhelms the dullness of the mind with stimulation. If the aspirant has been properly prepared, this increased mental energy can assist his or her spiritual evolution. An ill-prepared aspirant will be overcome by stimulation and will descend into debauchery.

Rajasic people (*Rajas* means mental activity) have active minds which must be properly channeled. They need less stimulation and more control, and use ginger, radish, boiled (as opposed to parched) grain, coconut milk and flowers in their Panchamakara. Sattvic people naturally enjoy ample *Sattva* (balance of mind and alertness) and do not require external aids to worship. They utilize the meat of silence, the fish of breath control, the grain of concentration techniques, the wine of God intoxication, and the coitus of one's ego with the Absolute.

The Sanskrit terminolgy used to describe the Panchamakara hides this meaning beneath its exterior. For example, "fish" stands for breath control because one's two nostrils are referred to in Yogic terminology as rivers since they are continuously flowing (the right is called the *Ganga* and the left the *Yamuna*). Just as fish swim in rivers, the breath swims through the nostrils, and holding the breath (*Kevala Kumbhaka*) is equivalent to "eating" the "fish."

Panchamakara is only one of many Tantric rituals but it illustrates well a fundamental Tantric concept: *Bhutashuddhi*. The physical universe is a permutation of five Great Elements: Earth, Water, Air, Fire and Ether, equivalent respectively to the solid, liquid, and gaseous states of matter, heat (which transforms matter from one state into another), and the field in which all activity takes place. To achieve universal harmony these Five Elements must be harmonized. Panchamakara is a fast, intense way to do this: meat stands for Earth, fish for Water, wine for Fire, grain for Air, and sex for Ether. When one reaches the stage of balance in which these inputs cause no disequilibrium of consciousness or metabolism it is much less likely that any other fluctuation in the Five Elements will cause disharmony, and a state of health has been reached, since health is balance and disease is imbalance. This health is infinitely more permanent than ordinary health.

To deal with only Five Elements, though essential in every Tantric sadhana, would be too mechanistic, and Tantric authorities advocate personification in accompaniment. Rather than seek to extirpate their emotions entirely as Yogic practitioners do, Tantrics magnify their emotions and transfer them entirely to a deity, a personified cosmic force. All the aspirant's natural propensities can spend themselves in this devotee-deity relationship, avoiding suppression of any desires which might erupt later to disrupt the harmony.

Thus Tantra insists, "There is no *Mukti* (freedom from delusion) without *Bhukti* (enjoyment)." "Enjoyment" refers to the acceptance of all phenomena which may occur to an individual, be they "good" (enjoyable) or "bad" (painful). The aspirant relies on the magnanimity of Nature (personified as the deity) to protect and provide. Yoga and Vedanta aim directly at Mukti, which was appropriate in earlier ages when the mundane world was less demanding. Tantra is more practical for today's world. Ayurveda is meant for those who desire only Bhukti, or unrestricted sensory enjoyments. It was promulgated as a separate doctrine because many today cannot comprehend health's spiritual aspects.

The doctrine of Kundalini and the Chakras is associated with that of the Five Great Elements. When the Elements have been thoroughly purified in an individual then the Kundalini Shakti, a goddess in her own right, has a free path upwards through the Chakras to meet and mate with Her Shiva in the brain. Each of the five lower Chakras is the seat of the subtle form of one Element, and only when they are purified and harmonized can the Kundalini free Herself from their grasp. Herbs can be useful to assist in this process, as can mercury. Even disembodied spirits can be useful since they churn the nervous system to the high pitch necessary to withstand the tremendous might of Kundalini, who is the individual equivalent of the cosmic Adya. Each aspirant's perception of Kundalini will differ according to their innate emotional make-up, and therefore many forms of the Goddess are available for worship. Whatever the form, the aspirant must interact with Kundalini on a personal basis. Some treat Her as sister, some as friend, advisor or wife. A few regard Her as a sixteen-year-old daughter, and the Aghoris treat Her as a servant. But my teacher Vimalananda opined that it is best to treat Her as a mother. In Her aspect as Adya She is Mother of all worlds and all beings. We emerge from Her, exist in Her and eventually dissolve into Her again. Moreover, a friend may fail you, a wife may quarrel with you, and a servant might rebel against you, but your mother will never desert you. Vimalananda told me, "Always sit in the lap of the Divine Mother. Let Her do everything for you, rely on Her totally, and She will never forsake you. If you try to do things on your own you will fall and hurt yourself. Only She can take care of you. The greater your *Bhakti* (devotional love) for Her the faster will be your progress."

Bhakti is essential because She is really *you*—you are a miniscule part of Her—and you must love yourself to make progress. Even the masculine deities are all part of Her. Whether the Tantric aspirant worships a male or female deity depends on the guru, but the outcome will be the same: Kundalini will reunite with her Shiva. First Mantra, Yantra and Tantra will be used to create the form of the deity in the aspirant's consciousness. Then the devotee and the deity will be together continuously, observing their stipulated relationship (son-mother, husband-wife or whatever). This is called *Tanmayata*. Eventually *Tadrupata* occurs in which all but a few vestiges of the devotee's original personality are eliminated and only the deity's personality remains.

For the Panchamakara ritual to be successful a couple who seek to perform it must first perfect *Shiva Lata Mudra*, a practice in which all sexual desire is eliminated. The male identifies entirely with Shiva and the female with Shakti, and this attitude must be held for three hours at a time to ensure success. The Tantras say, "Shivo bhutva shivam yajet": First

become Shiva and then you will be able to worship Shiva properly. When this self-identification with the deities is complete
then the consumption of fish, meat, grain, wine and the sexual
act are no longer acts of indulgence but become sacraments
because the deities themselves partake directly.

The merely curious have no business dabbling in Tantra, but
some so-called gurus in the West encourage their half-baked
followers to do so. Such self-delusive activity reinforces the
crystallizations of the personality which prevent spiritual progress. Tantric rituals are sacrificial rites. Though herbs, minerals, and animals are used as offerings, they are secondary to
the true offering, the sacrifice of one's limited self into the sacrificial fires of penance. In the Panchamakara ritual the female
is the fire into which the male offers semen, just as clarified
butter is offered in orthodox fire worship.

Ordinary sex is no sacrifice. When two people come together
to copulate they usually seek gratification for themselves, the
slaking of their lust. Perhaps indirectly they will try to satisfy
their partners. Tantric sex becomes possible only when one has
totally effaced one's own personality and offers oneself for the
gratification of the deity, the universe incarnate.

This is one reason Tantra has always been a closely guarded
secret. The danger of abusable knowledge falling into the hands
of the unworthy has limited its spread. One should never seek
to practice classical Tantra without a guru because no Tantric
texts exist which provide thoroughly accurate details of any
ritual. Each text omits an essential step, or includes false information, and only through a guru can the reality, handed down
from teacher to disciple over generations, be known.

Even if pure Tantra is beyond the reach of most Westerners
the Tantric attitude has much to offer. To consider some of
the topics already considered, Western psychology can learn
much from the Tantric concepts of personality and ego. The
concept of individual constitution—not merely in the Ayurvedic
sense of Vata, Pitta and Kapha but also the mental constitution of Sattva (Divya), Rajas (Vira), and Tamas (Pashu)—suggests
that people can be categorized according to what sort of approach will suit their temperament and would therefore be more

likely to work. Tantric herbal and mineral preparations are part of Ayurveda and can be evaluated for their efficacy. The whole physiology of sound and light can be revolutionized by examination of Mantra and of visualization.

Some of these Tantric attitudes are already being employed in the West, perhaps unknowingly. For example, cancer patients are sometimes instructed to visualize to encourage remission. One such visualization might be a school of piranha devouring the dead meat of the tumor mass. This is Tantric in nature; the sacrifice of an undesirable personality (the cancer) to an objectified projection of nature (the piranha). Such visualizations are often effective but because they are inherently combative they are not as useful for promoting health, which is non-aggressive, as they may be for cure. Tantra can suggest new and better visualizations which could positively increase the individual's stamina, vigor and happiness while simultaneously eliminating the disease.

Visualization can also be extended to other auto-immune diseases besides cancer, since auto-immune disease occurs when the ego loses its ability to distinguish what is part of its organism and what is alien to it. Psychologically this process is already being used in Neurolinguistic Programming. Undesirable habits or personality quirks can be altered thereby without analysis, guilt or trauma, and new traits can be added. Because there is no limit for self-improvement Tantra can be repeatedly employed to assist in adjustments.

For those who are already relatively healthy, Tantra can create deeper levels of harmony and health. Immortality may be generally unobtainable but a long healthy life is not, for which good immunity is required. In Sanskrit, immunity is *Vyadhikshamatva*, which means literally "forgiveness of the disease." By improper lifestyle and attitudes we create conditions in our bodies and minds which are agreeable to certain beings, which accept our (unspoken) invitation and move in. Most of us despise the disease without realizing that we have invited it to ourselves. When one learns to forgive oneself, and to forgive the disease its depradations, then the disease's return is effectively barred.

Unfortunately, even the Tantric attitude can be dangerous. As one accumulates power, the ego will balloon out unless the personality is continuously incinerated simultaneously. Hence Tantra's insistence that power be objectified and personified. Since Tantric ritual can be used to create emotions which did not previously exist, perhaps adoption of the Tantric attitude can prove therapeutic for those many today who suffer from emotional paralysis. Hence Vimalananda's insistence on the greatness of motherly love.

From the strictly spiritual point of view a study of true Tantra would provide Westerners a proper perspective with which to consider their own spiritual practices. For example, they might begin to regard Kundalini with greater respect after learning of the effects of Her complete awakening. Or, consider the millions who repeat Mantras daily. Most are ignorant of the requirements for Mantra Siddhi and so will repeat the Mantra sincerely for years with very little result, whereas with a little attention to Tantric teachings they could make quick progress by learning such things as:

   a) The location in the vocal apparatus where the Mantra should be recited along with its proper pronunciation.
   b) The process of Bhuta Shuddhi and the practice of Nyasa (which prepares the body and mind to act as a fit receptacle for the deity).
   c) The Dhyanavidhi, or specific visualization appropriate to the Mantra.
   d) The five great restrictions, which are reciting the Mantra daily the same number of times, at the same place, at the same time, with the same offering, while observing strict sexual continence during whatever period is set aside for this purpose.
   e) The total number of repetitions required, which differs for each Mantra (100,000 is often cited), plus the appropriate number and variety of offerings to the Five Great Elements.

Though Tantra may sometimes seem hopelessly complex and impractical one is unavoidably filled with awe at the amazing thoroughness and attention to detail which the ancient sages showed while promulgating this science. Even if it cannot be instantly commercialized or otherwise exploited in some mundane fashion, surely Tantra deserves appreciation for its very existence.

The greatest benefit of the study of Tantra and Aghora is perhaps an enhanced appreciation for motherliness. The doctor who cannot take a motherly attitude toward his patients is a mere pill pusher. My teacher insisted that all males should learn motherly love. Tantra is the worship of Mother; it is the most advanced method for inculcating maternal feelings. It is undeniable that as you look to the world, so the world will look to you. If the world is your Mother and all its inhabitants your family there is never need for loneliness, fear or despair. As my teacher Vimalananda observed frequently, when speaking of the Mother, "What more does one need to do once the Mother has accepted him? She will do everything without being asked. *She* is the being to be realized."

# INTRODUCTION

This is the story of the Aghori Vimalananda. An Aghori is a practitioner of the spiritual discipline known as Aghora. The word *aghora* can be interpreted as "deeper than deep," or as "gentle," or "filled with light, illumined." Aghora is the apotheosis of Tantra, the Indian religion whose Supreme Deity is the Mother Goddess.

Tantra has thus far been glimpsed in the West only in its most vulgar and debased forms, promulgated by unscrupulous scoundrels who equate sex with superconsciousness. Sex is indeed central to Tantra, the cosmic sexual union of universal dualities. The aim of Tantra is Laya, return of the seeker to the state of undifferentiated existence. Actually Tantra cannot be termed a religion, because it is bereft of tenets and dogma. It consists only of methods for achieving this Laya, or union of the individual with the infinite. This union is described with a sexual metaphor: the union of the personal ego (which is female) with the absolute (male). Under special circumstances sexual rituals are employed in Tantra to hasten spiritual progress, but the concept of licentiousness is totally foreign to the Tantric tradition.

Tantra has been divided into Right-Hand and Left-Hand Paths. The Right-Hand Path involves a search for the Unlimited Reality via the road of external imposition of purity. While its practices may seem strange to some, its emphasis on personal purity

will be familiar to those in the West who know of Bhakti Yoga,
Karma Yoga, and Raja Yoga, all of which conform more or less
to orthodox ideals of religious discipline.

The Left-Hand Path has attracted attention to itself by the
actions of those unwise souls who seek quick and easy spiritual development without any preliminary renunciation of sensory gratification. The result of such rashness is invariably
indulgence of the worst and most blatant sort, which has dam-
aged the Left-Hand Path's reputation.

The Left-Hand Path relies on its practitioners' absolute internal purity to protect them while they practice rituals which
may involve necromancy, intoxicants, sex, or other "forbidden" practices. Most serious aspirants automatically shun the
Left-Hand Path because of its potential for misuse, which is
indeed great. It is truly treacherous for the unwary: one text
observes that "walking on swords or riding a tiger is child's
play by comparison." Ironically, those undisciplined individuals who cannot succeed at the Left-Hand Path are naturally
attracted to it by the potential for unbridled indulgence it seems
to proffer, while those sincere seekers who might eventually
succeed at it are frightened away by its temptations.

There are a few, though, who do dare and who successfully
complete the rigorous Left-Hand training of Tantra and Aghora.
Strict renunciation is the prerequisite, extreme enough to purify the aspirant through and through. Only when purity is perfected is the aspirant assigned rituals which to the untutored
observer might seem hedonistic or "sinful." Aghora is not indulgence; it is the forcible transformation of darkness into light,
of the opacity of the limited individual personality into the
luminescence of the Absolute. Renunciation disappears once
you arrive at the Absolute because then nothing remains to
renounce. An Aghori goes so deeply into darkness, into all
things undreamable to ordinary mortals, that he comes out into
light. Sects in India are often distinguished by color of turban
or drape of robe. Popularly, Aghoris have been stereotyped as
ash-swathed ascetics with long matted hair who walk through
life wild-eyed, skulking about in charnel grounds, wrestling

with jackals for carcasses. The title *Aghori* is claimed by some groups who even assert an exclusive right to it.

Vimalananda had his own definition of Aghori which was independent of any doctrine or dogma. Indeed, his usage of terms like *Vedic* and *Tantric* may also be devoid of detectable textual support, for he never cared for texts. He believed — and it is a noble Indian tradition to do so — that a lineage's practices prevail over textual injunctions. Whatever you believe yourself to be you are, if you are sincere and honest enough. You are responsible for yourself, and your opinion of yourself is authoritative. This attitude often irritates those who have invested heavily in the infallibility of any one text or group of texts, but then Vimalananda had no use for organized religion anyway. As you read his story, remember that what he called Vedic might not necessarily be Vedic to a temple priest, but that both opinions might be equally valid, according to context.

Throughout his life Vimalananda resisted any attempt to fit him into any mold. He guarded his originality jealously. He was without doubt distinctly individual, but simultaneously he was exceedingly difficult to pin down and define. What we speak of in this book as *Aghora* is solely according to Vimalananda's teachings. He studied many systems and selected elements from each — Bhakti Yoga, Kundalini Yoga, and others — and melded them into a tool which he employed to advance himself. He believed that each individual should "carve out his own niche": study what he or she could understand, select those practices which they could sincerely do, and do them faithfully. So by this definition Aghora would always be different for everyone; only the Aghori's attitude would be held in common. Each Aghori would follow different practices, but all Aghoris follow them with the same intensity and disregard for self-preservation.

To Vimalananda, the true Aghori cannot be recognized by any external sign or mark. Experience in the world of ascetics had taught him that many fake Aghoris lurk under outward appurtenances. And he stoutly maintained that the true Aghora is wholly internal. Sectarian Aghoris might well take issue with this opinion, but Vimalananda lived up to it. He lived in an

ordinary flat in Bombay and went about his business incon-
spicuously. Inside, he was pure Aghori: as hard as diamonds or
as soft as wax, as the situation demanded. To his spiritual "children" he was the perfect mother — a combination of friend,
philosopher, and guide. To those with inflated spiritual egos
he was merciless.

One immutable tenet of Aghora is that death is to be personified and deified. Aghoris crave not for physical death but
for destruction of all their limitations, "killing" themselves
by internal or external processes. Aghoris do not fear death;
once embarked upon a course of action the true Aghori either
succeeds or dies trying, for there is no middle ground and no
retreat. Aghoris love to spend time in cemeteries and burning
grounds (collectively called smashan in Hindi). An Aghori is
never happier than when he is seated intoxicated in the smashan
performing a ritual near a funeral pyre, flames shooting up to
lick the midnight blackness. Vimalananda, so concerned with
external propriety in other ways, never hesitated to visit the
smashan when he had rituals to perform.

Some of the events described in this book may well offend
the reader's sensitivities. Part of this was Vimalananda's intention. He wanted Western holier-than-thou renunciates to know
that "filth and orgies in the graveyard" (as one American once
described Aghora) can be as conducive to spiritual advancement
as can asanas, pranayama, and other "purer" disciplines. But
another part is intrinsic to Aghora. In many ways it is and must
remain totally incomprehensible to the ordinary person, and
for some people no amount of explanation will satisfy when
they question the wisdom or the spiritual benefit inherent in,
say, consumption of human brain. Aghora is mysterious and
deep — deeper than deep, in fact — and only those who can
lay aside all their cultural clothing and plunge into it naked
can dive into its depths.

When Vimalananda and I were in America one of my friends
asked him, "As much as I have read about you and heard about
you and now listened to you, I still cannot understand what
an Aghori is. Would you please try to explain it to me?"

Vimalananda told me later, "She asked me so honestly and

earnestly that I felt I had to reply eloquently, even though this is really not something you can put into so many words."

He told her, "An Aghori is beyond the bound of the earthly shackles; nay, something above the elements which shape the universe, and you. He takes a sort of intoxicant and thus gets intoxicated in Supreme Love which emanates from the innermost recesses of his heart. Shall I call it interiority? It is that which is beyond awareness. He gives off the best part of love. Why part? Part of the Supreme, Universal Love, where one experiences, with the help of perception, All-in-One/One-in-All. When you, the finite, merge into infinity what dost thou not know? During this stage he merges with his own deity so that he becomes Him — capital H. That is why he is said to have gone from darkness to divine enlightenment. This is an Aghori."

Vimalananda was an extremist. He was certain that anything worth doing was worth doing well, and he was ready to stake his all to ensure that whatever he began was completed. For him, Aghora was the doctrine of no return, a personal creed which demanded relinquishing all in exchange for divine love. He wanted to warn spiritual dilettantes in the West that the frivolity with which they treat discipline and the self-delusion they attempt to pass off as enlightenment is merely a cheating of their own consciousness which leads only to the pit. For example, when I was once unwise enough to comment that a certain guru was supposedly awakening his disciples' Kundalinis by boffing them with a peacock feather duster, Vimalananda exploded in reply: "Has the Kundalini Shakti become so cheap that some so-called godman can awaken it in multitudes of people all at once? Oh, no! Were our Rishis (ancient seers) fools to spend decades out in the jungles working at hard penances to awaken Kundalini and to perfect Aghora? No, the people who think they can buy Kundalini are the fools. Westerners think they can purchase knowledge, but all they get for their money is fake teachers from India who dish out any slop to them and get rich on their gullibility."

Vimalananda conformed to none of the usual "guru" stereotypes. When at the races he dressed like the horse owner he was, and when at home he dressed like an ordinary Indian. He ate meat on occasion, used intoxicants frequently, and smoked cigarettes incessantly. He did all these things for specific, but hidden, reasons. Most of the people who knew him only formally never suspected that he might be of a spiritual bent. He cultivated this carefree image deliberately to avoid attracting attention to himself. This led me to early skepticism of his spiritual prowess, for I had been brainwashed by "spiritual authorities" to expect a certain role from a guru.

Fortunately for me I soon learned that Vimalananda's revulsion toward hypocrisy and posturing was exceeded in strength only by his obstinacy. At one time he had actively attempted to speed certain persons along the spiritual path but was unsuccessful with them due to their unpreparedness. He thereupon determined to provide real tools for spiritual cultivation only to those students whom he had first thoroughly tested and prepared. Hence, he never referred to himself as a guru, nor did he act in the way we have come to expect gurus to act. For example, when he chose to call me Ravi he did so because it is cognate with my nickname, Robby, and it was more convenient to use while speaking in an Indian language. It was not because he wanted to impress me by giving me some Sanskrit name.

He made a show of complete disinterest in teaching while actually spending much time evaluating the strengths and weaknesses of each of his spiritual "children." This Indian tradition is known as *Kurma Guru* (literally, "Tortoise Teacher"). After a mother tortoise buries her eggs on a sandy beach it is said that she retreats a certain distance and then concentrates on those eggs with such an intense current of love that the warmth of her love reaches the eggs and causes them to hatch. In the same way, a Kurma Guru seems to pay no attention to his disciples' progress but in reality monitors them closely and sometimes pulls their strings from afar.

Vimalananda's entire life was teaching and being taught. He was always ready to learn something new, and always ready to teach — in his own way — if a student was sincerely willing to learn. His day-to-day life was a lesson for whoever could understand it, a continual resubmission of his will to the Divine Will.

He was not easy to fathom, and he deliberately made his lessons hard to understand. When he decided I should learn something he would deftly insert it into a flood of mundane trivialities directed at others in the room and would expect me to be alert enough to pick it out. Weeks or months later he would question me about it, suddenly and without warning. I would be expected not only to have noted and remembered the datum but to have processed it internally to fit my own situation as best I could. He often observed, "What sort of educational system do we have nowadays? They announce their examinations in advance so that any idiot can mug up a bunch of notes in preparation. The key to testing someone is to test them when they least expect it and are least prepared for it. Then you have an accurate idea of how much they really know."

Sometimes just keeping up with Vimalananda's talks was test enough. Depending on his mood and audience he might speak in very fluent high British English, in colloquial Gujarati, or (most commonly) in Hindi. When the mood struck him he could switch to high-flown Urdu, and sometimes stabbed at Marathi or Bengali. He was an actor by inclination and he had an incredible command over a wide variety of language styles, which he could permute at will to obtain precisely the right effect on his audience. Over the eight years and nine months that I was privileged to know him he repeated each of his favorite stories a dozen times or more, but never the same way each time. Each repetition was uniquely flavored by his delivery.

Translation was thus no easy task. I have rendered all his words into English, approximating in his usual English style the intent which flowed through whatever vocabulary, syntax, and diction he was employing in whatever language he was speaking at the time. Working from memory and from the brief notes I would jot down after our conversations I decided it would be most effective to leave the narrative in his own words throughout, so that readers can imagine if they like that they, too, sat with Vimalananda and heard him tell his tales.

There is another reason for presenting his words as they were spoken. Vimalananda's impression on people was achieved primarily not by what he did, but by how he did it; not by what he said (though this was important), but by how he said it. Who he was was more significant than what he did, but he made people dig for his interior reality and most often they would come up empty-handed. Those few who knew him well — at least superficially — could never agree with each other on who he was, because his personality differed for each of his friends. He was a multitude of different people, all in one body. Once, before he had met me, he had a desire to jot down his musings and to accompany them with testimonies from his close acquaintances. He asked several of his friends, "If you had to write down something about me what would you write?" One replied with a single word, "Versatile." Another said, "Words just cannot express the reality." A third opined, "I would just turn in a blank sheet of paper because by saying nothing everything is said." His foster daughter had the last word by informing him, "No one has any business to read about you because unless they have experienced you they could never know the reality."

She was motivated by possessiveness, no doubt, and in fact knew him no better than did any of the rest of us, but her point is well-taken: How does one convey in two-dimensional print a multidimensional being? And it was not that he had anything to hide. There was nothing inscrutable about him; he never put on airs. He was available for everyone's scrutiny. He would talk to us in the way a child talks to its mother, neglecting to alter or hold back anything for the sake of self-image. He was a true innocent at heart, a child in many ways, never ashamed to display his innocent wonderment or admit to his mistakes. And like a child, he could equally well be a bad loser at games; the Aghori in him expected to win.

Perhaps it was because of this "child" within him that he could be such a good "mother" to all those around him. Or perhaps his concentration on the Divine Mother engendered the child in him. Whatever the causation, he was like a truly incorrigible child, a prankster from birth, always out for a gentle practical joke, ready to laugh at anything funny and to make anyone else laugh if he could. Nothing was bland around him. He could be miserable, overjoyed, or profoundly taciturn; he was never merely sad, happy, or quiet. His Aghora training had taught him to succeed or die. He never played any role half-heartedly but threw himself fully into everything he did, no matter how minor. There was not a phony bone in his body.

The personality "Vimalananda" was indeed amazingly versatile. His family once owned most of Bombay, and his early life was princely, but the life of idle riches never tempted him. He knew by turns fabulous wealth and wretched poverty, and served variously as an army officer, textile machinery manufacturer, dairy owner, quarry operator, race course gambler, and anchorite. He achieved high academic qualifications and observed strict spiritual disciplines.

Experts at Indian music regarded him as both an instrumental and vocal maestro. Among those who knew him he was renowned for his expertise at astrology, his ability to diagnose disease by merely looking at a patient's face, and his capacity to interpret the body markings on horses and elephants. In his youth he was a semipro wrestler and won his last bout at age 38, defeating a boy half his age. I never saw him beaten at arm wrestling even when his opponent was a powerful young wrestler one-third his age. His friends regularly demanded that he cook for them, so tasty and unique were his culinary concoctions. He could move each and every muscle in his body, including his ears and eyebrows, in time to music, as a result of his training in Indian dance.

He was an artist. He liked to say, "Here in India we believe in watching the artist at work, not in looking at the work of the artist. Artistry is not what the artist produces but is the artist himself, producing. A great composer's music may be transmitted from generation to generation in the West. Our great musicians do not concentrate on creating compositions; they create new musicians to maintain the progression of the artistry."

How can one then transmit Vimalananda's artistry to anyone who has not seen it at work? The use of his words is transmission of his art, but only alert readers will be able to detect the subtlety of his artistry at work there beneath.

Vimalananda could learn from anyone and would make whatever he learned more artistic. He put the stamp of his person-

ality on everything he said, did, and created, and it is my hope
that this stamp appears on these pages as well. He was charm-
ing and profound, and sometimes it may seem that he was in
awe of himself. In a way, he was. He was not conceited; he
was in awe of what was within him. Chapter Eight on Avishkara
explains this more fully.

He could be egotistical, and some of that ego is reflected in
these pages. He maintained that death of the ego meant certain death of the organism and so never tried to expunge his
ego, preferring to keep it tightly under his control. He equated
the ego, the individual's power of self-identification, with the
much misunderstood Kundalini Shakti. His control of his Kundalini enabled him to disengage his consciousness from his own
limited (if versatile) personality so that he could self-identify
with unlimited, divine personalities. Often when he spoke it
was with the awesome confidence of divinity speaking through
him, and this sometimes seemed arrogant to those humans who
heard but could not or would not comprehend it.

He could be maddening to deal with when he thought he
was right but happened to be mistaken. There were times I
found it difficult to respect Vimalananda, and other times when
it was difficult to like him very much. But it was never difficult to love him. When first we met I analyzed him, dissected
his opinions, and attempted to preserve the objective aloofness
I felt was appropriate for a Western scientist. All in vain, for
the current of warmth which flowed continuously over whoever he took into his circle of "children" was irresistible. My
distrustful Western nature balked at first but eventually my
doubt dissolved in spite of itself, and he and I settled into the
seemingly preordained role of father and son. Or perhaps I
should say "father and mother" and son, for never did his love
lose its motherliness.

Two principles guided his teaching: compassion for all beings,
including the seemingly insentient such as rocks; and perpet
ual awareness of *rnanubandhana*, the bondage of karmic debt
His compassion for his friends led him to ruin his health and
exhaust his wealth to insulate them as far as possible from their
own karmic debts. His shoulders were unusually wide, perhaps

from his wrestling, and he used to say, "Since Nature has given me such broad shoulders I should support whomever I can. Why should any child worry about rnanubandhana when its mother or father is there to repay its debts?" He treated all who came before him, even the buffoons, as a fond and indulgent mother would treat her beloved children. Women found him irresistible because he projected onto every female the same tremendous devotion which he directed in his worship toward the Mother Goddess. Until his dying day Vimalananda's sole refuge was the Motherhood of God.

He and I selected the name "Vimalananda" for use in his book from the many names he used during this lifetime. Its variety of meanings makes it appropriately representative of who he was. In Sanskrit *Vimalananda* equals "Vimala" (pure) plus "Ananda" (joy, bliss), or, literally, "the bliss of purity." "Malam vidvamsayati iti vimalah": The absolute annihilation of filth is Vimala. "Filth" is here the filth of attribution, the limitations imposed upon pure existence as a result of its incarnation. When the cosmic play of creation, preservation, and destruction is transcended all limitation is transcended, and that state is Vimala.

Or, when an aspirant has gone beyond the ego's flaws, when the ego is completely naked, cleansed of its accretions of personality and its stains of desire, then it perceives pure consciousness and knows that pure consciousness to be both "Thyself" and "Myself," and that is Vimala. Or, the "Ananda" an Aghori receives from his rituals cannot be purer (Vimala) because he sees the face of his beloved deity in everything and everyone.

"Vimalananda" can be derived in many different ways in Sanskrit, but its special significance here is that Vimalananda's physical mother was named Vimala. Vimala + Nanda = "son of Vimala." Vimalananda told me, "When I was a wandering ascetic I thought it would be wonderful to appear at my home one day and have the servant announce to my mother, 'Vimalananda has come.' What joy it would have given her!"

So 'Vimalananda' it was for this book, in lieu of such other names as Aghora Nath (master of Aghora), Shah-e-mauj (king of bliss), or even Bandal-e-aftaab (sun among exaggerators). This last is significant in that Vimalananda was, well, "larger" than life, and some of his stories may seem expanded beyond the bounds of plausibility. We Westerners ordinarily equate truth with the "objective" reality of sense perception. Vimalananda was concerned only that the subjective reality of the stories he told exert specific effects on the subjective realities of his listeners, for he held that objective reality is continuously being altered by our perceptions of it. Thus it is immaterial if, for example, someone really does cut off his limbs and throw them into a blazing fire, only to have them reattach spontaneously after several hours, or whether he merely visualizes the scenario so intensely that he thoroughly convinces himself that the events did indeed occur. The result, increased stability of mind regardless of external irritant, will create increased physical stability as well. For the mind, reality is defined by its perceptions. Aghora is total control of perception.

When Vimalananda felt it essential to make a point to some "child" he would unhesitatingly exaggerate or magnify his stories, just as we might do for real children. Also, Vimalananda spoke mainly for Indians, who often inflate the content of events they report. Indian listeners have learned to automatically compensate for this expansion by mentally scaling down whatever is said. Thus Vimalananda's exaggeration would be perceived approximately accurately by an Indian listener.

I mention this because I was continuously aware of this cultural trait and have accounted for it. The stories you read here have been calibrated for maximum veracity, at least in the system of reality in which Vimalananda lived. Also, the language of this book has been slightly sanitized at his own request. He used to make regular use of vulgarity, but only when he spoke with people whose normal speech is vulgar, in order to be coherent with them. In addition, each cuss word was spoken with a hidden meaning behind it, a hoary Tantric tradition called *Sandhya Bhasha*. But that is another story.

No idle tale ever escaped his lips. Each was aimed at a specific listener and might change its form according to the lesson he felt the listener needed to learn, though all his stories were based on incidents which actually "happened" to him, at least subjectively. As noted above, however, he transcended the blasé factuality of objective reality and ascended to the mythic. His tales were carefully textured with deep meanings available to the clever pupil who could properly interpret the words and the intonation and emotion with which they were spoken, ignoring the minor detail which Vimalananda himself scorned.

Vimalananda would unveil a story and present it to an assembly of people in his living room when the conversation seemed completely innocuous, and someone in that company would hear it and realize that it referred to a situation about which he had intended to ask Vimalananda but had thus far been unable to do so. There was a thrill in sitting quietly and suddenly realizing that a story was being directed at you. Vimalananda would not often target anyone by name, but a word here or a clue there would give his intention away. Vimalananda loved to play consciously with his "children" just as a mother plays abstractedly with hers, all the while maintaining awareness of the pot on the stove.

Vimalananda likewise manifested "otherness" continually: an eternal sense of other spheres of activity and other levels of awareness which operated in him simultaneously. He acknowledged this and often said, "To be really aware you must be able to know simultaneously what is going on thousands of miles away today, what may have happened here centuries ago, what will happen anywhere in the world decades from now, and what is occurring, has occurred, or will occur on other planes of existence. And you must still act as if you know nothing. You must just sit and talk with other people and play the part which Nature has assigned to you." In his music, his conversation, his chess, and even his sleep, he was always aware both of what was going on around him and also, effortlessly, of some "other" reality.

Or at least he made it seem effortless, though it surely involved tremendous strain which occasionally showed through. He credited tobacco with his ability to function in several planes of being at once. After close observation of him for years I can state confidently that though he was addicted to cigarettes, a fact he made no attempt to conceal, tobacco certainly did seem to exert a markedly beneficial effect on his consciousness, infinitely more than I have seen in any other smoker. Modern scientific research has demonstrated that small doses of nicotine have a positive influence on brain function, and Vimalananda was such a veteran of intoxicants that he could easily imbibe more nicotine than anyone else without deleterious effect.

Smoking did eventually kill him, or so his doctors said, from cardiac failure. Those of us who knew him knew he decided exactly six months before dying that he intended to die. His excuse was that he had finished everything in this life that he was expected to do, and to live any longer would be to attract new karmas. He also predicted, for years, that the day he gave up smoking would be the day he died. For as long as I knew him he smoked at least one cigarette daily until December 11, 1983, a day on which he refused a cigarette whenever it was offered, fully aware of what he was doing. The next morning he died. At sunset I cremated him.

From the day we met, Vimalananda had been telling me I would cremate him, in spite of his natural son who still lives in Bombay and who, according to Hindu tradition, should have cremated his father. But Vimalananda always said, even eight years before the fact, "My son will not even come to the smashan to watch me burn, nor will my wife." Indeed, they did not. When once I asked him about this he told me, "There is no escaping the Law of Karma. I have told everyone the truth, that you are destined to cremate me, and all of them have become jealous of you because they think they deserve to be involved themselves somehow. They don't know what they are talking about or else they wouldn't act that way. I may have a physical son, but you are my spiritual son, and I will have my death my way. Do you know what is an Aghori's profoundest expression of love? It is these four words: 'You will cremate me.'

"You will assist me to return to my Beloved. And when I am burning I only desire one thing: play a tape recording of Jim Reeves singing 'Precious Lord, Take My Hand.' I know all the Hindus will think it is a sacrilege, but pay no attention to them. That's all I desire, no rituals, no phoniness. I only want to go back to where I belong, and to have my Big Daddy take me there by the hand."

Vimalananda was cremated on the same pyre which had previously hosted his father, his mother, and his young son, Ranu, years before. Jim Reeves's voice did sing at his funeral to help release him from his "earthly shackles." Most of his ashes were consigned to the Arabian Sea, whose surf pounds the outer wall of the Banganga Smashan in Bombay; the rest were collected for ritual immersion in India's sacred rivers.

This has been a difficult book for me to write. I have spent months groping for direction, writing and rewriting, hoping to locate the best angle from which to approach to freeze Vimalananda in prose. Eventually I realized that he cannot be portrayed justly from a single angle, just as it was never possible to capture him definitively on film. He always avoided the camera, and none of his photographs which do exist resemble each other. In fact, it was always difficult to recognize the living Vimalananda from his pictures, because his entire face would change moment by moment according to his state of consciousness at the moment. He was loathe to part with photos of himself, which is why none adorns this book. He would say, "My friends will not like it if you don't take care of my photo. They will view it as a sign of disrespect. I don't care; I am just a nobody. But some of my ethereal friends are very orthodox and very strict and will not think twice before they punish for disrespect."

He certainly was not confined by the restrictions which confine most mortals. His eyes, for example, refused to remain the same color at all times. Sometimes they were a light blue; often they were light green, the color of the grape known as *anab-e-shahi*. At some moments they could become nearly colorless. People meeting him for the first time would point it out to him incredulously and he would disclaim in agreement, "How ridiculous! Is it possible for anyone's eyes to change colors?" At other times when he was feeling playful he would adjust his eye color to match mine and would then call everyone in the room over to see and comment. He loved to watch people react to an out-of-the-ordinary event because he felt he could gauge them better when they were caught off guard.

An enigma, a puzzle, a paradox, a riddle, a "mark of interrogation," as he himself put it: Who was Vimalananda? The more I remained in his company the less I knew about him. He really was "no-body": there was no one personality present perpetually in his body which could be pinned down and categorically identified as his. He could be hard and soft by turns, alternately refined and coarse according to his environs. One memorable night we started off dining elegantly at a posh Turf Club party and ended up, as fate would have it, listening to music in the middle of Bombay's red light district. Vimalananda finally took up an instrument himself and taught the delighted prostitutes a new song, just for fun!

Psychiatrists would probably classify Vimalananda as schizophrenic. Vimalananda himself used to say, "Either I must be mad or everyone else is; there are no two ways about it." Though no psychiatrist I am a licensed physician, and, in my opinion (an opinion shared by those who lived with him for many years before I met him), he was far saner than the rest of the world. Facile formulae cannot describe him.

I wrote this book knowing well that some of what is written will be offensive or at least incomprehensible to some, and that other passages will impel the curiosity of others to try out some of the more daring procedures. The natural reticence I felt for permitting Vimalananda to be introduced to an unprepared audience would have prevented this material from any publication had I not had clear instructions to do so. It began years ago when a man dressed as a medieval Rajput warrior was invited to Vimalananda's home in Bombay. After some preliminaries the spirit of a hero centuries dead, Kalaji Rathod, entered this man's body, broke open coconuts with a cavalry saber, and made predictions from the pieces thus formed. He advised me, when my turn came, to note down everything Vimalananda spoke. Vimalananda, who was not usually impressed with such performances and who had assiduously refused to allow anyone to record any of his words up to this time, mysteriously agreed and even encouraged me in this. He never read any of my writings on him until the first draft of this manuscript was ready. When I presented it to him he turned through a few pages, made a few comments, and lapsed quickly into his former seeming disinterest.

Vimalananda cloaked his meanings more thoroughly than ever before after making this assignment. His asking me from time to time if I had noted down some particularly intricate comment suggested to me that he still expected me to continue in my role as scribe. He continued to engineer situations, a pastime at which he was expert, and he would make use of the situations which developed spontaneously around him in his home, which was a veritable circus. During and after the unfolding of the situation he would test me on what I had learned.

As soon as Vimalananda felt he had dispelled my major doubts on a subject he would usually refuse to talk about it any longer, expecting me to learn more about it from direct experience. He explained that this would preserve the keenness of my spiritual hunger, to prevent me from ever losing my alertness or pausing in my pondering. He never spoon-fed me.

Gradually I accumulated a heap of information, enough to fill at least four books. The writing and rewriting of this book has enabled me to digest Vimalananda's teachings more efficiently, and I understood that Vimalananda's real intention in making me write was for the writing to act as a *sadhana* (spiritual exercise) for me.

Summaries and conclusions are supposed to close the books they serve, but I am listing mine here in the introduction. I cannot summarize Vimalananda, nor can I conclude anything at all about him. During the last visit of the Emperor Akbar's personality into Vimalananda's body, His Majesty told us, "Do you think you know the possessor of this body? You know nothing! If he is your friend and loved one, well, we spirits love him too. But don't be so stupid and insolent to think you can comprehend him. I do not know him, you cannot know him, no one knows him. This is the sort of man who allows you to play about with him, you fools! Apart from knowing him in his entirety you will never, never be able to know a single hair from the head of Vimalananda!"

Vimalananda himself requested me to compile my notes into this book and publish it now. He wanted Westerners to be exposed to Aghora. In his own words, "I once wanted to go to the West to demonstrate the practical uses of Aghora, the real spiritual science of India. I know I can deliver the goods, but whenever I tried to go my mentors always prevented me. They didn't want me to be tempted by glamour and power. They knew I could be a better businessman than anyone else — it is in my genes, after all — but they didn't want to watch me fall so low. I am not destined for commercialization; I am destined for something different.

"It is not necessary to publish this while I am alive. I have not achieved all I have achieved in this life merely to capitalize on it. I don't want the last years of my life to be spoiled by curiosity-seekers who want to meet me to find out if I am for real. I know who I am and don't care what anyone else thinks.

"Besides that, if I become too well known I'll have to sit on a throne and say things like, 'Blessings be upon you,' which is bull because you can't give blessings away like that. I won't be able to move about freely in society and play about as I do now. No more jokes, no more laughing sprees. I'll have to become stern and solemn. Why should I give up what little peace and quiet I have now, just to be worshipped by a bunch of people who don't even know what they are doing? How do all these so-called saints stand it, I wonder?

"Publish this book after I am gone. Let people know the truth. Let them know what is what. Out of the thousands who may read it at least a few will be sincere. They will try to learn more, and then Nature Herself will make arrangements for them to learn just as She did for me, and they will be taught according to their capabilities. The progression will go on; there is nothing to fear.

"I have never gone out and tried to attract anyone to me. People have come and gone. I don't ask them to come and I don't object when they go. What is it to me? I only want a few. If I love one or a few I can love well. If I try to love all I will just be cheating myself. Only Jesus could love all."

From Vimalananda's select circle of loved ones I was awarded the commission to try to explain to those who never met him just who and what he was. Hence this book. No one can disturb him now. His story can be told and his privacy will be preserved. I am pleased to offer this volume to those who can read it: I regard it as an offering to him, an offering which is also a promise I have kept, an obligation I have requited, a long-standing desire of his I have finally fulfilled.

Here is Vimalananda as I knew him. Even after hundreds of meetings he could baffle me with the incredible variegation of his knowledge, charm me with his ever-present effluence, and infect me into a smile with his good humor. I even almost got used to his anger. But having charmed and enthralled me and his other listeners he never tired of telling us, "Don't take anything I say as gospel truth. I am human, I make mistakes. Test on yourselves what I've told you. Try it out, experience it, and then you will know whether or not I'm telling you the truth. When you examine a gem you must evaluate it from all its facets before you can decide on its value."

Here then is Vimalananda, for your evaluation.

# CHAPTER ONE

# MA

*To be a guru you have to say, "I know and I can teach you." But if I say that, well, I'm finished. I can never learn anything else. I have shut myself off from anything new. If I remain a student all my life, though, I will always be ready to learn new things.*

I never call any of the people who come to me for spiritual guidance "disciples." I am just an ordinary person. I have lived unknown and I will die unknown, except to a few. I am not interested in anything the world can offer me and even if I die tomorrow I have no regrets. I have lived my life to the fullest; I have done enough. I'll always be thankful to Nature for permitting me to achieve so much. I will never have disciples, only "children," because that is the way a real guru should treat a disciple: as a spiritual son or daughter. And the bond between them is far more intense than that between a physical parent and child.

Even if the child is wicked or wayward, do the parents stop loving it? No! In fact if they are true parents they will love the child all the more, because that child gives them an opportunity to demonstrate their generosity and love, just as in the case of the Prodigal Son. The parents have a chance to forgive the child, and that feeds the ego. So no matter what a child might do, its parents are always bound to love it — if they are true parents.

It is the same way with a guru and his disciples. No matter where the "child" goes or how much he curses the guru, the mentor knows the child must return eventually. Where will he go? The guru can afford to wait for the child and forgive him when he returns.

Once there was a guru who made one of his disciples put on a loincloth and then sent him out into the world. Tying on a loincloth symbolized that the boy was meant to be a celibate mendicant. Everything went fine for the boy until one day when he washed his loincloth, and while it was hanging up to dry a mouse came along and chewed up part of it. The boy said to himself, "This will never do. I need a cat." So he got a cat to save his loincloth from mice. But then the cat had to eat, so he made arrangements for a cow to provide milk for the cat. Who will look after the cow? A cowherd was engaged to cut grass to feed the cow. But then how to pay for the cowherd? A field was taken and farming was begun so there would be produce with which to pay the cowherd. The farm in turn required labor, and in addition the boy had to live nearby in order to oversee it. So a house was constructed. Who is to run the house? A wife is necessary. So the boy married and threw away the loincloth, which was the cause of the whole mess in the first place.

When the guru returned to that area after some time to check on his disciple's progress he was amazed to see a large farmhouse and cultivated fields where he had expected to find jungle. Outside the gate of the house was a watchman who asked the guru what business he had in the neighborhood, When the guru asked where his boy might be the watchman replied, "Sahib? Oh, he is in his house." The guru said to himself, "Wah, wah, my boy, so you have become a great man, a sahib," and went into the house to meet the boy. After the usual greetings he told his disciple, "Look how you have got yourself reentangled in the world. Now don't worry, I am here to save you. Forget all this and come back with me to the jungle."

The boy replied, "Oh, no, Maharaj, this is much more to my liking; I intend to stay here."

The guru didn't say anything else, but just went off a little distance to meditate. Within a short time the disciple's mind changed completely. He realized the cage he had created for himself, and he left everything and returned to his guru. This is the kind of guru to have: one who once he accepts you as his disciple never forsakes you until the end, come what may. The bond between guru and disciple is stronger than any other, which is why the guru is to be respected even before God.

People come to me for many reasons, you know. Basically, though, they come because they are miserable. Most of them have worldly miseries and are satisfied with worldly happiness, which is why I don't talk to most people about spirituality. Most people are just not interested in experiencing anything other than food, sleep, and sex, no matter what they may claim. I'm sorry, but it's true. And the few who are after more in life are mainly after the happiness which the world can provide them: fame, money, possessions, children, whatever. Very, very few are really interested in spirituality.

And this is the way it should be. If everyone became spiritual and lost interest in the world all our society would grind to a halt. So the Yoga which teaches you to go out into the jungle is not meant to be taught to everyone. This is why I have not been able to find language foul enough to express how I feel about the so-called Yogis, Swamis, and godmen who India has been exporting to the West to teach spirituality. Yoga is not a system of physical jerks; know it once and for all. Yoga is meant to make every home a happy home. When every family member is giving out his or her best to unite the family and make it a success, that is real Yoga. And I don't mean the family you were born into or married into, necessarily. Whoever you live with is your family. As we say in Sanskrit, "vasudeva kutumbam" — we are all members of God's family.

So when people come to me for instruction I don't tell them to do exercises or to pay priests to do some rituals on their behalf or to go on pilgrimage or anything else like that. I tell them to first clear up their personal lives. Most people are not destined to become truly spiritual in this lifetime and there is no use in trying to force them to; they will just become miserable. If they are downright materialistic, well, I always say, "For those who believe in God no proof of His existence is necessary; for those who do not believe in God no proof is possible." If they are partly materialistic and partly spiritual, the true guru will see that they marry happily and live contentedly and observe simple spiritual practices. This will ensure their progression for future lives. The ones who are destined for it, the ones who have already done plenty of preparation in past existences, will be taught fully.

The guru does not need his physical body to guide you, remember. He may use other teachers or he may work directly through Nature. The first year of my life I took mother's milk; the next five years, nothing but cow's milk. For the next eight years I lived on nothing but three fistfuls of chickpeas. I would soak them overnight in water and then take one fistful morning, afternoon, and evening. No one told me to do it; it just seemed to me to be the right thing to do. Then for three and a half years I ate nothing but green chilies and water. When I finally started eating what people would call "normal" food I began by taking only raw vegetables because I wanted something crunchy, something to bite; you know how animals always prefer their food to be raw. For twenty-three years I never tasted salt, just because I didn't want to.

One day during my boyhood I was standing alone doing nothing in particular when suddenly, like a bolt of lightning, I heard a mantra. I liked it and started to repeat it. No one told me to do so, but I got such a good feeling from it that soon I was repeating it most of the time. You see how Nature works?

When I was in the first year of college my classmates and I went to Benares on a university tour. I met two saints while I was there. One was Bhaskarananda Saraswati, the sadhu who predicted to Lady Willingdon that she would become Vicereine of India. He was honored with a formal reception by the grateful lady when this occurred. Imagine — a naked ascetic, walking through a cordon of honor composed of troopers with drawn swords!

The other saint I met was Telang Swami. He has now left his body, after a life of more than 370 years. He weighed only about 300 pounds, and he had short white hair and a short beard; he never had anything to do with clothing except for a 1,008-bead rosary. He is the only person in the history of Benares ever to perform a ritual bath of Kashi Vishveshvara, the presiding deity of Benares, with his own urine and feces. When he did this one of the temple priests was so outraged that he came over and slapped Telang Swami, who didn't bother in the least about it and merely went off. That night the King of Benares saw Kashi Vishveshvara in a dream. The god told him, "Telang Swami is my very essence; how dare anyone insult him?" The next day the King tried to locate the priest to punish him, but learned he had died suddenly during the night. Telang Swami was a wonderful Aghori.

When I met him, he motioned to me to come over and sit next to him — he never spoke for almost 100 years — and he started playing with my hair and rubbing the back of my head. I left, and I don't know what he did to me but back in Bombay I began experiencing some queer things. One night Telang Swami came to me in a dream and requested me to return to Benares to visit him again, which I did. At that time I had no inkling of the nature of the relationship between us; later when I met my Junior Guru Maharaj I learned that Telang Swami was his disciple. This made us guru-brothers, and in his magnanimity he was helping to prepare me for what was to happen next.

After some time a few of my classmates took me to see a Jain ascetic by the name of Jina Chandra Suri. The old man peered at me and after a close inspection requested me to bring my horoscope to him the next day. I did, and, after carefully perusing it, he inquired about my willingness to learn astrology, palmistry, and physiognomy from him. I don't know what made me agree, but I agreed, and I studied with him for three years. He taught me how to construct Yantras and perform rituals; I enjoyed it.

One day he casually asked me to accompany him on a trip outside Bombay. He took me to Janakpur, up in the erstwhile Darbhanga State which is now part of Bihar. I thought we were just on a holiday, and for two or three days I had a fine time. The villagers were very hospitable, and I enjoyed a good rest.

On the new-moon night, though, everything went wrong. Jina Chandra Suri came and met me and started speaking very sweetly to me. I wondered what had come over him. There was certainly no need for such ingratiating behavior. I now know he was just fattening me up for the kill, because after all the preliminaries he told me, "Now you are going to do Shava Sadhana."

I had no idea what he was talking about. When I asked him he explained that a fresh corpse, or Shava, had been obtained and that I was to sit on the corpse and perform a ritual. Apparently he had looked into my horoscope and realized that I could succeed at this sort of sadhana. He must have planned out the whole drama over the last three years.

Well, I told him I had no intention of doing anything like sitting on a corpse and performing sadhana. I had done some Yoga before, but our family worships Krishna, and for us it is unthinkable to have anything to do with dead bodies or spirits or anything like them.

Besides, since childhood I could never see a corpse without breaking out in a sweat and falling into a faint, all because I so strongly self-identified with the dead individual. Once or twice when I was out driving I met a funeral procession and actually lost control of the car and allowed it to run onto the footpath; it was very dangerous. So I couldn't even imagine what would happen to me were I to sit on a corpse.

Jina Chandra Suri started to try to convince me, but I was adamant. Finally he lost his temper; it was the first time I had ever seen the old man get angry. He told me, "If you refuse to do it I'll perform the ritual myself on *your* corpse!"

I flared up: "Who do you think you are threatening?" I assumed he was talking through his hat. To show he meant business he motioned to a group of drunken tribals who were standing nearby, holding knives, clubs, and other weapons. At his signal they walked over and surrounded me.

I was really in a fix. If I did the sadhana there was a very good chance I'd die of sheer terror, or because some spirit would catch hold of me, or maybe the deity Herself would decide to take me as a sacrifice. But if I didn't do it, it was definite I would die. I decided that if I was going to die either way then I might as well perform the ritual, since there would be at least some minor chance of survival that way.

When I informed the old man that I would do it he immediately brightened up and became cheerful again. He started explaining the details of the ritual to me: how to position the corpse, how to sit on it, how to tie the lifeless thumbs and toes. Then he made me drink a full bottle of country liquor. I am the son of a Hindu merchant, and until that moment in my life I had never even touched an egg, much less a piece of meat or a drop of alcohol. But there was no choice; I took a big pull from the bottle. My God! I thought my throat was on fire! Tears came to my eyes; after all, it was my first time. Jina Chandra Suri was so overjoyed by my agreeing to do the sadhana that he became very solicitous about my condition. Seeing the effect of the moonshine on me he was so concerned he actually picked up the bottle and started feeding it to me a little at a time.

By the time I had finished the whole bottle all my fear had gone. This was the first time I had ever felt real fear in my entire life and, let me tell you, I was really scared. The only thing left for me was to foul my pants, I was so desperate. I was sweating, my hands were shaking, I was overwhelmed with terror. By the end of that bottle, though, I had lost every iota of my fear. I had made up my mind that I would either succeed at that sadhana or die trying: there was no way out. Challenge and response, the law of the jungle. I was ready.

This is the beautiful effect of alcohol: you never fear or hesitate once you've taken it. It has a number of side effects, no doubt, and very few people use it for the right purposes. But for certain practices it is essential. It was really a good thing that I drank that moonshine, because it helped me out in several ways.

Then I was taken to the corpse. It was that of a young girl of about fifteen, very pretty. She belonged to a tribe whose members pressed oil from seeds to earn a living. She had been dead only a few hours and was so lovely that I forgot the ritual, the danger, the fear, and everything else and started thinking only of her. She was beautiful in the way only primitive people can be beautiful. Not an ounce of excess fat, not a wrinkle on her skin. Her thighs? Solid like trees. Her breasts? Absolutely firm. I found myself wishing she were still alive so I could take her off alone to a quiet place and we could enjoy together. I was even ready to marry her, she looked so lovely. This was not necrophilia or anything perverted; I was just very drunk and I was sorry she was dead and unable to play about with me. I am telling you the truth about all this so you'll have some idea of what it was like.

While I was drinking they had taken her to the appropriate spot and pointed her head in the correct direction. Jina Chandra Suri, who was looking very pleased with himself, handed me an object and explained: "I am giving you my Yantra which I worshipped for forty years in Assam. It will take care of you. There is nothing to worry about. I am going to sit over there," he said, motioning to a spot about a hundred yards away, "and repeat mantras for your protection."

He then took a black thread and did Kilana in a big circle around me. *Kila* means nail, and *Kilana* is meant to "nail off" or seal off an area to prevent any troublemaking spirit from disturbing your concentration. As long as you remain within the circle you are safe. The moment you step outside the circle you've had it: you become a spirit yourself unless there is some ethereal being nearby who can come to your rescue, which is highly unlikely.

After the Kilana the old man told me which mantra to recite, gave me a *japamala*, or rosary, to count the repetitions, and shoved a dish of raw meat and a bowl of wine in front of me. The idea was that when the Goddess appeared, in the form of an animal, I should offer the meat and wine to please Her. Satisfied with my worship, She would tell me to ask for a boon, and I should reply, "Do whatever my guru says to do," meaning Jina Chandra Suri. This was all the old man's idea, of course, and I had no intention of saying anything like that. First I wanted to see whether or not the sadhana would actually work, and then if it did I would think about what to ask Her for.

Jina Chandra Suri walked off and sat down to start doing japa for my protection, and I knelt on the corpse in the manner I had been shown. The supine girl's mouth was open and had been filled with oil. The old man had showed me how to make a wick of raw cotton, and I lit my wick from one of the torches the tribals were carrying. Since it was a new moon night there was absolute blackness except for this lamp, and I could see nothing but the poor girl's face, which looked ghastly, grotesque in the flickering light of the flame. All my previous desire for enjoyment with her melted away as I peered down into her open, fixed, unstaring eyes. Both of us were stark naked, and her cold body underneath mine caused a sort of creepy feeling to spread through my body and mind.

Here again the alcohol saved me. Being drunk I was able to shake off the dread and begin my japa, gazing full into her face to concentrate my mind there. The old man had warned me that if she tried to get up I should knock her down and pin her firmly, so I was intently watching for the least twitch or flinch in her body to alert me to the danger. I suppose this is the most terrifying part of Shava Sadhana, because it is an immense strain on your nerves if the corpse suddenly tries to sit up and begins to growl and scream at you. Many people have died of fright at this stage. One old fellow died right in front of me. He was trying to show off and challenged me to a contest. We procured two corpses. The idea was to see who could bring life into one most quickly and control it most firmly. I warned him that he was too old to be trying such stunts but he was beyond reasoning with. As soon as the corpse started to sit up and he tried to control it, the spirit which had been forced to sit in the corpse caught hold of him. His nerves failed, his heart failed, and he died.

But I didn't have this problem on that first night, which is good since otherwise I probably would not be sitting here telling you this story now. I sat and did my japa. I don't know how many I did, but it can't have been too many before I suddenly began to get a very eerie, extremely queer feeling, and I saw a pair of eyes watching me from the darkness.

The animal, a jackal, approached me, snarling and baring its teeth. I don't know what came over me — it must have been the alcohol, because I was so drunk I didn't care for man or beast — but I became furious. I forgot everything I had been told to do, I forgot the wine and meat I was supposed to offer. I reached out of the circle which had been drawn on the ground to protect me and I grabbed the jackal. I was really incensed, and said to it: "So, you want blood, do you? Take this!" And I stuck my hand into its mouth. That liquor really did me immense good; I don't know what I would have done without it.

The Goddess, who was temporarily in the form of the jackal, was interested only in blood. One of the beast's teeth pricked my hand between the thumb and index finger, and the jackal licked up the drop of blood that oozed out — and then all of a sudden there was Smashan Tara standing before me, smiling, asking what I wanted from Her.

Tears come to my eyes whenever I remember that scene. For years the scar remained on my hand as a reminder of the night when I was there in that cemetery sitting on that corpse, and I caught my first glimpse of Smashan Tara. I don't know what your condition would be if you were to catch sight of Her. You might even die of shock. She is very tall, and Her skin is a beautiful deep midnight-blue color. Her eyes are beautiful; that's the only way I know to describe them. She has a long red tongue lolling from Her mouth. Blood, the blood She is eternally drinking, drips slowly from the tip. She is *ghatastani*, or pot-breasted, and *lambodari*, or full-bellied. Around Her neck there is a garland of freshly severed human heads which are freshly bleeding. She wears wristlets and armlets of bones, and anklets of snakes. Her four hands grasp a pair of scissors, a sword, a noose, and a skull. She wears a skirt of human arms, and to me She is one of the loveliest beings in the universe, because She is my Mother.

I suppose I should have been frightened at this terrific vision, but actually when I saw Ma for the first time I felt as if I had known Her before, perhaps in some previous birth, and that this was just a continuation of that previous sadhana. I am sure this is the case because otherwise it would have been impossible for me to achieve so quickly.

Anyway, She asked me what I wanted and I told Her, "Look, I never did this for myself. I never wanted to do anything like this. That fellow sitting over there made me do it. I don't want anything except to go back to Bombay."

"Don't worry," Tara assured me, "I'll see that you get to Bombay, but first you have to ask for something."

"But I don't want anything except to go back to Bombay."

"But you have to ask for something," Tara insisted, smiling.

"Just get me out of here first. Take me to Bombay and then I'll ask for something."

Tara laughed and told me to close my eyes. I did, and when I opened them again I was in my bedroom in our family mansion in Bombay, soaked in sweat from fear and shock. I was stunned for at least fifteen minutes and did not even know where I was. I walked from room to room like a zombie, trying to convince myself I was really back home. Gradually I realized that I had indeed returned to Bombay, and that thought gave me some relief. I was still drunk, so there was nothing to do but go to sleep.

When I woke up at 11 A.M. I had a terrible hangover. Of course I didn't know then it was a hangover because I had never experienced one before. All I knew was that my head was splitting open, bursting at the seams. I called my servant Dhondu and told him to bring me some Bayer aspirin. It came as a powder back then, so I took two teaspoonsful, and after half an hour or so I started sweating and my headache disappeared.

I felt good enough to start planning my revenge on Jina Chandra Suri for daring to lie to me about the purpose of our jaunt and getting me into such a situation: "I'll never see his face again. No — I'll butcher him. Let him return to Bombay and we'll see how long his head remains on his shoulders."

Thinking in this way I suddenly remembered the Yantra and rosary which were still with me. I said to myself, "Wait, I'm safe here in my own home. Let me try this out." There was some doubt in my mind that I had imagined or dreamed the whole thing. Just as an experiment I sat down and started doing japa. I had not finished even one hundred repetitions when Tara appeared in front of me again and asked me what I wanted from Her.

I said, "Ma, I really never had any intention of doing Shava Sadhana, and I don't want anything."

Again She smiled and said, "Ask Me for something." When Ma wants to give you something She creates a situation so that you must accept it. I finally had to tell Her, "Ma, I never wanted any of this, but now that I've succeeded I would most like for You to come to me every day and permit me to worship You."

She said, "But I can't come here. You will have to go daily to the smashan."

And that is just what I did. At that time Bombay was not so crowded as it is today, and the smashans were very lonely places. I began with the Worli smashan. A friend of mine would drive me there every night and wait in the car while I did my work. I had arranged for a man to provide me with fresh coconut water nightly. After offering it to Ma I would drink the rest as Her prasad, a gift from Her to me. There was an old fakir, a Muslim ascetic, named Mishkin Shah, who lived nearby and who knew why I visited the cemetery nightly. After we met we became good friends and I would have tea with him every night.

Ma would come to me nightly and we'd talk. After some time, when I knew Her better, I asked Her to show me all Her forms: Chinnamasta, who carries Her head in Her hands and drinks Her own blood as it gushes from Her neck; Bagalamukhi, who has the head of a crane, or heron; and all the rest of the Great Goddesses. Many rituals were involved in achieving success at the sadhanas for them all. I also had to perform Shava Sadhana twice more, each time with a different technique. For instance, the second time I did Shava Sadhana I did it on the corpse of a man instead of a woman, and the third time I did it on the corpse of a woman who had died while pregnant.

Jina Chandra Suri was not there to "assist" me those next two times I did Shava Sadhana. A few days after my experience in Janakpur he returned to Bombay and came to meet me. He began by praising me: "I am so pleased with you, my boy. I knew you could do it from the first time I saw your horoscope

Now do just as I say and we'll be able to collect plenty of money from all the maharajas and merchants."

I told him, "I will do nothing of the sort. You forced me to go and do a sadhana which I never would have done willingly. I will allow you to leave with your life only because you introduced me to my Mother. I must show my appreciation to you for such a boon, even though your wicked, dirty mind had different plans for me. Were it not for this I would ask Her to make a nice mince of you, just as you had planned to do to me. Now please get out."

First he pleaded a little. Then when he saw I was intransigent he got wild: "I'll perform a death ritual on you!"

I lost my temper, but I just laughed in his face and said, "Now I spend twenty-four hours of the day in the lap of my Mother, so your puny threats do not worry me at all. But my Mother may not like to hear you abusing Her son; I suggest you keep quiet."

This only infuriated him further: "Give me back my Yantra!" he shouted. I told him firmly, "I am not going to give you anything. It is time for you to leave," and I had him bodily ejected from my house. And what happened? After some time he raped a little teenaged girl, and that was the end of all his spiritual power. Thereafter he earned his living by making Yantras for rich Jain merchants, charging them 10,000 or 15,000 rupees each (about $1,000 to $1,500).

We kept up our relationship, however. I guess it was because he knew the power of Smashan Tara, since he had worshipped Her for forty years, and he probably still thought he might be able to get some benefit from Her through me. Sometimes he would come and meet me at my house, but the connection between us was strained.

He was unique, really, in his own way. As far as astrology, palmistry, and physiognomy are concerned he was a master. He had been able to dig up a number of buried treasures and texts. I have never met anyone in this world who could exceed his ability to make other people rich. "Why do you want to waste your time on spiritual things?" he would always tell me. "Do your penance, then cash in on it, make money, and enjoy your life. You are from a merchant's family, which means you are meant to make money, not be spiritual. Spirituality is for Brahmins."

He had himself owned tea estates earlier in his life and had fallen in love with an English girl, the daughter of a fellow tea planter. Everyone was against them and succeeded in breaking up the relationship. He was so disgusted with the whole situation that he left everything and became an ascetic.

Although he had worshipped Smashan Tara for forty years he never dared try to perform Shava Sadhana himself; he knew he could never succeed. He did attempt to make one Rati Bhai do Shava Sadhana, but as soon as Rati Bhai reached the smashan he got such a fright that he fouled his pants and then fainted. He has not fully recovered from the effect, even today.

Unfortunately for Jina Chandra Suri, I was a very different sort and paid no attention to him. I was listening only to my Mother, Smashan Tara. It is only by Her grace that I have achieved whatever I have achieved in this life.

I never told Ma that he should rape that little girl, mind you. I don't like rape; it makes me furious. It is one of the three acts which supposedly can't be atoned for or forgiven, along with murder of your guru, and gambling. What happened to Jina Chandra Suri was that Ma withdrew Her protection from him, and his mind was overcome with desire. He could have satisfied his desire in other ways but he could not restrain himself and this is what resulted. And besides, there must have been some karmic connection there, otherwise there never would have been an opportunity for him to be alone with her long enough to rape her. Had this old man been in his senses he could have postponed the repayment of this karmic debt for some future lifetime, but because his balance of mind was lost, his natural underlying lust which had been suppressed all those years suddenly spurted out. It is a fine thing to collect great spiritual power, but you are headed for trouble if you ever lose control over it.

You know, one person may do sadhana for years and years and still get no result, whereas someone else may only do a very small amount of penance and get a very great result, as was the case with me and my Shava Sadhana. It looks unfair, doesn't it? But the person who achieves easily in this lifetime must have spent many, many lifetimes of tough austerities, just as Kalidasa did, to reach the point where only a small further effort will bring results. Someday I'll tell you the story of Kalidasa. Right now I have a better story for you. Listen!

One time an Aghori decided to perform Shava Sadhana. Naturally he couldn't do it in the city because the people there would be scandalized and would accuse him of black magic and attack him. To avoid this he procured a corpse, carried it out into the deep jungle, sat on top of it, and began to do his japa.

A woodcutter happened to pass nearby and, seeing the Aghori and the corpse, took fright and climbed a tree to hide. While he was in the tree the woodcutter overheard the mantra which the Aghori was repeating. He was repeating it aloud to improve his pronunciation, which was proof he was still raw, because a real Aghori never speaks a mantra aloud.

Suddenly from out of nowhere a tiger appeared and with one cuff from its paw killed the Aghori. Immediately it began to lap up the freely flowing blood. Tigers always do that to a fresh kill. While it was busily engaged in slaking its thirst for blood, the tiger was frightened by a sound nearby and plunged into the deep underbrush.

The woodcutter knew well that a tiger always returns to its kill, but he had become curious about the whole thing and in spite of the danger got down from the tree to investigate. Then he wondered to himself, "Why shouldn't I try this out?" He sat on the fresh corpse of the Aghori and started to repeat the mantra he had overheard. After less than a hundred repetitions the deity suddenly appeared in front of him and said, "Ask for a boon!"

The woodcutter told Her, "Ma, I have only done this out of curiosity."

Ma told him, "That doesn't matter. What does matter is that I have come to you. Now ask for something."

He said, "All right then, tell me which law states that this fellow should not succeed even after long penance and that I should achieve within seconds?"

Ma smiled and said, "Close your eyes." When he did he saw that he had been doing this same sadhana for the past ten births. Ma continued: "Do you understand now? If you hadn't done this before, how could you have remembered the mantra? How would you have developed the courage to attempt the sadhana knowing the tiger would return at any moment? I was the tiger who killed this Aghori. I made him come here, where I knew you would be waiting. I gave you the intelligence to remember the mantra and do the sadhana. You had only a few japas left remaining from your past birth in order to get Siddhi, and now you have it. This Aghori must still go through two more lives before he gets an opportunity like this. Now ask me for something!"

The woodcutter said, "Ma, all that I desire is that you should keep me forever in Your sweet gaze." In that instant, he was made.

When I said he was made, I mean he obtained Siddhi. Not *Kaya Siddhi*, which is immortality, or *Maya Siddhi*, which is control over the mundane world. When you have one of these, of course, you have the other as well. No, I mean the Siddhi of having Ma with him twenty-four hours a day. Ma took possession of him. Not of his body, because if She had come for his body he would have become immortal. She possessed his mind; She plugged him into the Universal Computer so that he was able to get answers for any question, and could continuously play about with Her.

Ma came to me in the same way. Only because of the efforts of my past lives did I get the desire to study with Jina Chandra Suri; I could have easily refused. And unless I had done it in some previous existence I would never have agreed to do Shava Sadhana, even under threat of death. Ma wanted me to do it, that's all. And what I have gained by succeeding at Her sadhana is beyond speech. She taught me how to move around in my subtle body; She made me clairaudient and clairvoyant. I can go anywhere in the world without leaving my chair; nothing can be hidden from me.

I am talking as if I do these things, but in fact it is beyond me to do anything. Only Ma can do it; She does it all. When someone who is afflicted by disease comes to me Ma tells me the treatment. Sometimes She will tell me, "This person does not deserve to get well," or, "It is not in this person's destiny to be cured." Whereupon I ask Her, "Then why did you send this particular individual to me, if you didn't want them to be benefited in some way?" And then Her compassion flows and something incomprehensible occurs and the person is cured. I always pray to Her, "Ma, make me a leper, ruin me, do whatever You like but don't ever remove me from Your lap." And I know She hears me. This is the foundation of all my confidence in my abilities. Do I have any capabilities? Ha! Everything is from Ma.

My ideas are individual, no one else knows about them. People sometimes ask me, "How can you have learned so much in such a short span of sixty years?" I tell them, "I studied at Jnanaganj at Manasasarovara." *Jnanaganj* — heap of knowledge. *Manasasarovara* — ocean of the mind. My knowledge is all *Nijajnana*, knowledge from within, from Ma. My mentor has taught me a wonderful method of being able to tune in on knowledge from anywhere, with Ma's help.

Other people have wondered, "How can you treat someone as terrifying as Smashan Tara as your Mother?" They can ask such stupid questions only because they are ignorant. Once you know the meaning of the form in which you see Smashan Tara you will be able to understand why She is the Universal Mother.

# CHAPTER TWO

# SHAKTI

*When I'm disgusted, fed up with the world, I always turn to my Mother. She comes to me in any form I request, and we play that way. Sometimes She comes as my Mother, sometimes as my wife, sometimes as my child. She's always with me; She'll never go away. Long ago we promised each other to stay together always. If She ever leaves me I will not live even an instant longer. Who is She? My ego, the Shakti which self-identifies with my body. If She leaves me I have to die. Most people don't know the true value of the ego, and they misuse Her. But I think I am the luckiest man in the world, because my Smashan Tara has taught me all about my own ego, and how to realize Her as Adya, the Original Shakti. She is the being to be realized.*

## MAYA SHAKTI

Ma is the source of all knowledge, the source of both delusion and release from delusion. She is the foundation and supporter of this universe and of all possible universes. She is called *Adya* because Adya means "that which is first and which is therefore eternal, which has no beginning and no end, which is ever-existent." This is the only way She can form the base of the cosmos. If She too were subject to creation and destruction, what sort of foundation would She be? No. She is beyond everything, and She is the source of everything.

Though She is without beginning and without end, She may exist in either the manifested or the unmanifested state. When manifested She acts as the source of the universe in Her kinetic form; when the universe dissolves She becomes quiescent, She ceases to exist. Energy is equally energetic whether it is kinetic or potential; only its form differs.

And remember, you may eventually learn a few things if you work hard enough, but you will never be able to discover the origin of the Universal Mother, Adya. You should not even try to find out about it, because it is not to be known. It is just not knowable. But when you become Ma Herself, then there is no question of any distinction between the knower and the known. How can there be any knowledge of Ma when you have become Ma Herself?

Ma, Shakti, Maya: These three words describe Her. But each emphasizes a different attribute. *Maya* is Her delusive aspect, Her capacity to bind one to limited forms. *Shakti* is Her aspect of power and energy. And Ma? *Ma* indicates Her maternal aspect, the Motherhood of God.

Everyone is afraid of Maya because her job is to entice, entrap, enthrall, to prevent people from escaping the cycle of birth and death. Why should they be afraid of Her unless they are not confident that they can resist Her blandishments? It is not as if She feels hatred or envy or any other selfish emotion for the beings She enslaves; how can She? She is just doing Her job.

All these so-called swamis who say that Maya is evil are absolutely wrong. How can She be evil? She is the Mother of all worlds. I shouldn't even call these charlatans swamis, because *swami* means "owner" or "master." A real swami is the owner or master of himself, and if you are really master of yourself, Maya cannot have any effect on you and you would have no reason to fear or hate Her. These cheats make such a mess of a thing that it becomes difficult to untangle the mess and explain the reality.

You must try to understand that Maya can exist only where there is duality. The universe is full of pairs of basic principles: male and female, positive and negative, active and passive. Our philosophy maintains that the Soul is only one, indivisible, in the state of *Sat-Chit-Ananda* (existence-consciousness-bliss). But the Soul cannot enjoy itself unless there is some observer, someone who can perceive the Reality. Observers cannot exist when the whole universe is in a state of nonduality because all is one; no distinction between observer and observed would be possible. To satisfy this urge for an observer, Shakti projects Herself. This Shakti is *Adya*, the undifferentiated form, the totality of all universes. She is as unbounded and absolute as is the Universal Soul or Atman, and the only difference between them is that She feels Herself to be separated from Him, the male principle, the unchanging Atman, and this gives Her the impetus to try to locate Him and reunite with Him.

Adya is Herself unaware of how She projects. The whole projection is spontaneous because of joy, the overwhelming joy of existence or Sat-Chit-Ananda. Because the process of this projection is unknown to everyone it is called Maya.

Eventually Adya Herself begins to become individualized. Within Her, separate egos develop and become individuals. At some point these proliferated forms begin to grope for the Ultimate; at this point the Universal Soul gets the observers He had yearned for. Every individual begins this quest hesitantly, but every individual will one day or another reunite with the Unmanifest. Separately the Soul and Adya are impotent; together they create a beautiful play. When the play is over the projection is reabsorbed into the "projector" until the next cycle of creation. Isn't it wonderful?

People still ask me, "Why does Maya entice us if She is supposed to be part and parcel of the Divine Motherhood of God?" It is not so difficult to understand. Each man and woman are part of the Cosmic Male and Female Principles. In each human, buried down deep inside, is the remembrance of the indescribable bliss of Unity, of the joy which caused the projection in the first place. However, this originally pure impulse of joy must pass through the causal, subtle, and gross physical bodies, which are like sheaths surrounding the indwelling Soul. As the impulse passes through each sheath on its way to our waking consciousness, it is slightly refracted or perverted by our limitations. The purity is deflected slightly in each passage so that by the time the impulse becomes conscious it is more or less impure, depending on the individual. That is the true Maya: a pure impulse filtered down into our limited conscious minds which incites us to perform karmas which, in turn, tighten our bondage to the samsara.

The individual personality, when it is overcome by joy, creates multiple thought waves which project for their own fulfillment. It is like the cosmic projection, but, because of impurities, it is limited. These thought waves are projected from the causal body as a result of past karmas and are therefore imperfect. Most people forget that these thoughts are simply temporary manifestations and they try to cling to them, or avoid them altogether should they be uncomfortable. But if you know something about them you can choose the way that they are destroyed. That is why my mentor taught me that complete gratification of desire is the only way to become free of Maya. When all the imperfect projections are eliminated then only can you see the real thing.

Maya is very terrifying, it is true. In fact, to frighten is really the function of Maya. Maya will always frighten you, or try to, but She will never hit you if you try to come near. People are afraid they'll be finished if they leave off whatever they are doing in their lives: "If I lose all my money, what will become of me?" But everyone is going to be finished sooner or later. If you tell Maya, "I came into the world naked and I will go out naked. Do whatever you please, I don't care," then you can succeed at sadhana. A spiritual aspirant must be fearless, because then no harm can come to him; all danger arises from his own fear. This is especially true in Aghora. The spirits in the smashan will try to terrify you, and believe me they know how to do it. As long as you keep your wits about you they can't do anything to you. One little doubt, though, and you are very likely to make a mistake in your sadhana, and even the slightest error may mean excruciating death, and then perennial membership in the fraternity of spirits.

Maya is the external garb of the universe. When a lady is well-dressed, ornamented, and made-up she may appear to be beautiful, but if you strip her naked you will be able to count all her flaws, scars, marks, excess hair, or whatever. When you see Maya, you must look underneath to find out Her real nature.

A green mango is very pleasing to the eye but quite sour to the tongue. However, with a little discrimination you realize the green mango is just a stage in its development. And when you see the golden ripe mango you know it must be sweet. You must become aware of the impermanence of the green state and not rely on it to remain.

The projection is dynamic; thus it is called *Shakti*. Shakti is energy. It emanates spontaneously and is then controlled. Shakti must always be controlled, otherwise it is worthless or dangerous, just like uncontrolled electricity. Shakti is of value only when it has been conditioned. Lord Shiva is the conditioner, the male aspect of the Universal Soul. He is always depicted with three eyes. As long as his third eye is closed Maya can exist because then Shiva has but two eyes, duality; and Maya is the essence of duality. But when the third eye (the eye of *Jnana* — transcendent wisdom) opens, He sees only unity. That third eye cannot differentiate in any way and so the cosmos, which can exist only through duality, must be dissolved. As long as Lord Shiva's third eye is open, nothing can exist but the undifferentiated condition. When it again closes then Shiva becomes subject to duality, and the cosmos can again arise.

And this is why Smashan Tara has three eyes. She is both the manifestation of duality and the possessor of Jnana, so loving Her will never bring you grief. That is why She is called Tara: She makes you cross over the sea of duality and reach Unity. Tara will never fail you — far from it! But if you love Maya, who is pure duality, you will become trapped in the manifested world for millions of births to come. You have the choice of loving Maya or Ma, the superficial or the deep. You can't do both. Ma is never cruel; She always gives you what you desire.

If you want Maya, Ma's skin, you get it. And Ma will see that you get it until you are satiated with it.

Ma believes in giving you what you want. She gives it directly from Her own being, because She is a Mother. A mother feeds her own essence to her child in the form of milk. When you ask Ma for gratification of your mundane desires, that is just what you will get. She will keep you in the mundane world drinking the milk of Maya as long as you ask to remain there.

If you dream of sex daily throughout your life it is likely that you'll be craving sex at the moment of death too, so Ma will say, "All right, my child, if you want sex take as much as you can." And She will help you enjoy plenty of sex by seeing that you are born as a pigeon or a cock or a sparrow. And when you have had enough, when you are thoroughly satisfied, when you cry, "Stop it! Please stop it!" then Ma will make you move on to new things.

Ma wants you to learn your lesson. That is why you find a meat-eater reborn either as a predator or prey or as both in succession. Human beings cry a lot at funerals of their own kind but they have absolutely no thought for the sufferings of the animals they slaughter. They never hesitate to kill and eat. Just think, first they kill the chicken. Often they will cut its throat and let it bleed to death, which is a most painful way to die. Then it will be cleaned, cooked, and eaten, and if it happens to be tough everyone will curse it for not satisfying their palates. How many humans would give beautiful tender lean meat if they were slaughtered, dressed, prepared, and served?

Meat-eaters conveniently forget that animal mothers too love their children. Do they ever think of the agony a hen goes through when her chicks are slain in front of her eyes? Or a cow, the embodiment of motherliness, do they consider how much she suffers when she sees the slaughter of her beloved calf whom she has grown in her own body and nourished with her milk, whom she loves more than her own life? Do these so-called humans ever think of the terrible pain they cause te the mother cow? Could they endure their own children being murdered before their own eyes?

How is Ma to teach such donkeys? They are not humans,

whose intellect is subtle enough to self-identify with another being of a different species and experience its personal joys and sorrows. Ma has no alternative but to make them suffer as they have made other beings suffer, allowing the animals they have tortured to torture them in return. Fair's fair, after all. If I cut your throat in this birth you have every right to cut mine in the next or in some succeeding birth. Experience is the best teacher, and a fool will learn from no other.

Actually Ma is not enticing us at all; we are enticing ourselves. We look at Ma and see what we want to see. All these deities are our own projections, and our existences are our own projections. If we project the desire for flesh onto Ma, She will provide us with flesh, whether it's for eating or copulation. That's why I say about most so-called humans today, that their entire cultural refinement consists of eating flesh and putting flesh into flesh. I believe in going beyond the skin, beyond the flesh, the bone, the marrow, and everything else, and getting to the essence.

If you want to progress spiritually you must forget everything except the face of the Mother. She will offer you the entire cosmos to make sure you have no desires left. But when you arrive at the stage where you can pass up all temptations, when you succeed and She accepts you as Her own child, then you never again have anything to worry about. Once when Ma came to me She told me, "I'll make you ruler of the world!" I laughed and said, "Ma, thanks to Thy grace I know some of my previous births, and I know I've already attained the most the world can offer. I don't need to do it again. All I want is Thee." And She smiled and accepted me.

# KALI AND KALIDASA

Ma taught me well. She let me know about some of my previous births, the ones that mattered most to my present existence. But she didn't want me to learn everything at once For a play to be well acted sometimes it is better that the actors have no idea of what they are doing. In this way they act out their parts with greater spontaneity and feeling. When you know who you are, it changes everything.

Kalidasa's poetry is taught in schools and colleges all over India, but only a few people know the story of his life, even though he was India's greatest classical poet. He was a great devotee of Ma, as his name suggests: "servant (dasa) of Kali." For nine incarnations he worshipped Ma, and he ended each life by sacrificing himself. He would cut off his own head and let the blood spill over Ma's feet out of his intense love for Her.

In his tenth birth he was born amazingly stupid and horribly ugly. He couldn't even take proper care of himself, much less worship the Goddess Kali. He was a woodcutter, and since everyone knew what a dud he was they would take advantage of him by buying his wood for two rupees when the other woodcutters would sell the same quantity for ten. But he was happy to have plenty of customers, and he had enough to eat, so he was satisfied.

Now, the king of the country had a daughter who was as clever as she was beautiful, and when the time came for her to marry she announced that she would only marry the man who could defeat her at debate. Anyone who tried and failed would be executed. Many princes saw her face and fell in love with her, and all of them were beheaded when they failed to outargue her.

The king lost his temper one day and called for his minister and told him to find for him the stupidest man in the kingdom. Just to teach her a lesson he announced, "I am going to marry my daughter to him."

The minister knew better than to protest, so off he went in search of the stupidest man in the kingdom. It did not take him long to locate Kalidasa, who was busily chopping off the branch on which he was sitting when the minister walked by. He told Kalidasa that the king wanted to meet him.

Kalidasa said, "Why? I haven't done anything wrong. Why should I meet the king?" This is the way he used to talk; he was something like a fakir, always in his own mood.

The minister said, "No, no. The king wants to meet you to present you with something." When Kalidasa replied, "If the king is so anxious to meet me, he can come here," the minister ordered the two soldiers who had accompanied him to grab Kalidasa and drag him to the palace.

When the king saw Kalidasa, he was amazed that such a stupid man could exist. He told him, "I want you to marry my daughter."

Kalidasa said, "Why should I marry your daughter? There are plenty of other girls in the kingdom to choose from."

The king was not amused and said, "If you don't agree to marry my daughter your head will be chopped off." Kalidasa shrugged his shoulders.

During the wedding ceremony the princess was veiled so she couldn't see her husband properly. Afterward she went to the bedroom which had been prepared for the honeymoon. It was a beautiful rainy night, with a light drizzle falling as she looked out the open window. It was the rutting season and many of the forest animals were giving full throat to their mating calls. She saw her husband sitting quietly nearby, and thinking him to be shy she considered how to awaken in him the urge for love play. Just then a camel delivered his peculiar rasping mating call, and she coyly asked her husband, "Who is calling for his mate?" Her idea was that he should realize she wanted him to come to her like the animals do, for sex.

The Sanskrit word for camel is *ushtra*, but even that single word was beyond the ability of poor Kalidasa to pronounce and he replied, "Utru, utru." His wife lost all her erotic intoxication in that instant and thought to herself, "Can my father have really done this to me?" Then she said to Kalidasa, "You can't speak Sanskrit; you can converse only in degraded language. And you couldn't even comprehend the reason for my question. Get out, you're not fit for me." For the first time in his life Kalidasa felt hurt and insulted. It was all Ma's doing, of course; She was calling him. He was so disgusted with his condition that he left his house and wandered into a Kali temple. He started beating his head against the feet of the image — remember the influence of his nine previous births — until a few drops of blood fell onto the Goddess's feet. That was enough; the Goddess Kali Herself appeared outside the temple and banged on the door. "Let me in," She cried, "I am Kali! Ask for anything!"

Kalidasa got up and stood behind the door so She wouldn't be able to open it and shouted, "I don't trust you!" He had suddenly become vaguely aware of his previous births, and now he was afraid that Kali would again refuse to save him.

Kali said, "No, you don't understand! Trust me!"

Kalidasa said in a hurt voice. "No, why should I trust you? I trusted you nine times before and look at me now!"

Ma said sweetly, "Trust me. Just open the door a crack and see that it is really your Kali."

Kalidasa said, "I will stick my tongue out the door, that's all." And when he did, Ma struck his tongue and immediately he received divine speech. Not only that; but he became tall and handsome. You may not believe that; I don't care. But it's true. From that time forward Ma was with him twenty-four hours a day. Spontaneously, a beautiful verse in praise of Ma fell from his lips.

When Kalidasa returned to the palace, no one recognized him. But it was easy enough to gain entry to the king by reciting a poem. Back then kings loved poetry. So Kalidasa recited a poem praising the great beauty of the princess. He described the wrinkles in her hips when she turned, her high projecting breasts, the curvature of her waist, her navel. Kalidasa is famous for his similes and metaphors, so he compared each part of her body to an appropriate image from nature. And during the recitation itself the king's daughter happened to come onto the women's balcony behind the throne, and when she beheld Kalidasa she instantly fell in love with him.

When Kalidasa lifted his eyes and saw the princess, he didn't other to speak; he expressed his emotions with a look and a smile. What subtlety there is in the old ways of expression! When the princess saw this, she could no longer control herself and she said to her father, "I must marry this man; he is the only man in the world who is fit for me!"

The king indignantly replied, "Do you realize what you are saying? You are already married."

The princess said, "I don't care, I must have this man."

Imagine the surprise in the court when Kalidasa said quietly, "I am your husband." Kalidasa thanked the king for giving him his daughter in marriage. The king in turn offered Kalidasa vast lands, which were politely declined. Then the princess came down to her father's throne and in front of the entire assembly kissed her father and said, "I thank you, father, for having given me a husband worthy of my qualities." And the king, heaving a sigh of relief, was vindicated for marrying his daughter off to that poor "idiot" Kalidasa.

Kalidasa left that kingdom and went to Ujjain, where he embellished the court of King Vikramaditya. Do you know his poem *Meghaduta* in which a lonely *Yaksha* (angel) pines for the wife who has been separated from him? Kalidasa based that poem on the experience of his wedding night. In his previous condition he had been unable to express all the misery of his rejection. But thanks to the grace of Ma he took his unfortunate experience and converted it into sublime verse. If he had not been ignorant in the beginning he would never have been selected to marry the princess, he would never have been driven by desperation to pound his head on the rock, and he might never have been saved by Ma so he could win the princess back.

Ma wanted him to live for a while in the world and provide us with his sublime poetry. Suppose he had realized Her right away; would he have had the idea to get married and live a householder's life? Never. The bliss of living with Ma is billions of times greater than all mundane pleasures. She wanted to entangle him partially in Her Maya and then to save him, so that while he was working out his entanglements he would amaze the world as Her tongue, Her mouthpiece. At other times Ma will let someone worship Her for years until circumstances force that person to relinquish the bondage of Maya, and then She comes to him. It is all Her play.

# VIDYARANYA

About 600 years ago, in the time of the Vijayanagara empire in South India, the prime minister of one of the kings was named

Vidyaranya, who was a great devotee of Ma. It came to pass
that in the course of time Vidyaranya was ruined. He lost his
position and was reduced to almost nothing. All his power and
most of his wealth were taken away, and as a result his family
began to hate and abuse him. He became so fed up with everything that he decided to renounce the world and become a
hermit.

He went out into the forest and made a pledge to this effect.
Then he worshipped Ma one last time. At the height of his power, the zenith of his glory, he worshipped with the best items
available. Solid gold dishes were set aside for Ma's use, priceless jewels adorned Her, She was offered only the choicest foods.
Now, reduced to poverty, he could do nothing but prepare
unleavened bread out of mud and offer it to Her saying, "I'm
sorry, Ma. Now I have nothing, and I can no longer worship
you as I did before."

Suddenly Ma stood before him, and said, "Speak your wish."

He looked at Her quizzically and said, "Ma, what are You talking about? If You had really wanted to give me something, You
should have arrived five minutes ago. Then I could have accepted something. Now I have vowed to renounce worldly things,
so I don't want anything, not even You. I want only God."

Ma smiled at him and said, "Don't you understand yet? Close
your eyes." When he did, he saw mountains and mountains of
ashes — and a small pile of something that was still emitting
smoke. He still couldn't understand, so Ma explained it to him:
"You have been worshipping me for many years," She said, "and
by my grace all the karmas of your previous births have been
burned to ashes except that little pile, which is all that remains. If you had not lost your position you would never have
renounced life, so it was essential for you to be ruined. Do you
see?"

Vidyaranya did full prostration to Her, and immediately went
into a state of divine intoxication. Afterward, he wrote a famous
Sanskrit treatise called *Jivanmuktiviveka. That* is what grace
can do for you.

You see, when you have learned your lesson and have only
the desire for Ma remaining in your heart, She will come to

you. Then you have a chance to achieve. But when Ma does come to you, don't ask for grace. Grace is Hers to give, according to Her own sweet will. You can't get it on your own. Ask for compassion, learning, Jnana, and when you get Jnana you will know how to obtain grace.

# SARVANANDA AND PURNANANDA

In the entire world so far only two people, when Ma came to them, asked for *Sarvavidya*, the knowledge of each and every aspect of Shakti. One was Sarvananda Thakur of Bengal. I can't tell you about the other. Sarvananda was a Brahmin, the son of the court astrologer of the king of Tripura. The astrologer was able to get a son only after long years of penance of Shiva, and the boy was actually something like Shiva incarnate, but he didn't realize it until later.

One day when Sarvananda was still a young boy, his father took him to the court to show him off to the king, in hopes of some largess because of his precocity. There was an assemblage of astrologers there in the court, debating on the lunar day. Actually it was the new-moon day, but when Sarvananda was asked he opined that it was the full-moon day. This drew guffaws from the conclave of astrologers, and a slap from the embarrassed father, who was concerned about his position and how to save his face. He forgot that his son was the gift of Lord Shiva; would he have dared to slap Shiva?

The boy became angry and ran home. His old servant, Purnananda, saw the condition of his young master and, wiping his tears, consoled him a bit. Then Purnananda sent the boy out into the jungle with a knife to gather palm leaves onto which he would copy part of some astrological texts and teach the boy himself. At that time all writing was done on palm leaves.

Sarvananda climbed a palm tree, carrying the knife, and let his anger boil over by slashing at the palm leaves. Meanwhile, Nature had sent an ethereal being of a very high order to look after Sarvananda. This Siddha took a physical body and then created an illusory cobra and sent it up into the tree in which Sarvananda was sitting.

When the boy saw the snake, all his anger focused on it: "So you want to bite me," he said to the snake. "OK, but I'm going to cut you first. How do you like that?" And saying these words he hacked the snake in two by rubbing it against a sharp palm leaf. He then threw the pieces down at the base of the tree.

Now, the Siddha was sitting there, and when he felt the blood and flesh of the dead cobra fall onto his matted locks he said, "Hm-*mmm*! What's this? Come down here!" The boy descended, expecting the worst, but the Siddha merely stroked his head and said, "I know all about it, my boy, and I want to help you out." Using the snake's blood he wrote the details of the type of Shava Sadhana which would please Ma if properly performed.

Then Sarvananda returned to Purnananda and told him the whole story. Purnananda read the details and then told him, "This must be performed on a new-moon night, which is tonight. Let's do this: we'll go together to the smashan. You kill me and then sit on my corpse and do as I tell you. Then Ma will come and ask you what you want. Tell Her, 'Please revive Purnananda and do as he says.' That way Ma will appear to us both."

That night they went to the smashan and the boy cut the old man's throat and sat on his body, repeating the mantra given to him. After a few repetitions Ma appeared and asked the boy what he desired. He told Her as Purnananda had instructed him. She revived Purnananda and he too saw Her. Then She again asked, "What do you want?"

Purnananda replied, "All the so-called great astrologers ridiculed my boy for saying tonight was the full-moon night. Preserve my boy's honor."

Ma smiled, and from the nail of Her little finger a ball of light emerged which was so bright that for miles around it seemed a full moon. All the astrologers back at the court were wonderstruck.

Sarvananda was just a child, innocent of the ways of sadhanas, but he was so overcome with love for Tara that he told Her, "Ma, You have been so kind to show me Your form, but I want to see You in all Your forms, all Your manifestations, because I want to know You completely so I can love You properly." Tara smiled at him again, and agreed. Sarvananda had no idea of the meaning of Sarvavidya, but by asking for all the forms of Ma, Sarvavidya was what he received. If Nature wants you to succeed at something a situation will be created whereby you will request the right thing, knowingly or not. Purnananda actually became Sarvananda's disciple and became himself a great pandit and scholar. It was in fact Purnananda's works that inspired the late Justice Sir John Woodroffe of the Calcutta High Court to introduce the subject of Kundalini to the West under the pen name of Arthur Avalon.

And Sarvananda? He became a householder and then one day he disappeared. No one knows what became of him.

Normally you will not even think to ask for Sarvavidya; that is part of Ma's play. But even so when She gives you knowledge you become the expert, the gem in your own field.

# THE MOTHERHOOD OF THE GODDESS

Sarvananda was very lucky. Ma came to him while he was still a boy so he automatically treated Her like a mother. Only one person out of millions develops a desire to experience the Motherhood of God. There is nothing higher than the worship of the Mother because only the Mother can show the child the face of its Father. Just as a child is taught by its physical mother the identity of its father, grandparents, and other relatives, even so the Divine Mother shows Her child the face of its Father: Shiva, the Universal Soul. That is why you should try to succeed at the worship of God with attributes first, and your chosen deity will then lead you on to the attributeless Ultimate Reality. Who is the source of all attributes, after all? Ma.

Not all Aghoris treat Ma as Mother, you understand. But I think it is wisest to do so. Always remember, to control any Shakti properly is not easy, and to control Cosmic Shaktis is almost impossibly difficult. To catch hold of Kali by the hair and tell Her, "Come to me right now!" is rather dangerous.

That makes it a contest of wills, and, unless your will is stronger, Kali will frighten you into insanity or heart failure. Not because She hates you; oh no, She never hates anyone, though of course no one likes to be ordered around. No, She loves you and wants to play with you, but if an elephant wrestles with a mosquito, what will be the outcome?

If you treat Ma like your wife — and I'm not saying it's impossible; I knew one saint who did it, who projected his worship onto a statue of Ma and worshipped Her as his spouse, and eventually succeeded — and then one day find a human woman who seems attractive to you because of some connection from a past lifetime, you might suddenly find yourself projecting your worship onto the Maya, onto the flesh and blood instead of into the essence. Because your worship has built up so much energy your descent into Maya will be all the deeper, and who knows how long it might take to drag you out?

The best way to treat Shakti is as a Mother. It can save you from so many karmas also. If you look at all women as your mother would you ever think of raping or cheating or deceiving one? And if you see the Divine Mother in all beings can you ever intentionally injure anyone? No, and this automatically draws you away from the cycle of action and reaction. Ramakrishna Paramahamsa saw the Divine Mother in everyone, including even his own wife, and look what it did for him!

You can go into all the world's religions but nowhere can you find anything so sublime as our vision of the Motherhood of God. Christianity has it to some extent with the worship of the Virgin Mary, but the worship of the Mother has been perfected only in India because India is herself a mother. India has sheltered so many foreign races and religions, Jews, Zoroastrians, Christians, Muslims, etc., and has allowed them to flourish in their own ways. Has any other country ever done this? Because of this the cow is the symbol of India.

The cow is the perfect mother. She has four teats: one for her calf, one for guests including birds and animals, one for use in rituals, and one for her master. The milk is automatically divided into four equal portions; everyone is provided for. And the cow is passionately devoted to her calf, just as a real mother must be to her child. Sometimes the mere sight of the calf makes milk flow from the cow's udders; not drip — flow. I have seen this more than once when I owned a dairy. And if the calf dies the cow refuses to give milk — not like our water buffaloes who can be tricked with the head of a calf on a stick. The buffalo is the symbol of Tamas, stupidity, dullness; the cow is pure Sattva, mental brightness.

And not just buffaloes, even your Western cows will give milk whether or not the calf is still alive. When I always say that this is the fundamental difference between East and West I am not just talking through my hat. What is so great about giving milk? All animals do it. The greatness in our Indian cows is that they give milk only out of an outpouring of love. That is the value of cow's milk. Won't at least a little of that love come through into the milk? It must. That emotion separates cows from other animals. So how are we wrong to worship cows? We are not worshipping the hide, hooves, and tail; we worship the essence. A few years ago I read in the newspaper that an American cow suddenly devoured five dozen baby chicks who happened to be playing about in front of her. No Indian cow would do that; Indian cows mother little animals.

You know that Lord Krishna was called Gopala when he was a baby. *Gopala* literally means "protector of cows." There are many esoteric meanings to this word, but even the obvious meaning is beautiful. Gopala was such a lovable little baby that all the cows in the vicinity loved him more than they loved their own calves. This is why I always say that you should treat God as your Mother. The baby is the best controller of Shakti because there is no desire, no desire at all except for the mother, and, therefore, the mother will be perfectly, continuously attentive to the child.

Always sit in the Mother's lap. When you get out of Her lap and try to protect yourself She says, "All right, go on. Go ruin yourself." How can you take care of yourself? You cannot. The Law of Karma is too big for anyone to tackle alone But if you stay in the Mother's lap and always rely on Her for everything you need She will always provide it. Can any real mother ever neglect her child, or not try to make it happy? As long as you treat Ma as your own Mother She will treat you as Her own child.

How does a mother know when her child is hungry? It cries. Whenever it cries in a particular way the mother knows, "Yes, time for feeding." I know this from my own experience. When I am really angry, disgusted with the world, Ma comes to me and taps me on the shoulder, as it were, and says, "Forget all about that. Do you know . . . ?" And She proceeds to teach me something new, something I had never dreamt of, something so amazing that I become speechless and forget my anger completely. What compassion! Was there ever a mother such as She?

When the baby is not crying, however, its mother knows that its little tummy is full, and she does not bother about it. It is the same way in the world. As long as you are quietly enjoying your life as a human, Ma thinks, "Well, he is satisfied. Let him be. What use does he have for me?" And when you decide you are finished with life and want to get out of the unending cycle of birth and death, then there is only one thing to do: scream, cry out, demand that Ma should come and take care of you. And that is the only way that Ma will ever come to you. You have to desire Her much more than anything else — and there are so many obstacles to that in this dark age, in this Kali Yuga.

But if you can identify yourself with the newborn baby, then what desires remain? A baby is too innocent to be aware of any but the simplest and most essential desires. In that state there is no question of temptation. If you give a baby a choice between a chocolate and a diamond, which will it take? The chocolate, of course. A diamond has no value for a baby. And if you learn that the world has no value you will never be tempted by anything and you will be able to avoid all the obstacles which crop up in Kali Yuga. But only a baby can do that. That is why I love the baby Gopala and the baby Jesus so much.

You know, we Vedics believe that the same Rishi who incarnated on the Earth as Rama, and later as Krishna, also incarnated as Jesus. We take Jesus as one of us. But look what has happened to Christianity, to the beautiful teachings of Jesus. They have slaughtered so many millions in the name of Christ, when Christ preached that one must always turn the other cheek. But Jesus! His eyes! And the image of the Mother and Child: the baby Jesus playing with His Shakti. It is so sublime. Christians are just such fools to have received such a teaching and then to make such hash of it. But this is the thing, as Kipling said, "East is East and West is West and never the twain shall meet." In a way he was right. We Easterners have value only for emotion. You Westerners, like your cows, are basically materialistic. Of course there are exceptions, mind you. But when Nature Herself has created such differences in people, how can the one race understand the other? It takes a lot of effort.

# THE VISION OF THE GODDESS

There is another good reason to become a baby in front of Ma. Babies love their mothers no matter how vicious or ugly they may be. To talk idly about Ma's form is one thing, but to actually see Her dripping with blood, Her fangs ready to devour you, is quite another. Your reaction to Her determines what She can do for you. If you don't react with fear, She will do anything for you, out of love. If you react with fear or disgust, She will become all the more fearsome and disgusting, and then where will you be?

Kali and all Her manifestations — Smashan Tara, Chinnamasta, Bagalamukhi, and the others — are not bad. No one wants to love them; everyone is afraid. Kali can't understand why everyone is afraid of Her. If you love Her enough, you will change Her natural destructiveness to such an extent that even the underlying thirst for butchery will vanish.

People think that Smashan Tara is the most terrifying of the Goddesses — and She is. One of Her names is Bhayankari, that is, "the Terrifier." But if you go to Her with a heart full of love for Lord Krishna, She becomes Radha, Krishna's greatest lover. If you treat Her as a mother, She loves you as a mother loves her child. But if you have no faith in Ma, the Great Goddess, and if you fail, then there remains nothing for you but to be born over and over again until you get it right.

You may go to an image of Ma and tell Her, "Wah, Ma, how lovely you are!" or "How frightening!" or whatever, but the emotion you feel is only a reaction to Her outer form. You must know what sort of being you are worshipping if you ever want to develop a real relationship with Her, if you ever want to get underneath Her skin and reach Her inner being.

Without knowing Her inner being, how can you know Her? And before trying to go inside you must first understand Her external form, because it is actually *your* external form. The Atman or Universal Soul is the orb of the sun, and you are the reflection. Just as the moon can be reflected in thousands of pools of water at once, the Atman can appear in millions of humans and still remain aloof, untouched. Most humans are imperfect reflections because they are enmeshed in the Three Gunas, the three principal qualities of existence. If a lake is disturbed it cannot reproduce truthfully the image of the moon. But when it is calm the image is perfect. When you see Ma you are seeing Her through the veil, the film of the Three Gunas, which explains why you cannot see Her in Her true form in the beginning.

Why is She blue? First ask that, and once you've understood it you'll be able to comprehend the rest. Why is the sky or the sea blue? If you pick up a handful of sea water it is clear, but the sea as a whole seems blue. Air is colorless but the sky is not. These are optical illusions, and the fact that you see Ma — or even Krishna for that matter — as blue is also an optical illusion, because you are seeing them with your physical eye. Were you able to see with the divine eye, you would see something quite different. But to you now, Smashan Tara is *Shyama*, a deep, rich, luminous, midnight blue.

Around Her neck is a garland of freshly severed human heads, what we call in Sanskrit a *Runda Mala*. There are eight grinning heads on this garland. They represent the eight "nooses," the emotions which cloud the mind and incite one to perform karmas, thereby creating a tighter bondage to the ever-spinning wheel of birth and death. These eight nooses or snares, *pashas* in Sanskrit, with which you could hang yourself are lust, anger, greed, delusion, envy, shame, fear, and disgust. While you are in a state of ignorance you possess one or many or all of these emotions or grinning heads. Smashan Tara tells you, "I chop off your head to cure you of this malady, to free you from the grip of these snares." Most people, unfortunately, are so attached to their snares that they shrink from Smashan Tara in fear, thinking She wants to kill them. She does want to kill you — the false you, the limited personality which has accrued over so many births. You fear Her because you identify yourself with this mediocre personality when your true personality is something quite different. When She cuts off your head, your mind becomes firm, unwavering in its concentration, which enables you to succeed at Aghora Sadhanas.

Smashan Tara is *ghatastani* or "pot-breasted." What is a more appropriate symbol of motherhood than the female breast? Motherhood is inherent in all women. Take a tiny girl of two or three and give her a doll. How she will mother it! She will fuss over it, feed it, put it to bed; you will rarely find any boy who will bother so much about a doll. Women are meant to be mothers; the instinct is inborn. But it is only potential until the woman actually bears a child herself or adopts one. Then the motherliness fully manifests.

Even this realization does not develop spontaneously. It develops along with the child. In the case of humans, as the child develops in the womb, the mother's breasts enlarge and the nipples darken. The breasts actually double in size and weight during pregnancy. Milk also begins to form. The body is preparing food for the child even before its birth. Isn't Nature magnanimous? Most men see the breast and think of sex, but you'll ruin yourself if you try to treat Smashan Tara as your sex partner; you are just not strong enough to do so. Only a handful are. So you must realize She is coming to you as a mother, to love and protect you, and welcome Her in that way. She is *lambodari* or "big-bellied" because She consumes and digests all beings in the universe: She brings them into Her before sending them out again.

Around Her waist She wears a skirt of human arms, freshly

severed. One of the Sanskrit words for hand or arm is *kara*, which is related to the word *karma*. These arms represent all the karmas of all your millions of births. There are both left and right arms, so they include all karmas, auspicious and inauspicious. Most people clothe themselves in their karmas, and She wants to cut them off, remove them from you completely. Why does She wear them as a skirt? Because they cover the navel and pubis. And are these not the two things for which the majority of karmas are performed, the belly and the genitals? Won't most people do anything for food and sex?

As anklets Smashan Tara does not wear silver jewelry, but tiny cobras. The cobra is always the symbol of the deceased ancestors. When you do sadhana you must always remember you are not doing it for yourself alone, but for all your progenitors, since had it not been for them you could never have taken a human rebirth. She tells you, "These are your ancestors who have come to me and taken the shelter of my lotus feet."

Smashan Tara has four hands. In one there is a skull, which symbolizes the coating of the Three Gunas which surrounds the individual soul. The noose in another hand represents the noose which Yama's messengers of death use to snatch the living from the world. By seizing this noose from Yama, the King of the dead, She grants you the boon of immortality, because then there is no way for Yama to take you. With immortality comes fearlessness, since the basis of all fears is the fear of death. The third hand holds a pair of scissors, with which She cuts the three Gordian knots that bind you to embodied existence. This is connected with Kundalini Yoga. And finally, in Her fourth hand She carries a sharp sword, called a *Khadga*, which is symbolic of the eternal play of destruction and creation of the universe. To you it means destruction of your doubts, your false ideas, and impressions. She strikes through them all with Her sword. And because people die of doubt, this ensures you will never die.

Finally, Her face. I think it's the most beautiful I have ever seen. She has lotus eyes. Remember, the lotus is the symbol of discrimination. And Her tongue lolls from Her mouth, dripping blood. All creatures, no matter how tiny, have some sort of blood-like substance. When She takes it from them She purifies the blood, as they say in Tantra, through the process known as *Rakta Shuddhi*. What this means is that She removes so many of the karmas which have forced the individual to be born into a particular womb that a higher rebirth is guaranteed. She actually alters the patterns of your personality, which is merely the aggregate of all your countless karmas in myriads of births. This is the *Adhidaivika Rakta Shuddhi*, that is, Tara's purification of your personality.

When you have realized — not just mentally comprehended but realized through your own experience in sadhana — all the qualities of Smashan Tara, then She is no longer blue to you. She loses all color, all attributes. When you come and rest on Her lap all your wrong ideas about Her are removed. You see Her as She really is. You can't see Her with the physical eye. In Sanskrit and most Indian languages the eye taken as a whole is a feminine noun, the eyeball is masculine, the pupil is feminine, and the retina, called the *pardah*, or curtain in Hindi, is masculine. So you see the dual nature of the external universe is mirrored in the physical eye. With the physical eye you cannot hope to see anything but duality. But when the "curtain" is lifted you see the absolute, undifferentiated Reality, what we call in Sanskrit the *Nirakara Tattva*. Not even the shreds of distinction remain. Can a blind man tell the sex of someone in front of him? Only if he gropes. The state in which you see Smashan Tara in the Nirakara form is *Nirvikalpa Samadhi*, self-identification with formlessness.

So, you begin with ignorance, unable to distinguish "e-y-e" from "I." You see Smashan Tara in Her terrifying form because you are possessed of the eight nooses, of eons of karmas, and all the rest of the filth of your false personality, and She wants to disconnect it from you in the fastest way possible. Then, you see both you and Her as one; when all differences disappear, you cannot be different from Her. Finally, if you are meant for it, you again return to Her lap, and see Her in Her old form — but how different it will look to you then! You can't imagine it, you simply have to experience it. You go from duality to unity and back to duality, just as Paramahamsa Ramakrishna did.

My Tara always stands on Shiva, Who is deep in samadhi. One foot is flat on His body while the other is prodding Him, "Wake up! Wake up! Come dance with me."

Why is Shiva in samadhi? Shiva here is actually Jiva, the Individual Soul plus its coverings of the Three Gunas and all the rest. Because of the heavy overlay of karmas and Gunas and what-have-you, the Jiva is always in a state of deep sleep, unaware. When because of hard penances and stiff sadhana you realize Shiva, the Jiva becomes Shiva. Then you can say, "Shivoham, Shivoham": "I am Shiva, I am Shiva." Then you see there is not the slightest difference between Jiva and Shiva. Some gurus tell their disciples to repeat "Shivoham, Shivoham," but it is really useless. They begin imagining they are Shiva without having any of His qualities.

Once Shiva awakens, He and His Shakti begin to dance together, and the dance ends with Her merging into Him again. When the projection of the Shakti occurs, Shiva sleeps because He has lost the part of Him which was aware of Himself, His true self. After Shakti wakes Shiva She ceases to exist. It is only when your ego forgets all the eight nooses and the rest which force it to self-identify with the body (the physical e-y-e, eye) and identify with Smashan Tara, because your ego is simply your own personal Shakti, that the ego awakens the Shiva (capital I) and the dance begins.

One final thing: Do you know why Smashan Tara is always depicted in the smashan near a roaring funeral pyre? It is not your physical body She is burning on that pyre, it is your causal body. She cremates all the billions of karmas filled in the storehouse which is your causal body, thereby freeing you from further obligation of being born in the world.

See Ma, evaluate Her from all Her facets, find out about Her yourself, and find out the way you can love Her best. Most humans are such idiots that they are terrified of Ma, because they are afraid to disengage themselves from their filth. You must see Her in Her playful form, Her terrifying form, all Her forms, and love Her.

# CHAPTER THREE

# SHIVA

*The world considers You inauspicious, O Destroyer
of Lust who plays in the smashan smeared with the
ash from funeral pyres, wearing a necklace of human
skulls, with ghouls for comrades. But for those who
remember You with devotion, O Bestower of Boons,
You are supremely auspicious.*

*(Shiva Mahimna Stotra, 24)*

## MAHAKALA

One day I said to Smashan Tara, "You are my Ma, my Mother, but who is my Father? I know the Mother always shows the child the face of its Father, so won't You show me mine?" We have a saying in Hindi: "Only your conscience knows all your sins, and only a child's mother knows its true father." Without Smashan Tara I could never have succeeded at the sadhana for Her Grand Consort, Lord Shiva. Tantrikas and Aghoris work this way: First they achieve success at sadhana for Shakti and then use that Shakti to move on to the Universal Soul, Shiva.

I spent three years at the Worli smashan in Bombay performing rituals before my Tara would finally agree to show me the sadhana for Mahakala, the Destroyer of the Cosmos. That sadhana was impossible to perform in Bombay. First I went to Neemtolla Ghat in Calcutta, and then I spent ten months on Manikarnika Ghat in Benares.

Manikarnika Ghat is called *Mahasmashan*, the Greatest Smashan. Not even one second passes there in idleness; there is at least one body burning at all times, around the clock. This has been going on for untold thousands of years. The fire which is used to ignite the pyres has been maintained continuously for centuries; it is never allowed to go out. People come for thousands of miles to Benaras just so they can die there and be burned on Manikarnika Ghat. Every day dozens of bodies arrive by train, the bodies of those who died outside Benaras but yearned to be cremated there. There are too many bodies for them to burn down all the way to ash, so as soon as the skull pops open and most of the flesh is incinerated the priests recite the appropriate verses and push the corpse into the Ganges River to make way for another one. As soon as the body hits the river, packs of dogs fight each other for remaining morsels, and then the turtles and fish devour whatever is left. If you were to stay there ten months at a stretch like I did, and still not realize that you are going to die, well, then, there is no hope for you. You'll never realize it; you'll die in ignorance.

I used to sit there all day and all night. I would cook my rice in a fresh skull each day, without even cleaning out the bits of brain. The smashan is the ideal place for the worship of Lord Shiva because death is the eternal reality and Lord Shiva is the Destroyer, the very embodiment of death. You will always find Him among the dead, amidst spirits, corpses, and the ashes of burnt bodies. Manikarnika Ghat is Shiva's favorite haunt.

While I was doing this sadhana of Mahakala there eventually came a time when I began to hear someone laughing in my ear and telling me, "You fool! Do you realize what you are doing? If I come and stand in front of you, you will have to die; there is no escape. No one can see Me and live because no one can see Me except at the moment of death."

I laughed and said, "I don't care. I have to die some day, so why not now? I am ready to die, but I want to see You."

This went on for several days. Then the voice said, "Listen,

I'm serious. If you keep this up it will mean your end." Again I explained, "I am ready to die; life means nothing to me. I am waiting for You."

Finally Mahakala became pleased with my sadhana and told me, "I know you want Me to come and stand before you but you will not be able to endure seeing Me and still continue to live. I will come and stand behind you, and I will always remain with you at your back."

Since that day I have never been afraid of death. How can I be, with the Destroyer Himself to back me up? I now know what death is and when it comes to me I will embrace it, because it is my own beloved deity Mahakala.

I started out talking about Shiva and then began to call Him Mahakala. Shiva and Mahakala are two aspects of the same being. Call Him Atma, Purusha, Universal Soul, Ultimate Reality, God the Father or what you will, Shiva is the One, the Absolute, the One without a Second, the embodiment of pure consciousness. All duality exists in the manifested universe, and Shiva is beyond all that.

Or rather, almost beyond all that. Shiva has a form, which means that His personality exists within Nature, created from Adya. Lord Shiva is not absolutely absolute because out of compassion He has taken on an attribute or two to enable us to comprehend Him. These attributes, though, do give Him certain limitations; very subtle ones, of course. So subtle that from our point of view they are no limitations at all. But they are sufficient to distinguish Him from Mahakala.

Mahakala has no limitation of any kind whatsoever, at least in the universe we know. He has no form at all, none. At least Shiva manifests a form we can concentrate on. Mahakala is utterly formless, which means He can assume all forms at will.

Mahakala is the God of Time. He is *Satya Sri Akala*: True, Auspicious, Beyond Time. He is Time: How can He be subject to it? Since time exists only for mortals, Mahakala must be immortal, which makes Him true because He is absolute, free of any taint of Maya. This makes Him auspicious, in the true sense of the word. Mahakala is the only being of all possible beings in the universe who never falls prey to Maya. Even Lord

Shiva, the same essence as Mahakala in a different manifestation with a different job to do, fell once or twice. But Mahakala never even looks at Maya. No one can persuade Him to. When He comes for you, no matter how hard you beg for five minutes just to put your affairs in order, "no" is the only answer you will get. When even Lord Krishna Himself could not induce death to wait for even a moment how will you be able to do it?

Why is this? Because Mahakala is the pivot on which the entire universe turns. On the one hand there is the Saguna Brahman, the samsara, which is the infinity of forms, endless. On the other, the Nirguna Brahman, which is formless infinity, absolutely no form, zero as far as form is concerned. Between these two, connecting them together, is Mahakala. He is the fulcrum, the tangent between Infinity and Zero.

# DEATH AND THE SMASHAN

If you know about birth you know about death, and vice versa. The best place to learn about death is the smashan. The smashan is the true temple, the place of Eternal Reality. When you go into an ordinary temple you go to ask for some benefit — and if you see a pretty girl or a handsome man there in the temple you will forget about the deity and start thinking about how to get hold of that attractive but very impermanent human body. In the smashan, though, all you know is sadness and tears. If a man sees a woman he has to think, "Yes, she will die and be burned or buried like everyone else."

When you go to live in the smashan you first lose repugnance as you get used to living among corpses and bones and all sorts of other filthy things. After repugnance goes, fear goes, because when you know what a thing is you are no longer afraid of it. You learn about death, and it can scare you no longer. After fear goes, shame goes, because you are no longer afraid to walk about nude or to do what must be done there. You care for nothing then. Little by little all the Eight Snares disappear.

Most people go to the smashan for only a day. For the next week or so they will have no taste for the things of the world, but gradually that taste will return. This is what we call *smashan renunciation*. It is false, fleeting, easy to forget. Mahakala causes them to forget. If you stay in the smashan long enough Mahakala will cause you to forget the world permanently. You will forget your family, your friends, everything, and everyone. All you will be able to remember is that you are going to die. This is true renunciation, which Lord Shiva alone can give you, no one else.

One day when I was sitting in the Banganga Smashan in Bombay I saw the state funeral for the Governor of Bombay, Girija Shankar Bajpai. Soldiers were firing rifles, politicians were making speeches: It was a big show. Right next to the Governor's body was the body of a washerman burning quietly on its own pyre. I thought to myself, "No matter what your position in life, everyone ends up here sooner or later." Another time I saw an old Jain sadhu on one pyre and a young child on another. "Age makes no difference to Mahakala," I mused. "When your time is up you pass away." After so many experiences of death you forget all about life; your renunciation is complete.

The smashan is called *Shahr-e-Khamosh*, the City of Silence. No one goes there to sing or dance or laugh or enjoy themselves. No one goes there without being forced to do so, and all those who do go there cry for their loved ones who have left their bodies. Everyone cries — except the corpses. They laugh, because at last they have been set free from their earthly shackles.

Many people are terribly surprised to discover they have died. It's not unusual; suppose you had been at work doing what you like best, and you had a heart attack and died. Your mind would still be engaged in your work and would take some time to disentangle itself from its worldly attachments.

When death comes very suddenly like this, from a sudden heart attack or an accident or whatever, the deceased becomes very confused after death and must hover about as a spirit until he or she can figure out where to go. This is why I always say that even though there may be great physical agony it is better for the individual to be alert at the time of death or even to be asleep and dreaming, to permit the personality to project inward and search out the desires which will determine the next rebirth.

My mother was well aware of her impending death; my father
had many weeks to prepare for his. But for most people even
the act of dying is full of terrifying uncertainty.

You may do your best to communicate with dying people
but it will not help much. They have already entered a different world. You will notice that a stage comes when the eyes
begin to move rapidly and the lips form unintelligible words.
If you know about death you will know that the individual is
seeing Chitragupta's account book. What a beautiful word:
*Chitra*, which means picture, plus *Gupta*, which means secret.
Secret pictures, images no one else can see. And what is it?
Only the subconscious memory, the causal body, the record of
all the life's karmas. While you are in there in the subconscious
seeing all the activities of your life flash before your eyes like
a movie, as you review all your past mistakes, can you be at
all conscious of the outside world? No. Your ego, which up
until then has projected outward through your sense organs
into the external world, self-identifying with the body, now
projects inward into the subconscious, trying to find something
to self-identify with, selecting the karmas for the next birth.
So, the son or daughter may be wailing, "Oh, mother, mother,
mother, please forgive me, I never knew," but it is too late,
because the mother is entirely unaware of what is being said.
She has had to leave all connections with her physical body.

There is a way to force a person to be alert at the moment of
death. You can actually force the ego back into the conscious
mind and then communicate with the dying person for a few
minutes. But it is very difficult to do.

It is always best to have gone through the process of dying
while you are still alive. This happens, for example, when someone dies on the operating table and is then brought back to life.
The scientists who are studying death nowadays have inter-
viewed a bunch of these people, and they have identified some
of the sensations which one experiences at death: the movement of the consciousness through a dark tunnel, the roaring
noise, and what-have-you.

My foster daughter Roshni once experienced this. She used
to drink *bhang* (a preparation of milk and cannabis) every day.

One day I was in a queer mood, and I gave her the bhang personally. She drank it, sat down in the armchair, and closed her eyes. Within a few minutes her pulse and her breathing had both stopped. She came out of it after a bit, and I asked her what had happened.

"I was sitting in the armchair and flying through a long tunnel. It took a long time to get to the other end, and when I got there I started to go higher and higher. I was so scared I held onto the armchair very tightly. It was a very big space, an immense space, that we — the chair and I — were flying through, and I could see so many stars and other things that I can't express in words. I felt myself being attracted to a source of divinity, of love, and just then someone made me come back to my body."

And ever since that day she has been different. In fact she complains to me, "Why did you have to bring me back?" It was just like death, and now she knows what it will be like to die, just as those other people who have already experienced death know. And all of them will be much better prepared for death than the ordinary person, and their deaths will be much easier and better, because they know there is nothing to fear. Death is not to be feared; birth is to be feared.

"Ante mati sa gatih" — whatever you are thinking about at the moment of death determines your next rebirth. If you are aware at the moment you die and you remember God you will definitely go to Him, there is no doubt about it. It is much more likely that you will remember God at the moment of your death if you have been remembering Him regularly all during your life. This is why you must lose yourself in love for your deity so that you'll die with His or Her name on your lips. So many of our holy books advise that in today's world the greatest worship is the simple remembering of God's name. The Sufis do it this way also. But do you think it is so easy to remember God at the moment of death? Oh no!

Once there was a guru sitting under a tree with his pet disciple. As he was relaxing the guru saw a mango growing on the tree, very near the ground, and thought to himself, "How much

I would like that mango!" And just in the act of asking his disciple to pluck the mango for him, he died.

The disciple didn't know what to do. He was distraught: "Guruji is gone! Now who will look after me and teach me?" Suddenly he had a thought: If it is true that you go to whatever you were thinking of at the moment of death, and since his guruji had asked him for a mango just as he died, then he must still be somewhere around the area trying to get at the mango to fulfill that last desire.

So the boy plucked the mango, and, not knowing precisely what he was looking for, inspected it carefully. He found an ant crawling on it, and from nowhere, seemingly, another thought came to him: "Why shouldn't guruji be in this insect?" He took the ant between his thumb and forefinger and crushed it.

Immediately his mentor was standing in front of him. "Thank you, my beloved boy, for what you have done for me. I was indeed trapped in that ant, desirous of tasting a mango. You have saved me from many lives of groping about in Maya." And he blessed the boy and disappeared.

This does not mean that you should go around squashing ants. You had better know what you are doing before you play around like this. The boy in this story was just lucky — or perhaps you might say destined for it. How did he know that the ant was his teacher? In fact, how did he even get the idea to investigate where his mentor might have gone? It was all the play of his guru. His guru inserted these two thoughts into the boy's mind. This is the beautiful play of guru and disciple. The guru always knows what is going on but pretends to be ignorant; the disciple is expected only to be sincere.

But if you are not in a position to know about these things then don't fool about with them. In this case the guru himself was lucky. Suppose the boy had been a dullard, or ignored his intuition? The guru might easily have become entangled in Maya again, through even such a small desire.

Here is another story: There was an old woman who was truly pious. She worshipped God regularly, daily for several hours, and in fact didn't do much else. Toward the end of her life she became blind and had to grope from place to place, but this made her worship all the more perfectly since she lost most of the distractions of the outside world along with her sight.

She was purely a vegetarian and ate very little. One day as she was preparing her food she accidentally stepped on a baby mouse, which she was unable to see, of course. The mouse died with a squeal. She was softhearted and thought immediately, "What has happened? I have killed something!" And with this in her mind she suddenly died.

Well, "ante mati sa gatih." That last thought at the time of death was for the mouse, so she had to be reborn as a mouse. Then, because of the eternal fight for food, greed and anger returned to her, and she was back on the downward spiral through the samsara.

So, even the slightest attachment can do you in. On the other hand, even the slightest attachment to God can save you. There was a man named Ajamila who had performed plenty of bad karmas in his lifetime. As he lay dying he could remember nothing but the name of his son Narayana. Now, Narayana is the name of Vishnu, the Preserver of the Cosmos. And at the moment of death the name of Narayana was on Ajamila's lips.

Two demons came to drag his soul down into hell so that he could atone for some of his karmas, but an angel stopped them and said, "How dare you try to carry this man away? Don't you know he died with the name 'Narayana' on his lips?"

The demons laughed and said, "Oh sure, he was calling his son. Is that devotion?"

"The fact is, he remembered Narayana, who exists in every human anyway. He is coming with me," said the angel, and Ajamila did get into heaven. Of course he must have done plenty of penance in earlier births to get an opportunity like that, but that shows the power of God's name.

Almost no one knows the time of their death. But, thanks to Mahakala, I can know everything about how my friends will die, when they are due to die, how death will occur, how many people will be present to witness it, under what conditions the death will occur. Since now I have a special relationship with Mahakala, sometimes He can be induced to show His magnanimity to them. Suppose someone's destiny mentions a lingering death after an accident. Mahakala can arrange to finish that person off immediately at the time of the accident — no suffering.

You cannot outwit Mahakala, but you may be able to prolong life. Mahakala always needs an excuse to take you, a concomitant cause. If you avoid the specific situation which is fated to cause your death you can go on and on — but very few can avoid it. Mahakala's effect on the mind is just too intense.

Just recently one of my friends decided to go to Talegaon, a town near Poona, on a holiday. I told him, "The next fortnight is extremely crucial for you; don't leave Bombay if you value your life." But he insisted upon going. When he got to the railway station the lines were blocked and no trains were moving. Instead of interpreting it as a bad omen and going home, he and his wife sat on the platform and waited several hours until they could get a train. They went to Talegaon, and a few days later he died. No matter how long you are able to evade it, death becomes inevitable eventually. You can't cheat death.

Only one person is excepted: the Yogi. If he knows enough he will know about his own death six months before it occurs, because then the *prana* will start to leave his body. Then, if he likes, he can decide the best day and time to leave his body, and when he is ready he will call all his "children" together to receive his last blessings. After he says good-bye to each one, and the auspicious moment he has waited for has arrived, he sits in the Lotus Posture and goes into a trance. Suddenly there is a loud pop — Phat! — and a jet of blood spurts up from his *Shivarandhra* (posterior fontanelle of the skull). That is it; he is gone, free.

Remember what Kabir says: "When you come into the world you are crying, and the world is laughing. You must live your life in such a way that when you go the whole world will cry, and you will laugh." And he did it too.

But it is very uncommon to die aware like a Yogi does.

If people could only know what happens at death and after death they would not make so many mistakes. My Ravi and I burned my father at Banganga, in the same place where I burned my mother and my son, Ranu, and where I will be burned one day. When my father's body was in flames, don't you think his spirit must have been hovering about it somewhere? Of course it would have. Suppose you came home from work one day to find that your landlord had thrown you out of your flat, and the building had been condemned by the city and then demolished. Wouldn't you hang around the area for a few hours or a few days to reorient yourself? Every dead person hovers about the body, wondering what to do next. Why do you think the Hindus cremate their dead only a few hours after death? Because the spirit may have some hope of returning to the body as long as the body exists. When that body has been reduced to ashes, though, the spirit has to find its own path. Burial encourages the spirit to hover about for quite a long time, especially if the body is well preserved. Muslims hold a forty-day reading of the Koran to which the spirit is specifically invited, but this is not good because it makes the spirit linger. The sooner the spirit leaves and begins to find its own way, the better.

The poor dead person wants to let everyone know he is still alive and may become quite perturbed when no one around his body is listening to him, which is only reasonable, of course. You too would feel offended if all your relatives suddenly started to act as if you weren't there, when it is obvious to you that you are quite present. You can't blame the friends and relatives for failing to respond to the deceased's calls. Humans, except those few who possess very subtle perception, cannot see or hear the dead.

This is why I say that very few death rituals in any religion have any significance at all for the dead person. The priests invented most of the ceremonies as a means of making money from people's gullibility, which is bad enough except that almost none of the priests know anything at all about spirits, nor can they see and converse with them. The Vedic religion is not composed of useless rituals; those which are meaningless were added later by greedy priests.

After death the corpse is to be bathed, according to tradition. This is a good example of a meaningless ritual. Is there any use in bathing a corpse? Have you ever heard of anything more ridiculous? What is the use in cleaning it when in a few hours it will become ash, or worm or vulture food? Is the deceased worried about feeling clean when he no longer has a body?

You know, one day I had an interesting thought: We Indians are mostly vegetarian, and when we die we are eaten by vegetables; that is, we are consumed by wood, which is a plant material. We eat plants all during our lives and when we die the plants eat us in return. This is the Law of Karma. Muslims and Christians are predominantly meat-eaters, and when they die they are buried and become meat for worms to eat. Parsis are also meat-eaters, and when they die they are exposed on the Towers of Silence, and the vultures come and feast on them. I tell you, there is no escaping karma at all, except by grace.

What is even more amazing to me than the way people hold tightly to tradition is the changes which come over the deceased's loved ones. I will never cease to be in awe of Nature, of the power She has over the human mind. Five minutes before he dies a man's wife hugs him, kisses him, and cries over him. Five minutes after he dies she is afraid to touch the dead body; that peculiar feeling is there. Of course she feels peculiar. Even when they used to enjoy sex and thought they were getting enjoyment from the body, they were really enjoying something else: each other. You never feel like cuddling or fondling a dead person because there is nothing within to cuddle or fondle; only the outer shell remains.

Shall I go further? After the husband dies his corpse is removed from the house, and even after his cremation the ashes are never brought home. Why? Because his spirit might come and trouble his wife. How absurd! Don't people have any common sense? They have been married for years, and they must have made love hundreds of times. If the spirit does come he will *love* her, he will try to help her out; isn't it logical? But when it comes to death, very few do what is logical.

When Roshni's father died I warned all his relatives not to waste money on any rituals. I told them frankly that there was no use and whatever could be done for him was up to me to do. His sister said to me, "You are a Hindu; what do you know about our Parsi religion? All the rituals will be performed and the family will pay for it; that is our way."

I told her, "This has nothing to do with religion; this is a case of looting my poor children of part of the money their father left and that too for something which is useless. If it could do some good I would never object."

But she wouldn't listen to me. Eventually I lost my temper and said, "Go ahead and do it and face the consequences." They did, and within a few months this lady and all the relatives who had abetted her injured their left legs. She broke hers so badly it had to be put back together with screws and a metal plate. Only my foster daughter, Roshni, was spared; I've always been fond of her.

When one of my Guru Maharaj's disciples died I was told that he was going to be burned on a sandalwood funeral pyre which would cost about $3,000. Isn't it the stupidest thing? When the spirit has left the body, is burning it on sandalwood going to make any difference? When you finally leave your body you see so many new things, you experience so many unique things, that you have no time to bother about how your old body is being destroyed.

At the time of cremation a *Pinda* (ball of rice flour) is put out for crows to eat. The crow is a very smart bird. If a good observer is nearby he will notice that sometimes no crow will take the Pinda. Now, crows are always hungry and they would like to take it, but that spirit is hovering around the Pinda and is refusing to allow any crow to eat it. The spirit is very frustrated. He has been calling and calling but no one can hear him. This is the only way in which he can draw attention to himself.

When you notice that the crows are not eating the Pinda, you must understand that the spirit has some Vasana remaining, some earnest desire that was left unfulfilled during his lifetime. Then, if you care for the peace of the spirit you must go to the Pinda and say, "If you have some unfulfilled desire, come to me in a dream or tell me in some other way," and the spirit will try to contact you.

This very thing happened to one of my "children" not too long ago. He did not talk to the Pinda, but one of his recently deceased friends came to him in a peculiar sort of dream and asked him to help provide a better home for his now fatherless children. And he is going to do that now, to satisfy the spirit.

Both the Hindus and the Parsis offer food to their departed loved ones, who consume it ethereally by smelling rather than tasting it. The external form of the food doesn't change. I caution everyone I know never to eat food offered to a dead person. Such food has been polluted by the spirit's intense desire to return to physical life, which has a ruinous effect on the mind. You can even make a practical demonstration of this. Find a saint in samadhi and put some of this food into his mouth; he will directly come down from his samadhi, the pull of the physical is so strong. Priests are well known for eating such food, and this explains why their intellects are so materialistic even though they worship continuously.

The rituals of death in their simplest forms have been propounded because there is some value in doing them. But you need to know what you are doing. Do you have any idea why we Hindus always lay the corpse out on the ground with the head to the north? You know that the magnetic lines of force of the earth run north and south. There are three important benefits in this practice. First, rigor mortis sets in quickly and decomposition is hastened. Second, the magnetic field reacts with the body in such a way that the spirit cannot reenter the body even if it tries. Third, in this position it is easier to perform Kilana on the spirit and do Pitri Tarpana immediately, which will help the spirit find its way to a new womb much faster and easier. After death the spirit is confused, uncertain of what to do. It is up to you as a loved one to do your utmost to give some direction to the after-death experiences to minimize the feelings of loneliness and terror of the unknown.

*Pitri Tarpana* is one of the after-death rituals which is *really* useful, if you perform it correctly. It is a process by which you invite your dead ancestors and attempt to satisfy their lingering desires which prevent them from making their way higher in the hierarchy of existence. Did you know that this can actually alter your genes and chromosomes for the better? Suppose one of your ancestors was a debauchee, very fond of sex. When he dies his lust will not disappear, he will carry it along with him. He will long for sex, but since his body no longer exists he will have no way in which to satisfy his desire.

However, his genes and chromosomes still exist. They have been passed down to his children and grandchildren and so on. There is no real difference between seed and tree, is there? One is in an unmanifested form and one is fully manifested. So this old geezer's lust will be felt by his descendants; so long as they have some of his genetic material in them they will vibrate at his wavelength, at least to some extent. You have millions of genes; not all of them work at once. How does the body decide which ones work? This is one way.

Now, if Pitri Tarpana is performed and this ancestor is made to take birth in a new womb — probably an animal womb since he is so overcome with the animalistic desire to copulate — he will have a nice new body with which to enjoy sex. He will self-identify with his new genes and chromosomes and will forget his old ones. Then you will be free of his influence on your own genes and chromosomes, because he won't be there broadcasting lust for you to resonate with. This will make your mind firmer, less sexy.

Your ancestor will bless you for giving him a means through which to fulfill his desires. Besides, you owe a debt to all your ancestors for having provided your physical body to you, and this is one way to pay off that debt and eliminate the karmic bond. Isn't this wonderful? Everyone is happy.

This is one of the many reasons I hate communism. Communists are taught to forget their parents, to denounce them if they work against the state. If you destroy your parents, who are your roots, how do you ever expect to prosper? On the contrary, you'll degenerate, become more primitive and barbaric. I hate communism!

Your ancestors are one of the reasons it is troublesome to be reborn. Every time you are reborn you have to cope with the idiosyncracies and whims of all your dead forebears, and by the time you are finished overcoming all those limitations your life is over. That is why once you reach a certain stage in your sadhana you begin to crave for freedom from the obligation of being reborn. And let me tell you: salvation, Moksha, freedom from rebirth, or whatever you want to call it is Shiva's grace, nothing else. Lord Shiva tells His Shakti, "All these fools You have created to play with should be put to sleep; make them unaware of the truth and let them grope about. Only a few will I allow to reach for Me and come to Me, and then merge into Me when they are perfectly aware."

This is why everyone who goes to the cemetery cries; in fact the smashan is also known as *Rudra Bhumi*, the place where tears flow. Ordinary people cry because they are deluded by Maya and are self-identifying with the relative or friend who has just died. Saints and immortal beings cry tears of joy because it is in the smashan that they see their true personalities, their true selves; because what is Lord Shiva but pure consciousness?

What state is Shiva in? *Samadhi nishto*: permanent samadhi, eternal oneness with the universe. Shiva's samadhi is different from ordinary states of samadhi because Shiva is aware of everything at all times. In ordinary samadhi you may lose your awareness of external reality: Shiva, though, is perfect awareness.

Shiva is almost never touched by Maya. He is the creator of Maya and allows Her to play about as She wishes. He can never die, because all other gods and celestial beings in the universe are subject to His jurisdiction; if He were to die how could He take them when their time came to cease to exist? The God of Death is the only being in the universe with the authority to take life; without that authority even He could not do it. An ordinary policeman can arrest a governor or a prime minister on the strength of his badge; without his badge he is powerless. Shiva has the right to kill.

Since Shiva cannot die He was never born, because everything which was born must die. Death treats all beings alike. This is why Shiva is called *Swayambhu* or self-existent, not subject to birth and death. You may have seen the icon of Shiva as Nataraja, Lord of Dance, where He is surrounded by the flames of dissolution as His dance creates, preserves, and destroys innumerable universes simultaneously according to the rhythm of His two-headed drum. Shiva is the source of that sound. He is pure rhythm.

You see, Shiva is absolute. Any form you worship is only a form, and your worship is worship of the absoluteness behind it. For example, take the Shiva Linga, the most commonly worshipped image in India for thousands of years. What is it really? It is absolute firmness, stability. What is firmer than a rock? You may beat on it, shake it or do whatever you please to it but it will never budge.

The Shiva Linga is Shiva's penis, and the base in which it is mounted is His wife Parvati's vagina. There is a saying in Sanskrit: "Bhagamukhe linga, agnimukhe parada," which means "no matter how well you discipline the penis or solidify mercury alchemically, the penis will always ejaculate when placed into the vagina, and mercury will always melt when put into fire." But this is not true of Shiva. He has completely burned lust from His consciousness. His penis forever resides in Parvati's vagina and yet He never loses control. This is why the Tantric alchemists worship Shiva, because mercury is Shiva's semen and only through His grace can they achieve the ability to solidify it so that it will not melt even when cast into fire.

Mount Kailasa in the Himalayas is said to be Shiva's abode. Why? Because it is intensely cold. Where there is no heat there is no mental turmoil. Heat is turmoil, which arises from desire. Lord Shiva has gone beyond all desire — but that is not so easy.

Life is only a memory. It may be a sweet memory or a bitter memory, but it is only a memory. As long as you remember that you are such-and-such a person with such-and-such an address and you have relatives and friends and whatnot, you can stay alive. When you forget — when your karmic debts have been paid and your warehouse of karmas is empty — you can no longer self-identify with anything. Without memory there is no life. In Sanskrit the word for memory and the word for the God of lust is the same: *Smara*. Desire is the cause of karma, and when desire is destroyed memory too will go, and you will be free. This is why Lord Shiva is called Smarahara (meaning Destroyer of Lust as well as Destroyer of Memory). *Sma* in grammar means "past." Memory is only of the past.

*Sma-rahara* is He who transforms you from present tense to past tense, He who kills you. *Sma-shan* is the place where you go from present to past, where you are transformed from existence into a memory.

What happens at death? During life the body is sustained by the ego, which self-identifies with the body, the relatives, the personality, and so on. Your ego is nothing but your Kundalini Shakti, your own personal fragment of Adya. All during life your ego tries to find Her mate, Her controller — Lord Shiva — and because we have forgotten the truth we find evidence of Shiva in other people, and convince ourselves that we have located what we have been searching for.

When Mahakala comes to a person He calls to the Shakti to come and unite with Him. This is why Mahakala has no form; He has every form. Every created being is only half and spends its entire life trying to reunite with its missing half, to return to the state of unity. Mahakala is like a master key which temporarily provides that perfect missing half, long enough for the individual to forget his or her previous existence and start on the road to a new existence.

When Mahakala comes to a person and the ego-Shakti sees Him face to face She suddenly realizes, "Oh, no! I am not the body, I am not this limited personality, I am the Grand Consort of my Lord, the unlimited, eternal Personality!" Because of overwhelming love the Shakti leaves the body to unite with Her Lord, and forgets who She had been self-identifying with. As soon as the ego forgets to self-identify with the body, the individual dies.

Some Yogis and some other higher beings exist in the Sadashiva form: Their individual ego-Shaktis are merged together with Shiva at all times, but they are not fully united since if they were, individual existence would have to be terminated. This is very rare, no doubt, but when it happens you can go beyond death.

Mahakala is a Rudra; He makes everyone cry. Do you know that He also cries, out of joy, whenever He takes anyone? He thinks, "By my magnanimity I have removed this individual from all the pains and miseries of existence, and the fellow was not even aware of my presence. Now he is truly at peace. People are fools to cry for their dead; they should cry for themselves."

Lord Shiva is Bholenath, the Lord of Compassion. He has not one atom of cruelty in His person. He is the kindest being there is because He relieves you of all your earthly agonies. Can anyone ever think of asking for more than that?

Everyone is afraid of dying, which explains why no one is willing to love Mahakala. Only two persons in all our scriptures have loved Mahakala and both of them became immortal: Markandeya and Nachiketas. Destruction is necessary, but, unfortunately, no one is willing to face death. Even for Rama and Krishna who were real incarnations of God there was one moment of shock, one tremor, when Mahakala appeared before Them. Some slight Maya was there, a momentary remembrance of Their children or whoever. So, you see, the sight of Mahakala is so terrible that even God incarnate quails before Him. Even Jesus had a moment on the cross when His faith almost failed Him.

Of course the sight of Mahakala is not terrible; it is wonderful. But the ego *sees* Him as terrible because He has come to rip Her away from all Her attachments, and some attachments go very deep. When She is free, She realizes who She is and who Mahakala is. To remain alert at the moment of death is the achievement of a lifetime.

People think death is to be feared. It just isn't so. Birth is to be feared, because when you are born you forget all about what you did in your past lives and you go out and ruin yourself. But death is release from your physical shackles.

When Shiva comes to take someone He is very gentle, especially to innocent and harmless people. And children! How He hates to take children! He'll do almost anything for a child just so it won't feel any fear; just so He can release it from its suffering. Why does He love children so much? Because of their innocence. They remind him of Gopala, Vishnu in the form of a baby. Shiva cannot do without Vishnu, nor Vishnu without Shiva; preservation and destruction go hand in hand.

# ANJANEYA

Once upon a time Shiva and Parvati were on Mount Kailasa in the High Himalayas enjoying the night air, the stars, and the intense cold. Parvati decided that it was a propitious time to ask a question. "Lord," she whispered, "on whom do you meditate?" Lord Shiva smiled and said, "O Goddess, my mind is always turned to Vishnu, and even now I am thinking that He is going to be born into the world as Rama. I have decided to be born along with Him to help Him out." And that is why Anjaneya was born, and why He was the servant of Rama.

Anjaneya is called Hanuman. Some say this is because Indra, the king of the gods, once broke Anjaneya's jaw (*hanu*) with a thunderbolt, but there is a hidden meaning there. Hanuman should be read as *Anuman* because he is the atomic force (*anu* means atom), the force which moves all matter in the universe. That is why He is called *Pavana Putra* or *Vayu Suta* (Son of Wind, wind being personified as the motile force). And we all know the power of nuclear energy! That is the power of Anjaneya.

You can also read His name as Hanaman. *Hana* means to kill, and as Maharudra, the manifestation of the God of Death, Anjaneya is a killer. He is called the *Ekadasha Rudra* (the Eleventh Rudra) because He has perfect knowledge of both the dual and nondual aspects of Reality. Eleven is 11, 1 + 1 = 2, duality. Once Anjaneya said to Rama, "If I look at you from the point of view of Jnana (absolute knowledge), there is absolutely no difference between me and you. But when I see you through the dual viewpoint, from the standpoint of a devotee, then I am your servant."

Anjaneya is extremely clever. On one occasion He was throwing stones into the water, and they would float; but when Rama tried to do it the stones would sink. When Rama asked why that was, Anjaneya replied, "Master, I throw stones in your name and they float, but you are God incarnate, and if you throw something down how can that thing ever stop until it reaches the bottom?" And Rama was amazed at his answer.

No one can match Anjaneya in Vira Bhava or in Dasya Bhava

He is the perfect hero and the perfect servant. That is why His devotees call Him Mahavir, the Great Hero. He could easily have taken Sita Himself and returned her to Rama without any war; after all, He burned down the entire city of Lanka. But no, the play had to go on.

It is always better for you to worship Anjaneya in His aspect as the perfect servant, because your qualities of service will develop and automatically your ego will be kept under control. If you try to worship Him in His heroic aspect you will have to endure great difficulties. It's worth it, though. I can't describe to you the feeling I experienced when I first saw Anjaneya. I was in a smashan late at night, and as my ritual reached its climax a tremendous electrical storm began. The lightning came closer and closer, striking the ground near me, and it seemed as if the thunderbolts were going to fall right on top of my head. The noise of the thunderclaps — *Meghanada* — was almost unbearable. Even the best of ascetics would run away; who would not try to avoid being struck by lightning? But, no! You have to sit. Thanks to His grace I was able to endure it, and I was able to see Him face to face. In fact, as the thunder worsened my mood became more exalted: "Ah! *Now* He is finally going to come to me!"

Anjaneya is high, no doubt, but there is no manifestation of Śhiva higher than Mahakala. He is the *Adirudra*, the First of all the Rudras, the Ultimate.

# SAGAL SHAH

When someone in India feels some overpowering emotion or has a fright he will touch his chest and say "Rama Rama Rama." He will never say, "Hara Hara Hara," because Rama is part of Vishnu and so preserves life, and Hara, being Shiva, takes it away. Only a very few ever say "Hara" under such circumstances. Whenever I think of this I think of my own mother. As she lay dying she was repeating the name of her guru Haranath Thakur: "Hara, Hara, Hara, come to me." How many people have ever died with the name of the God of Death on their lips, even inadvertently as in my mother's case? That is why I always say I am most fortunate to have had her for my mother.

The word *Hara* comes from the root "Hr," which means to snatch. Mahakala is He who snatches your life away. He has also been described as Lord of Thieves, because He robs you of your most precious possession: your life.

What is life, anyway? The worlds, the gods, the demons, everything has been created by the Rishis; it is all their play. New creation can only appear when the old disappears, which is why the Rishis never allow Death to cease to exist. Otherwise, their play would suffer. Death is essential for life. The Rishis don't like to interfere directly — even if your child is a criminal do you destroy it? Never! — so Mahakala is there to do the dirty work of disposing of all the old forms.

The Rishis are actually in charge, though; they pull the strings, and the universe dances. For example, they give Lord Shiva the badge which allows Him to kill. Even Mahakala, who comes as close as any being can to existence without manifestation, exists at the whim of the Rishis. And the Rishis are beyond human comprehension, totally.

I have always advocated worship of God with form. But you should realize that when I say this I mean that you should worship the One who manifests through the deity. All deities, all forms of God are mere aspects of the One, so instead of saying, for example, "Wah, Lord Shiva, how compassionate You are," wouldn't it be subtler to say, "Wah, Lord, Your creation Lord Shiva is the epitome of compassion." All deities are merely playing their assigned roles in the great cosmic drama. You should respect them for how well they play their roles, and love the One who manifests through them. It is so much easier to get to the One by worshipping God with form.

Mahakala is the absolute manifestation of Shiva, but there are others who are almost as terrifying as Mahakala. I had to perform Shava Sadhana twice more before I was able to complete the sadhanas for all of Shiva's manifestations. The last time I did Shava Sadhana was in the Sunderbans, the jungle islands which form the delta of the Ganges. I went there not out of curiosity but in response to a telepathic request. I ignored it for a few days until it proved too strong for me, and I had to make my way to the jungles.

The Sunderbans jungles are impenetrably thick. They are the home of the Royal Bengal tiger, "Mr. Stripe," who can grow to a length of twelve feet. Tigers make a jungle exciting. While I was there I was well looked after by the Santhal tribe. They would bring me fruits to eat; occasionally I would even get a hunk of raw meat. I learned some useful things from them also. Primitive people are really wonderful in some ways. These Santhals act together as Bhairava and Bhairavi; can you believe it? And they have the utmost respect for their guru; they treat him as God himself.

Although I was enjoying myself I began to become restless after two or three days, and one night I decided to return to Bombay the next day; whoever had called me probably would not show up. That night while I was sitting at my dhuni he came: It was Purnananda, the same Purnananda who was the disciple of Sarvananda and later initiated Justice Woodroffe. It was at the insistence of Purnananda that I did Shava Sadhana again. By this time I had done it a fourth time after the three I had done for Shakti, and I was an old hand at it; it was just a formality to me. But it was essential for Batuka Bhairava. Batuka is a little boy only about eight years old in appearance, although he can be terrifying when he wants to be. The corpse was that of a handsome young man, and I succeeded without any ado. I am still thankful to Purnananda for enabling me to complete my sadhanas of all the manifestations of Mahakala.

Perhaps I was meant to do sadhana of Mahakala. I have always felt very lucky that I am a descendant of Sagal Shah, who was a merchant and a devotee of Lord Shiva. He had a little son who, you may believe it or not as you wish, was actually Mahakala in disguise.

Sagal Shah had taken a vow that he would not eat each day until he had fed a sadhu. One day during the rainy season he had not eaten for three days, because he lived on an island and no sadhu would venture out there during a heavy storm. On the fourth day he learned that an Aghori, who was really Lord Shiva in disguise, had come to visit the island. Sagal Shah accompanied the sadhu to his home. The Aghori declared that he had not had food for three days and demanded something to eat.

"Of course, Maharaj," said Sagal Shah. "Will you have some sweetened milk or yogurt, or . . . ?"

"You fool of a merchant! I am an Aghori. Am I meant for sweets? I eat meat. Bring me meat." Aghoris are always wild and uncontrollable.

Sagal Shah, remembering the old proverb "atithi devo bhava" (treat your guest as God), said to himself, "Lord, who have you brought into my house today?" because he had never even brought meat into his house before, much less cooked it there. But the guest must be satisfied. That was part of his vow.

The Aghori continued: "And I don't want mutton or chicken. I want human flesh."

Sagal Shah, resigned to his fate, said "All right, Maharaj, l will have myself killed and cooked and served to you."

This only made the Aghori wilder. "Dunce! You are an old man. Think how stringy and tough your meat will be. I want a young child. Take his brains and fry them for me."

Sagal Shah said, "I have a young son who is in school right now. I will go and bring him and have his brains cooked for you." His wife, who was pregnant, also realized that it had to be done, to fulfill the vow.

Sagal Shah went and found Chelayya, his son, and asked him to come home with him. Before he could explain why, Chelayya told him, "So that old fellow wants to fry my brains and eat them? All right, let us go there and I will see how he does it."

His father should have suspected something when Chelayya knew all about the Aghori before being told. But Sagal Shah was too distraught over his son's impending death to notice. How could Chelayya know about it? He was something different; his own father had not realized who he was.

They went to Sagal Shah's house and Chelayya told the Aghori, "So you're trying to be funny, eh? All right, *do* it! Go ahead!"

And he was slaughtered and his brains pulverized, and the

dish was prepared. The mortar and pestle in which his brains were mashed can still be seen on that island.

When the meat was set before the Aghori, he became wilder still and refused to eat it, saying, "How can you expect me to eat food prepared by a barren woman? Shameless wretch!"

This was too much for Sagal Shah's wife, who said to him, "You damned Aghori! Who do you think you are? I am pregnant, so you dare not call me barren. Now I am going to make you eat and I am going to watch and see how you do it!" Ma in Her kinetic, Shakti form.

Suddenly the Aghori said to the corpse of the boy, "Get up!" and immediately the boy was standing there alive saying, "So?"

Then the Aghori instantly bowed to Chelayya — the Aghori bowed to Chelayya, mind you — and said to Sagal Shah, "Request a boon!" Sagal Shah replied, "Lord, what can I ask for? In Kali Yuga no one is tested like this, and you have graced me by being born into my family. Now all that I can ask is that all in my family and all of my descendants should have pure minds. Anyone who develops *Durbuddhi*, perverted intellect, should be destroyed."

And so it has been until today. For fifteen generations in my family no one did any work, but the family was fabulously wealthy. And anyone, like my father's own brother, who tried to act funny and become a criminal, died. Our family was the agent for the East India Company and we used to own all of Bombay. Because we would not cheat at business we have lost much of what we once had. But that doesn't matter one bit because we still have the real treasure: the blessing of God. Take the example of my father. Just before he died, no one could tell the difference between him and his guru; he had concentrated on the form of his guru for so long that his own form had changed. He must have done billions of japas in his life; so did my mother. And that is just one effect of japa and meditation. With such a background is it so amazing I turned out like this?

# CHAPTER FOUR

# RNANUBANDHANA

*Punarapi jananam, punarapi maranam, punarapi matrdareshayanam: Birth and death and living in a womb, over and over and over again.*

## THE PRIMAL DEBT

What is the purpose of being born? To recognize yourself, to realize that you are neither the body nor the mind but rather the Eternal Soul which is the Ultimate Unity — call it Atma, Parampurusha, Brahman, or what you like.

How is one born into the world, though? What makes an individual take birth? Some say that karma is at the root of everything, but when they are asked the origin of karma they say that karma is eternal.

But how is that possible? If karma was eternal how could anyone ever escape from it? Actually the Law of Karma is nothing else but Newton's Law of Motion: Each action causes an equal but opposite reaction. There is no fundamental difference between action and reaction since their relationship is such that whenever one occurs the other has to follow; this is simple cause and effect. This is why I always say, "Cause is Effect concealed, and Effect is Cause revealed." When you know one you know the other. If you know the potentiality inherent in the seed you can predict what sort of tree it will produce. If you know the egg, you know the bird.

If there is no end to action and reaction how could anyone ever hope to get out of the whirlpool of life? How could you ever hope to realize yourself? There must be a way out, and there is. God is never cruel or unjust; humans are, and we project our limitations onto Him. To get out of the grip of karma you must first realize that all karma is due to *rna* (debt). Karma can occur between two individuals only if there is some bondage of debt between them. I call this *rnanubandhana* (from the Sanskrit *rna* "debt" + *anubandhana* "bondage"). For example, if I steal something from you in this lifetime the opportunity for me to steal from you can arise only if a debt exists between you and me; only if you owe me something. If there is no bondage, I will not be able to locate your home, or will not find what I want even if I do burgle it. And if I steal from you, instead of receiving from you as a gift the thing I want, of your own free will, it is highly likely that you must have stolen from me in the past. Your past action creates a like attitude in me. This is a very much simplified example, of course, but you can get the idea from it.

My theft from you is not a karma: it becomes a karma only when I identify myself with the act of stealing. As long as I do not self-identify myself with the robbery it is not a karma for me. It may be unwise — it will hurt your feelings, it may land me in jail, you may beat me up or shoot me in return — but it is no karma: It is only a past rna working its way out. Self-identification with one's actions converts them into karmas by binding the ego down more tightly to the limited, temporary personality.

If I write a check for 10 million rupees and fail to sign it, it is valueless, even though I performed the action of writing it and giving it to you. Once I sign it, though, and you present it to my bank to be honored, well, I'm in trouble unless I have at least 10 million rupees in my account.

Remember, only the ego has the power to self-identify. Your ego is continuously self-identifying with your body and your personality: "I have black hair, I like race horses," whatever.

Thanks to the ego we are all able to remain alive because as soon as the ego ceases to self-identify with the body an individual dies.

The difficulty is that the ego not only self-identifies with the body, it also self-identifies with all the actions performed by the body. The ego tries to protect itself by preventing the repaying of karmic debts which have fallen due. Thus, new karmas are created.

Suppose I know I have a rnanubandhana with you. If I am wise I will ensure that the debt is paid off; it will mean one less bondage to the world and will bring me closer to my goal of self-realization. People enjoy being repaid but usually balk when it comes to paying out. The result is karma.

In my case I am very anxious to finish off my cycle of births and deaths so I allow every person who has any rnanubandhana with me to take from me whatever they are entitled to. Whether they are destined to make my life miserable, or to make me poor, or whatever, I don't mind. Let them do it; they cannot take from me any more than the value of the debt I owe them. The moment I object in any way, even mentally, then karma has begun. Likewise, if I have to take from someone I take only what I know I am entitled to, no more and no less.

Now, I know I have the advantage of knowing about my rnanubandhanas. But anyone, even someone who has no idea at all about whom he owes and who owes him, can make good use of this attitude. The more you scheme and plot to snatch from others the farther you bind yourself down in karmas. The freer you are, accepting when it is given and giving when it is requested, the more of your rnanubandhanas are effaced and the closer you come to your goal.

This is why I always say that life is only a memory. It is the memory of all one's rnanubandhanas of countless births. This memory is stored in your causal body, from which the rnanubandhanas project for their fulfillment at the appropriate moment. If you have given a lot in your past births then you will have many people to act as your debtors in this birth and you will have "sweet memories." If you have taken ruthlessly from everyone in the past they will take from you ruthlessly this

time around and your life will be filled with "bitter memories." However you look at it, life is nothing but a memory, be
it bitter or sweet.

And remember that the sweet memories can also get you
into karmic trouble. Suppose someone owes me money and I
demand it from him, or kill him for it, instead of permitting
him to pay me in his own time, according to his own sweet
will. Or suppose a woman owes me sex, and when the rna is
over and she wants to leave me I try to force her to remain, or I
rape her if she refuses to provide me with immediate gratification. Or suppose I am a doctor, and a loyal patient suddenly
stops coming and I react with indignation or with insulting
behavior. The moment you act to protect what you feel to be
your self-interest, your ego, karma adheres to you like mud.

People ask me, "But how did all this start? How could there
be a first rnanubandhana, a first debt to start the whole ball
rolling?" The first rna, the source of rnanubandhana, occurs
when Shakti has emanated from Shiva. After emanating She
feels She must return and reunite with Him. She owes Her existence to Him and because She feels incomplete without Him
She craves reunion. The period between the emanation and the
reunion is the time when karma is performed. When the union
is complete there can be no karma; there is no individuality
left to self-identify.

The job of Shakti is to irritate, prod, awaken Her Shiva. Once
Shakti has emanated, Shiva becomes quiescent. Shakti incites
Him to action so They can dance together and by Their dance
create the play of existence. Shakti provides the energy for the
sublime cosmic dance, Shiva provides the control and rhythm.
This is the meaning of the pictures in which you see Kali dancing on the prostrate body of Shiva: She is awakening Him out
of samadhi so He can dance with Her. My Tara does the same
thing.

Look at the atom. The protons are like Shiva; they remain
still at the center, attracting the electrons to themselves pas-
sively. The electrons, forms of Shakti, whirl incessantly about
the nucleus trying desperately to reunite with the protons.
Shakti is dynamic because it is She who emanates; She moves

outward and then tries to move back, like the protons. The neutrons represent what happens when Shiva and Shakti reunite. All dualities like polarity and charge are finished; the manifestation is dissolved. This is why the authorities say that the Absolute Reality has no gender or attributes. All the attributes are contained within it — otherwise how could they manifest? — but in the absolute state they are only in potential form. When a neutron splits to form a proton and an electron then the manifestation begins all over again: Duality has been created out of unity. If a physicist is asked why this happens he can only answer that it is in the nature of matter to manifest and redissolve like this. And we Vedics say the same thing, that it is simply in the nature of the universe to manifest and redissolve periodically.

But why the atom? Consider human beings. Birth and death, death and birth: two sides of the same coin. You can't have one without the other. If you know birth you know death, and vice versa. Birth came first: Shakti emanated from the Unified Unmanifested Reality. When Shakti returns to Her controller, Lord Shiva, that is death. Birth and death occur only so long as the causal body exists, because only when there are sufficient karmas with which the ego has self-identified will there be enough impetus for birth to take place to create situations in which the karmas can be worked out.

All the karmas in storage in the causal body must be burned away before one gains exemption from rebirth. But it is so rare for the causal body to burn that only a few over the course of centuries and millennia ever get to experience it. Besides, out of a million people perhaps only one even wants to experience it. Why? Because most of your karmas must first be burned away before you can even develop the desire to do away with desire. And, as long as even a few karmas remain, your body will remain and your ego will continue to self-identify with your form and will continue to relate to the universe in terms of form.

The Ultimate Shiva has no form, no attributes, nothing. When you aim for the ultimate you can't expect to carry form along with you. Remember, all forms, even the form of Shiva, exist within the manifested universe, which is nothing but the Adya Shakti. When you are ready to go beyond Shakti to Shiva you must be willing to turn from form and go beyond everything. Which is another reason I say over and over again: Worship God with form first and only then go for the Formless Absolute. Convert your own self into your deity so your ego self-identifies with the deity's form and not your own, and then your deity can carry you across to the Ultimate.

# FATE AND RNANUBANDHANA

Unless you work very, very hard and obtain immortality you can be certain you are mortal. All created beings are mortal, because they are merely projections of energy, of Shakti. When Shiva and Shakti unite, millions of beings and universes are created by the overflowing of their bliss: This is on the cosmic scale. On the small scale a man and a woman copulate, and when the sperm and the ovum unite, they, two cells, proliferate into billions of cells out of the exuberance of their joy. Men and women procreate; Shiva and Shakti create.

Whether it is creation or procreation, every projection is limited. The limitation is one of time. Even at the creation of the universe the projection of Shakti is limited; otherwise how could any forms be created? The idea of form is nothing but the idea of limit. Shakti is the force of limitation, which is why some so-called holy men fear and despise Her. But they don't realize how limited they are themselves.

The moment anything is created its life span is determined. Call it trajectory or atomic clock or anything you please, but the seeds of destruction are planted at the instant of creation and grow at a fixed rate. And that is why I always say, the moment of death is fixed at the moment of birth.

Some people say, "Oh, but you can always commit suicide and cheat death," but it's not true. If you decide to commit suicide it is because you are meant to commit suicide. As they say in Sanskrit, "Purvadatteshu maranam": you get the same death again and again, for at least seven births in succession. If you are meant to die by your own hand the idea of suicide will come to you just at the time that Mahakala is ready to come for you. So it is not as if you have any free will over selecting your time of death. Every death, in whatever circumstances, is decided at the time of birth; you may do your best to avoid it but you will be unable to do so.

Even if you could know when you would die — and only a few Yogis can know — there is no likelihood that you'd be able to alter the time or the circumstances because even if you try to make some changes Mahakala will make use of your rnanu-bandhanas to create the situation as He desires it. He will pervert your mind and the minds of those around you to force events to occur as He pleases.

Here's an example. Once there was a childless couple who prayed to Shiva for many years before being blessed with a son. When the father, who was the local king's astrologer, cast his son's horoscope he was horrified to learn that the boy would die on his ninth birthday after paying his parents 100,000 rupees. This was the rnanubandhana between the boy and his parents, the reason why he had been born into that family.

The boy's father was mystified as well: Where could a nine-year-old boy come up with 100,000 rupees? He felt secure in the absurdity of the situation but just to make sure, he never let the boy out of the house, even to go to school, so he could never amass any money. Still, the boy learned something of astrology almost by default, because his father was an expert and people came regularly to consult with him. Off and on the man would warn his wife, "Never take anything from this boy!" and his wife would assure him she wouldn't.

When the boy became eight years old the astrologer warned her again: "Make sure you never accept anything whatsoever from him!" His wife replied, "I told you once, I will never take anything." At age eight years and eleven months the astrologer delivered yet another warning to his wife and received the same assurance.

Three days left. The father thought, "When this period passes the dangerous conjunction will not recur for at least 100 years. Nothing to worry about." One day left: again he cautioned his wife. But he didn't realize that he was living in a fool's paradise. Mahakala always possesses His victim six months before the appointed time of death and makes the individual perform the actions which cause death to occur in the prescribed manner. It was no different in this case.

The wife of that country's king had finally become pregnant after many years of barrenness. Just before the delivery was to occur the astrologer's son was strolling through the palace garden when he saw a gardener's wife collecting flowers. He asked her in childish innocence, "Where are you going with all these flowers?"

She replied, "I am to take them to decorate the queen's bedchamber, where she is about to give birth to a child." The little boy said, "I am coming along with you." The lady told him, "Only women are allowed." The boy said, "Make me wear a sari so I can come too," and looked at her so mournfully that she had to agree. Mahakala had taken possession of him and was ordering her; otherwise the gardener's wife would never have dared to take him along, knowing the stiff penalty she would have to face if the deception were discovered. Some rnanubandhana had to exist between the boy and the gardener's wife, of course, to give Mahakala a field in which to operate.

Off they went to the palace like mother and daughter. There, just at the moment of the child's birth the little boy got inspiration — from Mahakala — and took a twig and wrote on the wall in the blood-red juice of the *paan* (betel nut and betel leaf mixture) he was chewing: "This boy will surpass his father in every way and will live for 125 years." Then he and the gardener's wife left.

Ten minutes after the delivery all the royal astrologers came, led by the little boy's father, and when they cast the horoscope they all agreed: "If the father ever sees the face of this child the father must die."

Well, what to do? The king could not afford to allow that to happen, because the welfare of the kingdom was at stake, so he called two butchers and told them, "Take this child out and kill him." The queen felt grief, but consoled herself with the thought that her husband would continue to live and she could have more children.

When the two butchers had taken the baby out into the forest they said to one another, "What has this child done that he should be murdered on the day he is born?" They could not do the deed so they left the child under a tree. They killed a deer instead and took its eyes to the king to prove that they had done the job. How could two bloodthirsty butchers become so compassionate? Mahakala, the god of death, and a complex rnanubandhana connecting the baby, the butchers, and the luckless animal.

By now the king was feeling remorseful — guilty of the murder of an infant and his own son at that — and he was wondering what to do. The remorse? Mahakala's doing. He went to the queen and told her, "I've done a terrible thing." She said, "You? What have you lost? I've lost my baby." Suddenly the king saw the horoscope written on the wall. When he read the words he was so astonished that he called all his guards and ordered them to find out who had written it. They interrogated everyone who had been there and when they reached the gardener's wife, she admitted that the chief astrologer's young son had come in disguise and done so.

Meanwhile the boy had gone happily to his home and had had his nice food and was resting, as if he knew what was going to happen next. Suddenly officers arrived and escorted him to the palace. The king confronted him with the writing on the wall, and the boy boldly told him, "What I have written cannot be wrong. The baby cannot be dead." A nine-year-old boy could never be so confident; Mahakala was speaking.

At this the king called in the two butchers, who confessed after a good hiding that they had not killed the infant. The king and his whole court rushed to the tree and found the baby alive, honey from an overhead honeycomb dripping into his mouth to satisfy his hunger. The astrologer's son told the king, "You have seen your son's face and yet you live." The king was wonderstruck and asked, "How could you be right when all my astrologers were wrong?" The boy told him, "I was present at the precise moment of birth; my father and all the rest were ten minutes late." The king was so pleased that he wrote on a slip of paper, "Pay the bearer of this note 100,000 rupees from the royal treasury."

The boy ran home as fast as he could, calling for his mother: "Ma, Ma, Ma!" When he got to his house his mother met him at the door. He jumped into her arms, thrust the note into her hand, and died.

His father came home a few minutes later, having heard the whole story at court, and found his wife cradling their son's dead body. He shouted, "You stupid wife! I told you never to take any money from him!" But she said, "How could I have known that the scrap of paper in his hand was a receipt?" And then, of course, there was nothing to do about it.

So there is no way to escape death unless you go beyond it. Please remember, the time of death is fixed for everyone. Even if you want to die earlier or later you will not be able to. I remember a newspaper report: As soon as some young bride left her new home to visit her mother her husband became so depressed that he decided to commit suicide. First he swallowed all the poison in the house. Then he sealed all the doors and windows and turned on the gas. Since he didn't like the smell of gas, he went and bought some cigarettes and returned to the kitchen where he lit one, and bang! He was so frightened by the noise and fire that he vomited out all the poison and ran for his life. He was miraculously unscathed by the explosion, and his wife had to get him out of jail for trying to burn down the house.

And then there was another true story not too long ago. Some primary school teacher had been so fed up with his life for the past ten years that he kept wanting to die but had never been able to do so. Then one day he was found dead in a Shiva temple, embracing the Linga. He had searched for Mahakala for so long, and had finally found Him. Why didn't he succeed for ten years? Because it was not yet time for him to die. No other explanation is possible. I have spent many long years of my life in the smashan and I think I have found out a little something about death.

You know, it is really a blessing that we do not have full

knowledge of fate and rnanubandhana, the workings of birth and death. If we did, a mother who knew that a certain son would take more from her than he would give would never love him; she would neglect him and might even try to kill him. We would be prejudiced against other people from the start and that would only increase our self-identification with our bodies, which exist solely because of rnanubandhana. And all this would only add to our already heavy load of karmas. That is why one does not get remembrance of past lives until a later stage.

# RANU

I have experienced all this myself, you know, which is why I can talk about it. I lost my first son, Ranu, in spite of every precaution; and I did not understand what was going on until much later, when my Guru Maharaj literally beat it into my head.

Ranu was meant to die young, that is all there was to it. I had plenty of warnings, I had my own suspicions, I did all I could, but there was no way to avoid Mahakala.

Jina Chandra Suri, the Jain ascetic who forced me to do Shava Sadhana the first time, was also involved in this drama. See how strange are the workings of rnanubandhana? My wife had had several miscarriages, and I was wondering if she would ever be able to have a child. Once when she was at her parents' home in Gwalior, Jina Chandra Suri came to me and said, "There is an ethereal being who has been coming to me daily and bothering me: 'I want to come to the world of mortals and play. Let me come. Let me come.' I have decided that he should be born into your family." Right in front of me the old man wrote out the horoscope and described exactly how the boy would look. He told me, "Your wife will conceive on such-and-such a day."

I thought it was all a big joke, and told him so: "Look, Maharaj, my wife is in Gwalior; how can she conceive there?" He didn't bother to reply but just left. I knew that even in his miserable condition he still had a few tricks up his sleeves, so I sent a telegram to my wife telling her there was no need for her to return to Bombay; she should continue her vacation with her family indefinitely.

But it's not so easy to prevent the unfolding of your destiny. Someone in Gwalior told my wife, "Your husband has just been operated on for his tonsils and he is hiding it from you." She took fright and caught the next train for Bombay. When I met her at the station I realized that it would all take place as Jina Chandra Suri had predicted. My wife conceived on the specified day, the pregnancy was uneventful, and the boy was born at the exact time required by the horoscope the old man had written out. What's more, the baby fit the physical description perfectly.

And so I have Jina Chandra Suri to thank both for introducing me to my Mother Tara, and for giving me a unique son. You know, Jina Chandra Suri's fate was somehow connected with that of Ranu. Three months before Ranu's death the old man came to me and said, "Your child is going to make you cry; he'll make you miserable." And three months after my son was cremated, the old man passed away himself. One day he was delivering a lecture on the Jain religion in one of their temples, and in the middle of the discourse he just keeled over dead.

What a boy Ranu was! My God, if he had lived he would have been the best! Sports, studies, you name it, he was tops in all of them. Not only that, he had innate spiritual powers. Sometimes when people would come to me to get some work done Ranu would meet them first and say, "Give me some chocolate and I'll see that your work gets done." And it would be done! No one ever understood how, and even I only found out how after he was gone.

Everyone who met him loved him. He was my father's favorite. And my mother! Here in India it is a tradition that when you take initiation from a guru you give up one food for the rest of your life; you dedicate that food to your guru. My mother refused to eat mangoes after Ranu's death, because mangoes had been his favorite food — even though obviously he was not her guru.

And even my gurus loved him! One day when Ranu was being too mischievous I raised my hand as if to slap him. I would not have done it; I never hit my children. I just wanted to scare him. But my Junior Guru Maharaj was in the room. He caught my hand and with real pain in his voice he said, "Haven't you ever looked in his palm and seen how short his life line is? Promise me you will never strike him." And of course I did promise it. Actually I had known from Ranu's horoscope that his life would be in danger early on, and as soon as my second son was born and I looked at *his* horoscope I saw that it predicted he would be the eldest child in the family. This certainly suggested that Ranu had to die.

So I decided to give him the happiest childhood I could. When he was wild and naughty I would tell him, just to punish him a little bit, "If you don't behave, your Papa will go to where Gopala lives," meaning that I would die. But Ranu would always tell me, "No, Papa, I will be going before you do." He knew, he knew!

Well, Ranu died at age nine. As the time approached my Senior Guru Maharaj decided to visit Bombay. Now I know that he came to say good-bye to Ranu; back then I was still hopeful that something could be done.

One day a couple of friends and I were sitting with my Senior Guru Maharaj and one friend said to me in English, "Why don't we try to get your Guru Maharaj to go to the cinema?" This fellow knew that my Senior Guru Maharaj would never patronize any thing like that because he hates the British, which mean to him Westerners in general. He used to say, "What have the Westerners ever done for us except to teach us to urinate standing up like donkeys?"

Anyway, my friend was still talking: "Let's take him to a really hot picture." My old man was just looking at him with his piercing stare — his eyes never blink — and then suddenly he said in Hindi, "Why don't we go to see a picture today? I'd like to see that new picture with Rita Hayworth in it."

I got the shock of my lifetime. I couldn't understand it. Why should he want to go see something he hates? And how could he possibly know or care who Rita Hayworth was? But we went.

And during the picture my Senior Guru Maharaj didn't even look at the screen. He sat with his head on his chest, covered by his arms, with his elbows together at the waist. Very strange. I didn't know what to make of any of this.

If you ever get the opportunity, see that picture. It was called *Down to Earth*. Danny is a piano player whose dancer quits him. He is in bad shape so his mother, who has died, gets permission to come down from heaven to help him. She becomes his dancer — of course he does not know who she really is — and then he rockets to fame. They are doing very well together when the first dancer Danny had employed comes back and asks to be rehired. Although his mother tells him, "But Danny, I only want to help you," he sends her away and rehires the first dancer — and straightaway plummets. Then he realizes his mistake and asks his mother to come back. She does, and up he goes again.

His mother is finally called back up above. There is a limit to everything, after all. She begs, she pleads, "No, I can't go, I have to look after my son," but then we see a big Gandharva or some kind of angel smiling at her, and he moves his hand and she leaves the earth and is drawn back up above.

As she is about to go she sees her son and cries, "Danny! Danny! Don't you hear me? Can't you hear me? I want to help you. Listen to me!" But Danny is drinking at a cocktail party in some producer's house and he can't hear her because she has become ethereal.

Up in heaven she is very unhappy — "My Danny, what will become of him?" — and someone comes along to talk with her about it. She is completely despondent, and he just strokes the back of her head and suddenly she says, "Oh, it was all a dream, wasn't it?" And she becomes happy again. But still for some time the memory is there, like the morning recollection of a dream.

After the picture was over my Senior Guru Maharaj asked us, "Did you understand?" I said, "No," because I couldn't understand. My old man left Bombay and sometime later Ranu died. About two months thereafter he returned to Bombay and asked me again, "Now, did you understand that film?" I still can't tell you how he knew that film was worth seeing to remind me of the story of Ranu's life.

Look how Mahakala works. I had gone out of Bombay to Mathruli near Surat in the Konkan for a short while with a certain sadhu — my wife's own guru, in fact; he was named Shankargiriji and lived to be about 125, though he was not quite 100 at this time and still looked like a sixteen-year-old boy — and I told my wife in no uncertain terms not to have Ranu operated on for his tonsils while I was away. But she ignored my advice and did it anyway. I had a peculiar feeling that something terrible was going to happen. Then when I learned of the operation I told her specifically that if she let him go to school while I was gone that it would be the end of him. Well, she didn't listen to me. She — or rather Mahakala — sent him to school and he developed polio. He was sick only four days.

While I was sitting out in the jungle I started seeing something funny. I saw that Ranu was dying. I told Shankargiriji that I had to go back to Bombay, but he said, "Don't be stupid, it's all your imagination; don't go back." I waited there for some more time and then I saw the same thing again. This time I forced Shankargiriji to come back with me to Bombay. By the time I got back it was almost too late. I quickly put Aghori Baba's stick under the mattress and laid my boy on the bed on top of it.

I then thought that everything would be all right, because if Aghori Baba's stick had stayed underneath him Ranu could never have died. That is the power of the stick. Aghori Baba gave it to me long ago, and I have used its miraculous powers on so many people. My foster daughter used it on me when I had my heart attack. I used to ask her, "Why is my bed so lumpy?"

But look how Mahakala works! Dinkar, my friend who was with me there, told me to go down and get some coconut water for Ranu. While I was gone Ranu — remember, it was Mahakala speaking through Ranu — asked Dinkar to put him on the other bed. Dinkar never knew about Aghori Baba's stick, and didn't move it along with Ranu. When I came back my boy was gasping. I lifted him in my arms, he said "Gopala," and he was gone.

He knew he would die. He even told the principal of his

school, "Now it is time for me to leave. I won't be meeting you again. I'm going to a place where it is very cold," meaning he would be reborn in America. And even my intellect had become perverted. At one point I had prayed, "Let my boy die rather than become a cripple," because he had been so good at sports like badminton that his spirit would have been crushed if he had been forced to limp around for the rest of his life; that is what polio does to you, you know.

In any case after my Ranu died I went mad. My position was pitiable. I actually had to borrow money to burn him. For six months I sat in the smashan with one small bone and some ash which I had retrieved from his funeral pyre. I was trying to revive him in the same body. Eventually someone promised me that he would come back to me after being born to different parents, carrying certain signs on his body so that I could recognize him.

I refused to meet my Junior Guru Maharaj for four years after my son's death. When I finally did go to visit him I gave him such a barrage of curses that he had no option but to sit and listen to me for two hours. I used all the foul language I know; in addition I was telling him things like, "You are a sadhu so you never had any children; what can you know of the grief of a father who loses his son?"

He listened to me patiently until I was through and then said quietly, "Wah, Babuji, wah; now I know how strong is the love of human beings. If you really loved your son so much how is it that you are still alive after his death? Why didn't you die of shock at the moment of his death or throw yourself on the funeral pyre with him? You are eating and drinking as if nothing had happened. You are going to the races and enjoying your life. So I understand that this was not real love but only rnanubandhana, just a debt which had to be paid."

I was ashamed, because I knew that what he said was the truth. Then he told me, "Come here," and he pressed a certain nerve on the back of my head, and suddenly I understood the rnanubandhana between me and my son, and why he had to die. Guru Maharaj told me, "There is no need for you to cry.

You know God exists in everyone's heart. If you see your Ranu in everyone you meet, you will have so many Ranus."

So, I lost one son but gained millions. Wasn't it worth it? And later I realized that by continuing to live I had been able to do some things for Ranu which benefited him immensely. I saw to it that he underwent thousands of births during the four years between his death and his reincarnation in human form. Thousands of births, in which millions of karmas were wiped out. And in so many of those births he was sacrificed. It is not necessary for the spirit to enter the womb and actually grow with the fetus. It is sufficient if the spirit enters the animal just a few minutes or hours or days before the sacrifice occurs. And the nice thing about it is that once you are sacrificed in one womb you never have to take rebirth in that womb again; never.

I can predict one characteristic of my son's personality in his new body, wherever he may be. He will never want to injure any animals; and there will be some species of animal of which he will be so fond that he will never be able to endure it if he sees them in pain; all because he has been sacrificed in those forms.

When you see a dead animal on the road and a shiver suddenly and involuntarily goes up your spine, somewhere in some previous birth you must have endured something like that. Perhaps it was not a car; you might have been crushed by anything, even an elephant or a boulder. But subconsciously the agony is still present. You "remember" the past experience and shiver uncontrollably.

And once you develop yourself spiritually you feel not only your own pain but you empathize with the pain of the being who is suffering. When you see God in every human, every animal, even the tiniest insect, and even in the vegetables you eat every day, you cannot bear to see their torment, because it becomes your torment. You see God suffering, and it is unbearable.

Whenever I drive past a certain mutton shop near Poona I see rows of goat carcasses, and I feel pity for the goats who were slaughtered merely to please someone's tongue. One day I got so wild that I said to myself, "I'll see to it that everyone in this city is burned alive!" just to make up for the sufferings of the little kid goats who are tethered near the carcasses. Animals can smell imminent slaughter, and they fear death like any other living being. How cruel it is to force baby goats to spend twenty-four hours with the dead bodies of their own kind, knowing all the while that in the morning they too will end up on the meat hooks!

I was so wild that day that I was ready to invoke any spirit just to finish off everyone in the town and teach them a good lesson in sensitivity. Suddenly some ethereal being sneered at me, "You fool! Who are you to pity them? At least they know when they are going to die; their suffering is limited to a day. But you have no idea when you are going to die, or how much you will have to suffer. Who deserves pity: they or you?" And then I had to keep quiet, because every word was true.

Let me assure you, though, that it is better not to know when you are going to die unless you are an advanced Yogi, and sometimes not even then. If I had not known Ranu was going to die I would still have felt the hurt at his death, no doubt, but how much more did I feel it when I knew it all beforehand and could do absolutely nothing about it? It is a real blessing from Nature that when we are born we forget our rnanubandhanas; otherwise most people would not be able to endure the misery of existence. Only those who need to know are finally permitted to know, so that they can go beyond rnanubandhana. And for those few who do know there is nothing more relieving than the grip of Mahakala, the grip which signals that soon they will be free of the responsibility of remaining alive, swimming in the shark-filled ocean of the material world.

# AUTHOR'S POSTSCRIPT

Ranu's story exemplifies Vimalananda's whole teaching about rnanubandhana, a true tale of how a being takes birth, plays about, pays off debts, and departs, once those debts have been paid. The story of Ranu would not be complete, however, without appending the story of Vimalananda's father to it. Since this tale involves me personally I have deliberately written it in first person from my point of view.

During the summer of 1978 Vimalananda predicted that his father would die in his sleep before the end of the year. I had already experienced Vimalananda's accuracy in predicting the date and time of an individual's demise. It surprised me then when the year was ending and the foretold death had not yet occurred.

We were in Bombay to celebrate Christmas and New Year's when on the night of December 30 I told Vimalananda, "You assured me your papa would pass on during this year. What happened? He is still alive."

Vimalananda replied, "There is still one day left in the year, isn't there? Let it go by first and then tell me anything you like." Suddenly, for no apparent reason, a dog began to howl piteously in the street below. We later discovered that he had been locked in the post office located in our building on the ground floor and was howling to try to attract attention to his plight. According to the science of omens, however, the mournful baying of a dog in the night is an exceedingly inauspicious sign.

The phone rang at 5 A.M. the next morning to announce that Vimalananda's father had died in his sleep during the night, about the same time the dog had begun to wail. As Vimalananda hung up the phone he turned to me with a big I-told-you-so grin and said, "Now what do you have to say?"

As we entered the old man's room to pay our last respects Vimalananda sighed contentedly and whispered to me, "Look at that face!" Then he pointed to a picture on the wall which was obviously one of the old man done just a short while before his demise, for the features tallied almost precisely with those of the dead face before me. "That fellow on the wall is Haranath Thakur, our family guru," Vimalananda continued. "My father concentrated on his picture for so many years that he became like his guru even in physical form. This is a practical demonstration of the Kita Bhramari Nyaya, the Law of Caterpillar and Butterfly: Whatever you concentrate on you will eventually become.

"Actually there is a better reason for this," he mused on. "In 1927 my father came down with meningitis and died. Yes, he died; I can show you death certificates signed by three different doctors. We received a message from Haranath immediately: 'Don't remove the body for twelve hours after death.' All our relatives said, 'Don't be stupid. He's dead now, let's cremate him.' But my mother had implicit faith in her guru and she was adamant. After six hours the corpse sat up. He lived for another fifty-one years.

"A few days later my father received a letter from Haranath: 'My son, you will have a long life, but you will never see your Haranath any more. Look after my boy,' meaning me; I was eleven at the time. A cover letter from Haranath's son was enclosed which stated that on such-and-such a day at such-and-such a time his father had gone to sleep in his garden after mentioning that he felt my father needed his help. Haranath never woke from that sleep. The time he went to sleep turned out to be exactly the moment my father revived.

"After this experience my father was a changed man. Although he had not had much interest in his business before, after this incident he lost all interest in business and would spend his time doing japa or discussing spiritual subjects with my mother. I think there must have been some connection between his revival and his guru's death."

Vimalananda made some further observations about his father's corpse, noting that there were no flies around the body and that abstemious living had made the body itself almost as light as that of a child. Both things he attributed to the old man's purity.

At the Banganga smashan Vimalananda insisted on arranging the pyre himself: "I always arrange the pyres for my family's funerals. It's my job; the smashan is my home. I think I should know best how it is to be done." After igniting the pyre Vimalananda called me over and he and I made offerings of clarified butter into it as if we were worshipping a sacrificial fire according to the traditional ritual. No one dared stop us, though there was visible agitation in the audience at the scandal of a son openly performing ritual worship on his own father's funeral pyre.

Later as we sat quietly smoking and watching the pyre burn I mentioned this to Vimalananda. He laughed a hearty laugh and said, "What does my family know about me? I have never shirked from doing anything I felt I needed to do. I don't know why it is, but I will do most anything just for the experience of it. I'll do it once or twice just so I know I can do it well and then quit so it doesn't become a habit. Aghora is my life, though. I have always lived in the smashan, and as an Aghori I cannot afford to distinguish between the funeral pyre of my mother or my father and that of anyone else. How can I? No; sadhana means sadhana, however you look at it. You must be ready to forget *everything* to become an Aghori."

"I had the same idea at my mother's funeral. In fact I asked my friends, 'Shall I perform a little sadhana here? It will give us great material benefits.' But they turned me down."

He fell silent. For a couple of hours we chatted intermittently. Apart from voices, only the hiss of the dying pyre's flames, the cawing of a few raucous purple and black jungle crows, and the splash of ocean breakers just beyond the retaining wall disturbed the stillness of the smashan. Eventually Vimalananda said jauntily, "Let's go see if the old man has turned to ash yet." On inspection only a few bone slivers remained among the piles of ash. After collecting some of these splinters for later rituals we walked back to the car to drive home. A broad smile illumined his face as Vimalananda told me, "Tonight we'll celebrate New Year's Eve with champagne! I feel I really have some reason to celebrate. My father has succeeded at his sadhana and had a fine death. As we head into the new year he has got a good head start into a new life, a life those of us who live in the smashan know very, very well."

# CHAPTER FIVE

# MENTORS

*Nature is very kind to me; in fact, as my friend Faram used to say, Nature is cockeyed to me. And that is because of my mentors. My mentors were very good. That's all I can say; my mentors were very good. Maybe it's true I was meant by Nature to succeed at all my sadhanas, but my mentors triggered me up and made me succeed. They were too good.*

## MY THREE MENTORS

You know, I met my Senior Guru Maharaj after I left Benares where I had been doing sadhana of Mahakala on Manikarnika Ghat. I had heard that in Girnar (a mountain in the Saurashtra peninsula of Gujarat), Dattatreya (an immortal ascetic) was still living, and that if you tried hard enough and were destined for it you could meet him. I had to go and find out if it could be true.

I went to Junagadh by train, and when I arrived at the foot of the mountain I decided to stay at the Nawab's guest house. At that time the Nawab of Junagadh had jurisdiction over Girnar. I would go out on the mountain during the day and return for my food and rest to the guest house. That is the sort of luxury I was used to; after all, I am a billionaire's son.

Then I decided that I should move out onto the mountain itself since I had not come to Girnar for a holiday but to do sadhana. I located an old deserted Shiva temple and moved in there. It was situated in such a way that by sitting in front of it no animal could surprise me from behind. In front of me I would build my *dhuni* (the sadhu's fire) so I was protected all round, because animals won't come near a fire.

I started eating only what the sadhus ate at the *Sadavarats*. These are places established by rich merchants to feed whoever comes by, as a sort of service. I took off all my clothes and walked around without a stitch. At first I covered myself with my hands, but after a while I lost all my shame.

Eventually I quit eating with the other sadhus and started eating nothing but fruit from trees in the jungle. Before long I realized that I was harming the trees by plucking their fruit, so I ate only what fell. Then, I ate the leaves from the wood I would cut for my dhuni; then only fallen leaves, then only water, and finally I was living on nothing but air until afterward an ethereal being told me to start eating again.

Just as I had been doing in Bombay and Benares I spent most of my time in the smashan. One day, a funeral party had brought the body of a young man to be burnt. While I was watching the tearful relatives arranging the pyre, I noticed a thin fakir standing nearby. Very thin; just like a skeleton. As I watched he walked over to the boy's parents and said, "What do you people think you are doing? This boy is not dead, he is just asleep."

The boy's father looked at him and said, "Why are you trying to interfere? Are you God or something that you can bring the dead back to life? Get out of here before I have you thrown out." But the fakir insisted that the boy was not dead, and I suppose that he insisted a little too much because then the boy's father hit him across the side of the head and a few drops of blood trickled down.

The old fakir wiped his forehead, saw the blood, looked at the man, and said, "So, you've made me red. Now I'll make this a red-letter day for you!" He walked over to the corpse and said, "Get up!" He gave it a nice kick. The corpse sat up.

Well, you should have seen the condition of the members of that funeral party. They ran as if they were being pursued by ghosts. I said to myself, "*Oh*, this fellow has something." The old man came over to me and took out his chillum and filled it with *ganja* (marijuana flowers). He offered it to me first, but I requested him to ignite it. When he inhaled, a flame a foot high leapt from the chillum.

When you are wandering as a sadhu you run into all types of people. Many criminals masquerade as sadhus or fakirs in order to escape the police, and the police in order to catch such criminals masquerade in the same way. Then there are men who run away from nagging wives or heavy debts or some other responsibility. There are magicians, and men who cheat barren couples with promises of children, and the whole flotsam and jetsam of society. When you become a sadhu, you must be able to know who is genuine and who is not. And the best way to do that is with a chillum of charas or ganja, because most sadhus are forbidden to drink.

Be sure to let that fellow light the chillum and take the first puff. You will be benefited in so many ways. First, he will get the fire going for you so that you don't have to inhale too hard. Second, by his technique of holding the chillum and inhaling you will know whether he is an old crony, or a beginner, or just what. And as soon as he starts to get into his intoxication everything will come out: who he is, why he is moving about as a sadhu, where he is going.

I'll give you an example. Once I was out in Girnar and I happened to meet a strange sadhu. As usual we sat down to smoke, and before long I began to collect information from him. When he told me he was from Rajasthan I immediately suspected something because people from that state are well known as misers instead of sadhus.

I shifted the conversation slightly and came up with the information that he hated to beg. Another clue: Would someone who had plenty of money and position in society ever stoop to beg? So he must have been a prosperous merchant, since people from Rajasthan are good at business.

My last bit of data was obtained when he told me, "This ganja

has made me hungry; let's go down and get something to eat."
I was convinced; here was a businessman who had left his family, perhaps because he lost his money, though that was not certain. I decided to rid Girnar of one more false sadhu and told him, "Swamiji, I am so pleased to have met you. I want to give you something in return. Take this number and bet on it."

He did, and he won a packet. He left Girnar and returned to his family and business. Would a real sadhu ever think of gambling? Never.

Anyway, when a foot-high flame rose from this sadhu's chillum I knew he was a veteran. He said to me, "So, you have come from Bombay," and then he went on to tell me about my family, my life, and most everything else, and then asked, "Do you know who I am?"

Now someone, some ethereal being, had told me who he was. And when I told the old man who he was, he was so amazed that he had to keep quiet. I became his disciple.

He eats sometimes, but only when he feels like it; he does love to drink tea, though. His eyes, which never blink, are the only things which would give him away; they are much sharper than an eagle's. Otherwise he looks completely nondescript. And he is the shrewdest old man possible. If he wants to trick you he'll do it in such a way that he'll have you admiring him for it. And if he wants to make you rich nothing can stand in his way.

There was a friend of mine who owned three cars and was a well-to-do businessman. As his destiny would have it he fell on hard times and had to hock all three of his automobiles. My Senior Guru Maharaj had come to Bombay then, and one fine day decided he wanted to go for a drive. I immediately thought of my friend and told him, "This is your golden opportunity. Take my Senior Guru Maharaj out for a drive and then he'll do anything for you."

My friend laughed and said, "I don't have a car anymore." I told him, "Beg, borrow, or steal, but locate one." Somehow he was able to redeem one of his cars, and we got it onto the road — without any fuel in it. He told me, "Look, I've come to the end of my money; how can we drive without any gas?" We considered the possibilities, then got in touch with someone we knew who had an account at a filling station. We drove over there and filled the tank on credit. Ready to go!

After his ride, my old man was feeling expansive, as I knew he would be, and he looked over to my friend and asked him, "How much money do you need?" He replied, "300,000 rupees." My Senior Guru Maharaj twirled his mustache for a moment, and then pulled off one of the rings on his fingers. He said to my friend, "This ring is for Saturn. Put it on and go to sleep for an hour, and then let me know what you see or hear." My friend and I had a low opinion of the whole drama, but he went off to sleep in the next room.

Meanwhile the old man and I were having a discussion. He was telling me, "I want you to go out and borrow as much money as you can at any rate of interest, even 1,000 percent per day." I thought he was up to his old tricks again. One of his peculiarities is that you can give him any amount of money, even 10 million rupees, and within half an hour he'll come back to you and tell you he has spent all of it and needs more. The last time he was in Bombay, I warned a certain Maharani about him. I told her, "Give him anything he wants to eat — meat, fish, anything he wants. If he wants clothes, give him clothes. Give him perfume, give him flowers, give him anything you please, but don't give him any money." I had to leave Bombay for some time, and when I returned she told me, "I lost 10,000 rupees." I told her, "Look, I even took an oath from you that you wouldn't give him a paise." She said, "I don't know what came over me." I know what came over her — but that's a different story.

So, I thought he just wanted some money and was going to leave me in the lurch again. You have no idea how I pacified the Maharani and eventually arranged to have her reimbursed; and I had no intention of doing it all over again. I told him as much, and he told me there was nothing to worry about, and while we were arguing in this fashion my friend came back from his sleep and announced, "I've seen two numbers."

At that time people used to bet on the opening and closing quotations of the New York Cotton Exchange. They would bet on the two numbers to the right of the decimal point, so we knew what the two numbers stood for. They happened to be the same double-digit number. My friend was impressed, because someone had told him the number over and over until he couldn't forget it. I was still doubtful.

My Guru Maharaj told me to go out and not to return until I had borrowed at least 10,000 rupees. I went to a moneylender, who explained all the interest rates and what-have-you to me, and I walked out of his shop with 9,000 rupees. That's the way they do things: They keep 10 percent as the first payment while they're charging you interest on the whole amount. When I got back to him my Senior Guru Maharaj told me to put all of it on the numbers. I flatly refused. Wasn't it enough to have contracted a debt of 10,000 rupees? If I was to lose all the money, I would be in a truly pitiable plight. My old man told me, "All right, I know you have no faith. Do one thing: bet 5,000 rupees, and 1,000 rupees more for me." "You?" I asked "What is the guaranty I'll ever be paid again? I know all about you."

He looked at me and twirled his mustache, and said, "I still have this, don't I?" My Senior Guru Maharaj was an emperor at one time, in this same body, long, long ago. I've seen his sword; I've seen coins with the imprint of his face stamped on them. And in this part of the world, a king's mustache or beard is equivalent to his honor; so to swear to me on his mustache that he would repay me showed the seriousness of the whole thing.

Still, I warned him: "Listen, if you are just going to mess everything up again I am going to cut your throat from ear to ear; this time I've had enough." He told me, "My child, I will cut my own throat if I fail to deliver for you."

There was nothing else left to say. I bet 6,000 rupees at 90 to 1. We sat around waiting for the results. I had lost all hope until the news came: The first number had come correct. I felt relieved and immediately said, "Let's cancel the bet," because you could get paid 7 to 1 or something like that if the first number alone came. The old man told me, "No, we've done it, now we're going to see it through to the end."

When the second number came my astonishment knew no

bounds: more than half a million rupees! Immediately my Senior Guru Maharaj said, "Repay your loan." After that, and after giving my friend what he needed and pocketing my share because I was also broke at the time, I tried to give him his part of the winnings. "Now do you believe I kept my word?" he taunted me. "Take the 1,000 rupees which were in question and hire a musician so I can enjoy a nice night. That's all I want." We had beautiful music all night long, and the next day my friend, who had been impressed with the old man's power, told him, "My sister has been in bed between sandbags for the past six months with a broken spine. Can you do anything about it?" The old man went to see her and gave her a hard slap — and in that instant she became well, perfectly healed.

After finishing all the work my Senior Guru Maharaj took his ring back from my friend — he is very careful about such useful objects — and then he told him, "I'll see that you get heaps and heaps of wealth, more than you can even dream of, but you must stop your whoring and wining." My friend looked at him and said, "What would I do with heaps and heaps of money? How would I spend it? No thanks; I prefer to enjoy." And then it was the old man's turn to be astonished at how perverse human beings can be!

Once he and my foster daughter and I and a few others were all sitting talking together. My foster daughter had been pestering him for days to show her his true form; and when she would ask, he would tell her, "I know who has been putting such things into your head," with a pointed glance at me. "Don't pay any attention to him; are such things possible? My real form is the one you see right here." But a woman never gives up once she has set her mind to something, and this girl pestered him and pestered him until finally he said to her, "How big was your father?" Now, her father was a very hefty man and fairly tall as well. When she told him all this he said, "Bring me one of your father's coats." She did, and he put it on. It fit him terribly, or rather we thought it would because he is so thin, but then we saw he had filled up the entire coat until it was bursting at the seams and he had become so tall his head was near the ceiling. Then he caught himself and said to her,

"If I show you fully, your ceiling will break, and you will not
be able to exist," and he became his normal size again. But she
had had her glimpse. Then he told her, "By seeing this have
you been helped in any way? Ask me for something that is of
some use to you."

Usually, however, you cannot convince him to do anything.
Even if you throw the filthiest language at him he will say,
"Those are all old words; why not try to think of some new
ones?" He loves to play about and can be really jolly sometimes, but look out when he means business. For giving spiritual knowledge, there is no one to beat him anywhere in the
world; even my Junior Guru Maharaj admits it. And if you ask
him for spiritual knowledge, he will ask you in return, "Are
you ready to be flayed alive?" meaning, are you ready for all
your karmas to be ripped from you? If you say yes, you will
suffer more terribly than you could ever dream you could suffer, but when you come through it you will be ready. Put
through the fire, gold becomes impervious to everything, and
so will you.

No one can fool him unless they play music for him. People
have made millions out of him just as they have from me simply by making him hear music. When he is overwhelmed by
emotion he might even give you the results of thousands of
years of his penance; then later he will realize what he has done
and beg some favor from you in return. He's really very sweet
that way. He should be generous, having been a king. Even now
some of that regality, that kingliness remains, despite the fact
that when he left his throne for his sadhana he renounced everything. Nowadays, you can't even meet him if you want to; no
one knows where he has gone, except me. He is by himself,
and he is no longer in his normal senses. He has gone mad with
love for Krishna.

He was the one to tell me that I would have to go to a guru
from the south, my Junior Guru Maharaj. I call him my Junior
Guru Maharaj because he is a disciple of my Senior Guru
Maharaj. So I am not only his disciple, I am his *gurubhai*
(co-disciple) also. He says frankly that when he was young my

Senior Guru Maharaj used to feed him and look after him. So imagine how old my Senior Guru Maharaj must be.

No one knows how old either of them are, but if you look in my Junior Guru Maharaj's mouth you will see two full sets of teeth, one row right behind the other. They say you grow a new tooth after every 100 years; I don't know. If I tell you his origin you won't believe me. When Lord Curzon was Viceroy of India at the turn of the century, archaeological excavations were going on in the state of Orissa, and in a cave in one hill they discovered the perfectly preserved body of an old sadhu. Someone thought to call a man from the Jagannath temple in Puri who knew about samadhi and such things, and after massage, and oil rubs, and I don't know what else he was able to bring the sadhu down from his samadhi and back into consciousness of the world. That sadhu is my Junior Guru Maharaj. I have met people who have known him ever since then and they say his looks have not changed in the least up to the present day, except that in some places his hair has grayed.

How I met him is a story in itself. I have always been fond of Maharajas, Emirs, and other rulers, and they have always been fond of me; there must be some link. I was trying to help a certain prince succeed his father as Maharaja, and one day I happened to ask an acquaintance if he knew of any sadhu who could help us out with his spiritual powers. He brought this sadhu to us.

At first glance he didn't look like much to me. Driving home from the railway station this prince was telling the old sadhu about how his father was ruining the administration of the state, and how well he would be able to rule if given an opportunity. Finally, the old man spoke: "So you want your father to die, eh?" And as soon as we got down from the car and crossed the threshold into the house, word arrived from Delhi that the prince's father had died very suddenly. I thought to myself, "Yes, this man has some power!"

I was broke at the time, and desperate, and there were races that day. I had decided to go and bet on the horses and sink or swim. When I told this to the sadhu he took my wallet from me and put a pinch of ash into it, and said to me, "Keep this with you and bet on whatever you see and hear." I laughed in his face and told him, "Maharaj, this is Bombay, people are not such fools here to believe such nonsense." See and hear, indeed! Still, I kept the envelope in my pocket and left for the races.

Because he had insisted on sitting and chatting with me, I was late to arrive and missed the first three races. I started cursing him because my choices had won two of those races. Unnecessarily I had wasted my opportunity to make money just because of some old fool and his ash! I decided to go back to him in the evening and beat him black and blue.

While I was mired in this depression, I was standing under a tree near the bookies' enclosure, and I suddenly heard something telling me to bet on a certain horse. At first I didn't believe I was hearing it, but once I believed, I decided to see what sort of a horse it was. Well, on the racing form it was hopeless; besides that, the jockey, Ghuman Singh, had never won a race in his life. I thought, "When he doesn't know what he's doing, why should the old man try to show off? How can I waste money on his guesswork?" I decided to bet on another horse, my own choice, and told the number, which was seven, to the clerk in the betting window. He accidentally gave me six fifty-rupee tickets on the horse whose number I had heard; his number was eight. When I realized this mistake I bellowed to change the tickets but it was too late; the race had started and the shutters on the betting windows had slammed down.

I started cursing the old man more vehemently than before: "My last 300 rupees, which I've been saving for an emergency, and I've wasted it! What did I do to be introduced to such an unlucky old man?" Running this thought over and over in my mind, I sat and watched the horse win. I couldn't believe it; I was rich! He paid 70 to 1. Incidentally, that was the one and only race Ghuman Singh ever won in his entire life.

I had to admit my mistake, and I started listening to the voice much more seriously. Over the whole day I made 59,000 rupees, and after the last race I went to a bar on Charni Road and had a few more than my quota of drinks. I had made up my mind: "I must keep a tight grip on this sadhu; he can make millions for me!"

It sounds ludicrous, doesn't it? But I was desperate for money. Of course I could have gone to the smashan and collected millions without working up a sweat, but I will never ask money from a spirit. Here was an old man, though, who seemed ready to provide me with winners just for the asking, and he would bear the karma! It seemed too good to be true.

When I got back to the sadhu he became wild with me the moment I stepped through the door: "Ha, how dare you drink, what do you think of yourself?" and so on. I coolly took the money I had made, laid it at his feet, and told him, "Maharaj, please take as much as you like; just agree to help me again next week."

This only made him wilder. He told my friends, "Go make him vomit and give him an enema." They worked me over so well that by midnight I was almost sober again. When I went back into the sadhu's presence he was still so infuriated that he took his fire tongs and gave me two whacks squarely across the right temple: ptak! ptak! And then he told me, "Did you take birth for things like this?"

I had to tell him no, because those two blows gave me partial memory of my previous births, and I understood why I had been born where I was and what was expected of me in this life. This is why I respect him as my guru: not because he initiated me into a mantra, but because he helped me remember who I am.

Maybe I should explain one thing here. Gambling has a catastrophic effect on the mind. Meat, alcohol, sex: these all cause temporary ruination of the consciousness, but the effects of gambling are permanent. If a man earns money at gambling what does he spend it on? Rich food, alcohol and other intoxications, and women. If he loses money what happens? Envy, hatred: "That fellow cheated me, he was out to get me, now I'll show him, I'll ruin him." The man becomes a cutthroat, literally, if he is of the lower class of men, because he kills to regain his losses. Or, if he is more refined he kills his enemy economically. Gambling is one of the three karmas which cannot be obliterated in the same lifetime. The other two are murder of the guru and rape.

This being the case, how can both my Junior and Senior Guru Maharajs have helped me through gambling? First of all, they never encouraged me to gamble, and they have always done their best to prevent me from doing so. But in both these instances they knew I was out of money and this was the most convenient way for them to help me; and they wanted to convince me of their abilities as well. And don't forget: this was really nothing like gambling. They knew ahead of time what was going to happen, and they just handed that information over to me. It's more like collecting interest on an investment than gambling. They do have to suffer for using their powers for such trivial things, of course, because no one is exempt from the Law of Karma. But they know how to minimize the penalty, and they don't bother about such minor troubles. And besides, they are not in the habit of doing it daily; once only, to serve their purposes. And very strange indeed are their purposes.

By doing this they saved me from an evil fate. I just told you that gambling is a permanent disease, and it was as true for me as for anyone else. But they cured me of it. Not that I gave it up altogether; I still bet whenever I see a good thing, or when one of my own horses is running, and I enjoy directing how my horses work and deciding which races to run them in. It's a wonderful sport — horse racing.

But I was an inveterate gambler, uncontrollable; and my Junior Guru Maharaj brought me under control. I gamble now, but gambling doesn't control me like it once did; I control it. This does not mean you should gamble. I have known only a handful of people to enter the racecourse and then leave it again before losing their money, character, or balance of mind. I was exceedingly lucky, because my Guru Maharaj was willing to take my evil karmas on himself. He knew exactly how to deal with them. Truly, my mentors are wonderful, and they have always been so gentle and kind to me, I don't know why.

My Junior Guru Maharaj can also be extremely strict when necessary; no mistake about it. There was one Behari Das who lived near him several years ago. Behari Das was a good Aghori, but something of a bully: he would trouble all the other sadhus in the area. They would come down with diseases, and Guru

Maharaj would cure them. Behari Das came to know what Guru Maharaj was doing and his ego was hurt: "Who is this fellow trying to undo what I do? I must kill him." But how to kill him? Guru Maharaj doesn't eat or drink, so there was no possibility of poisoning him that way. Does he smoke ganja? Yes.

So, one day Behari Das came to meet Guru Maharaj and told him, "Maharaj, I have decided that I must make you smoke this chillum of ganja as a token of my respect for you." I happened to be there at the time and I immediately knew what Behari Das had in mind. I said, "Why should Guru Maharaj take anything from you? I will smoke it."

Behari Das got wild: "Who are you to interfere? My desire is to see Maharaj smoke this chillum." Guru Maharaj said to me, "Don't worry, Babuji, I'll smoke it." The chillum was lit, and in two puffs — only two — Guru Maharaj finished the whole thing and then put it big end down on the ground.

Then Guru Maharaj said to Behari Das, "Behari Das, I know why you wanted me to smoke that chillum; I know what sort of love you have for me. Unfortunately for you your time is up. You have only five minutes left. Now get out of this ashram." And in five minutes he was dead. As for Guru Maharaj, he had to suffer terribly for six months: boils on his body, dimness of vision, and so on.

I have also been troubled by such people. There is a fellow in Bombay who has tried to poison me three times with ganja mixed with arsenic, aconite, and so on, and each time he lands himself in the hospital and then begs me to cure him. But I also have to suffer for some time; that is just the way things work.

My Junior Guru Maharaj is really an unusual old man. He has roamed all over the world, but no one knows how he does it. When one fellow asked if he had been to London he replied, "Yes, they have a railway there that goes under the ground; I've seen all those things." And when this fellow asked him how long ago he was there he told him, "Four hundred years." What can you say about that?

He is a type entirely different from my Senior Guru Maharaj: a miser. He will not let anything out; he is just like a stone. In fact, he will advise you, "Become just like a Shiva Linga." What he means is, don't let anything affect you. No happiness, no sorrow, nothing: absolutely firm. When he goes anywhere he will sit in one room only, never going out or moving around. Sometimes he stays in one place for twelve years at a time. He never eats or drinks; at the most he takes cow's milk if you really force him to. And once he leaves a place he will never go back there. He is still very old-fashioned and believes strongly in purity and impurity, because he is still doing his sadhana every day. You see, he has done terrific sadhana all his life. He has done such penances that even my Senior Guru Maharaj has admitted that there is no one in India, and that means in the world, to beat him at doing penances.

He is very strict, but he loves to play about in his own way. His play is of a different age. He believes in sacrifice and he expects everyone else to also, so he will frequently cause trouble for someone in order to pull that person out of some entanglement. Of course, he doesn't actually cause the trouble. He just causes certain karmas to come out of that person's causal body and be projected. Since he always causes the bad karmas to be projected, to purge the causal body of all its evil influences, this will always lead to misery.

No one wants to accept responsibility. They want to enjoy all their good karmas and avoid all the bad ones. One day a man had a nice dinner of very spicy food full of chilies, followed by ice cream. Next morning when he squatted to defecate, he screamed, "Ice cream first! Ice cream first!" Only when you are miserable will you remember God; you will never think of Him otherwise, unless you are a true saint. Guru Maharaj is here to make people remember God, not to make them rich or famous. I will give you a written guaranty, if you like, to the effect that after you meet Guru Maharaj *everything* will start going wrong in your life. That's just the way he works, the old, crude way. But that's the way he is.

Once a friend of mine came and asked me to take him to Guru Maharaj. I knew what sort of person this fellow was. He was called *Bala Yogi* ("Child Yogi") or *Kaviraj* ("King of Poets") and he used to sing devotional songs in praise of the Divine

Mother: "Jaya Ambe, Jaya Ambe" and so on. He liked most to have plenty of female disciples: you know what I'm getting at. His brother was dead, and he made a big show out of taking care of his brother's wife. Actually, he developed an illicit relationship with her. I thought it only fair to warn him: "Watch out — Guru Maharaj may do something." He told me, "Ha, you only want to keep him for yourself; why not let other people get the benefit of his powers? I'm sure he'll give me something." I had warned him; my job was over.

You know, when I visit my Guru Maharaj I don't say anything. I sit in one corner. When I feel like it I get up and walk out. Everyone else thinks that I am very rude and insolent and very foolish for not sitting with him. Only he and I know what is going on. When he was last in Bombay he would make everyone go to sleep and then we would exchange the notes in our own way, a way in which words are not required.

I am most shameless; I fight with my Guru Maharaj. I tell him, "What is the use of an ashram? The whole world should be your ashram." Then he gets wild on me. It is only in the past few years that he has had an ashram, and only now his hair is starting to turn grey. It was always jet black before.

So, this friend and I went to Guru Maharaj, who was in Bombay at the time, in 1959. Now, you don't need to tell anything to Guru Maharaj: all he has to do is look at you and he knows every bit. And this fellow made another mistake; he started to recite Sanskrit verses to Guru Maharaj, trying to show off his wisdom. Guru Maharaj is a man who after being dug out of that cave spent twelve years on the branch of a tree doing japa, never touching the ground even once; could this man teach him anything?

Suddenly Guru Maharaj smiled, scribbled something down on a piece of paper, and handed it to my friend, telling him, "Keep this with you always. Wave incense before it daily, when you sit for worship, sit on top of it, then put it under your pillow when you sleep." As we left, my friend smiled knowingly at me and said, "So Guru Maharaj did something good for me after all." But I knew better. I could see that Guru Maharaj was going to have this man's hide.

What happened? Kaviraj went directly to his sister-in-law's house to celebrate with a little sex. But as soon as she saw him she shouted, "How dare you drink bhang and come here? Get out!"

He looked at her and said, "But I never drank any bhang today." She screamed, "Don't say anything to me, just get out. I never want to see you here again!" and she gave him a beautiful pair of slaps, and shut him out of the house. He spent the night on the front steps and had to do without his morning tea as well.

The next morning he came crying to me: "Look what that Guru Maharaj of yours has done to me!"

I told him, "What did I tell you before?"

He replied, "You must take me back to Guru Maharaj so he can free me from this."

We went back to Guru Maharaj, who heard all the complaints and then said to Kaviraj, "I did it to clean out your karmas." Kaviraj said, "But I never asked to have my karmas cleaned out!" Then Guru Maharaj told him, "If you are tired now, take that piece of paper and throw it into the sea." He did, and afterward he was reconciled with his sister-in-law and continued with his life as before. And whenever anyone would ask him about Guru Maharaj, he would say, "Please, he really put me in the soup. I don't want to hear about him."

After Kaviraj left the room, I asked Guru Maharaj, "When you know these people can't take it, why do you do such things?"

Guru Maharaj laughed and said to me. "No, Babuji, that was a Yantra I gave him. If he had kept it he would have broken off from that lady for good and would have quit all his evil ways. Then he would have had to turn to God. He knew so many verses and sang such nice songs, he should have been made a saint."

It's useless trying to argue with Guru Maharaj. He thinks he is still living in a previous era, and he expects everyone else to act accordingly. It is true that when your plans go wrong you have to turn to God, but that is the old, crude method; no one will put up with it today. Nowadays only those people who can't be successful at anything else turn to God: "Asamartho bhavet sadhuh" (A man fit for nothing else becomes a sadhu), but what is the use of that? Still, Guru Maharaj goes on feeding bitter medicine to whoever comes to him. People curse him, but he never bothers about it. Very few will ever be able to understand his play.

In spite of all this, I still fight with my Guru Maharaj. Once when I went to meet Guru Maharaj, he was talking to a businessman from Bombay. The businessman was sitting there with his mistress, ignoring the fact that Guru Maharaj is very strict about those things. His morality is of another age. Why, when he came to Bombay and saw a woman driving a car, he was so shocked that he told me, "Babuji, now I know Kali Yuga is really here." I don't know what he would do if he ever saw a woman flying an airplane.

As I was about to enter I saw a lady crying on the steps outside the room. I have done sadhana of Ma all my life, and I just cannot bear to see a woman cry; it is as if my own Mother is crying. So I asked her, "Ma, why are you crying?" She told me, "Sadhugaru (meaning Guru Maharaj) will not allow me to enter his presence today." It was because she was in her periods.

Then I lost my temper. I stormed into the room and asked Guru Maharaj what he meant by forcing the lady to sit outside like that. I told him, "She is only menstruating. I am an Aghori. I worship menstrual fluid because it has the power to create. Though you have performed Aghora sadhanas you seem to have forgotten all that. A woman cannot conceive before her periods commence or after they cease, so the power of creation lies in that only. Can you create?

"Not only that, you are sitting here with a woman who is no better than a prostitute, and you have the nerve to tell this poor lady who has come so many miles to see you that she may not enter the room. Who do you think you are?"

The fellow whose mistress I had insulted tried to protest, but Guru Maharaj told him to be quiet and said to me, "Wah, Babuji, you have really become a true Aghori now. Your Aghora has become perfect. I only told her to wait outside because I am doing a certain ritual for which I needed to observe purity, that is the only reason. Please don't misunderstand." He just smiled at me and shook his head, and then I lost all my anger also. He is really a wonderful old man.

I can afford to argue with my Senior Guru Maharaj as well as with my Junior Guru Maharaj because they are something different from all the saints and sadhus that you will ever find in India. But even they have to respect my real mentor. I won't tell you His name; I will just call Him "my Mahapurusha," because I love Him as my own. Even though I have treated those two as my gurus, they have never given me a Guru Mantra. My Mahapurusha is my real guru.

You know, I have seen all the big so-called saints, but none of them interests me after knowing Him. If you ask my Junior Guru Maharaj about my Mahapurusha, Guru Maharaj will say, "He is God Himself." If you ask my Senior Guru Maharaj about Him, tears will come from his eyes and he will say, "If you can give me only a glimpse of Him, I will make you the richest man in the world" — and he can do it, too. My Mahapurusha is thirty feet tall — yes, thirty feet. His eyes are the size of your hand. His head is as wide as your chest. I used to sit in the palm of His hand very comfortably, as if I were a pygmy, and we would play together — at a time when I weighed 210 pounds. Once He said to me, "I want to sit on your lap." My God, what a fright I got; I was afraid my bones would break! But when He sat down He did not have the weight of even a rose petal; it was just as if a feather was there.

My Mahapurusha believes in gratification, satisfaction, so that no stain of desire is left. Sometimes we would be sitting in Girnar and He would say, "Let's have lunch at Maxim's. Close your eyes." I would close my eyes, and when I would open them we would be at a good table in Maxim's in Paris appropriately dressed, He reduced to ordinary human size. We would have a delicious twelve-course lunch there, and then — back to Girnar.

One day I had just finished a tough ritual, and I was sitting around kind of bored when He came up and said to me, "What are you doing, moping around like that? Come on! Let us have our worldly enjoyments!"

I asked, "Where are we going?" He said, "You be quiet and

close your eyes." I did, and when I opened them we were in Spain. I got the shock of my lifetime. We were both dressed like Spaniards, and we went to a night club. So many beautiful senoritas were there. We danced the tango with them all night long. All the men gathered at the sides of the club and glared at us! So jealous they were! And La Paloma was playing. After tangoing for some time, my Mahapurusha looked at me warn- ingly, and then we went outside and zip! Back to Girnar. World- ly enjoyments along with sadhanas; what a guru!

He is far, far ahead. I used to smoke twenty pounds of ganja a day, because I know the mantra which nullifies the bad effects. But He has no need of mantras. No one can know Him. Don't even talk about it. When He would sit with the sadhus in Girnar, He would take His pipe — an elephant's tusk — and fill it full of ganja. He would light it and finish the whole pipe- full in one puff, throw the pipe high into the air, shout "Jai Girnari!" and vanish. He has no limits at all.

Once we were sitting together in a circle, and one old fakir began to complain that there was no one around who could do miracles like the great saints of the old days could, especially the art of creating gold.

My Mahapurusha didn't say anything to him, but pointed at the Nandi of a nearby Shiva temple and said, "Get up!" The bull, which was made of stone, stood up. My Mahapurusha told him, "You've been hungry for so many ages. Now eat!" And the bull ate some of the green grass growing near him. Then, "Drink!" The bull took a long drink of water. Finally the bull was told, "Go over to that old fakir and give him what he wants!" The bull ambled over to the fakir, who had opened his mouth wide in amazement in the first place. He turned his behind to that astonished old man and defecated — pure gold. When he had finished he was told, "Now go back and wait," and he went back to his pedestal, sat, and became completely stone again, waiting for the next time he would be awakened.

The old fakir had tears in his eyes, but my Mahapurusha was gone. His method of teaching is something else also; some- thing quite different. First He makes you sit down, tells you to close your eyes and then gives you a good slap with His left hand. You go into a trance and when you wake up, after a few hours or a few days, He is gone, but you have learned everything about the subject He was teaching you. Don't ask me how. Of course He never eats or drinks; His only enjoyment in life is to smoke ganja. Once a poor girl came to Him. Her parents had been beating her because she was hungry and had been stealing food from them. He told her, "Ma, why do you worry? Take this, and you will never have to eat or drink again." He gave her a pinch of ash from His bag, and what He had said happened. When I was in Girnar, I met her, and she had never eaten or drunk anything from that day onward.

But my Mahapurusha has left Girnar, and no one knows where to find Him, except me. He belongs to me, and I belong to Him; we are pals.

It is thanks to my Mahapurusha that I have achieved whatever I have achieved in this lifetime. He has looked after me well since I was born, through the medium of Haranath Thakur, my parents' guru. Years before he ever met my parents or became a guru, Haranath was traveling in a one-horse shay through Kashmir when at a stop along the way he suddenly fell down. He knew he was dying, and he did die.

When he was dead my Mahapurusha came to him. He never knew who my Mahapurusha was; I was told the whole story later by my "Big Daddy." My Mahapurusha said to him, "Do you know you are dead?"

He said, "Yes."

"Do you have any desires left?"

"Yes, I want to meet my Mother."

Then my Mahapurusha cut his body into sixty-four pieces and threw three pieces away. Can you guess which three pieces were thrown away? The Three Gunas: *Sattva*, *Rajas*, and *Tamas*. He put the other sixty-one pieces together again and suddenly the man came back to life, and was given instructions by my Mahapurusha. Eventually he became my parents' guru, and in that way my Mahapurusha could look after me while I was growing up. Haranath always used to tell my parents, "My boy," meaning me, "will move about in fine suits of clothes and no one will ever know him."

It is only thanks to my Mahapurusha that I have survived for so long here in the world. It was He who sent me back here from Girnar, otherwise I would never have left. And now, whenever I hear "La Paloma" I am reminded of Him. People have made millions of rupees out of me just by playing "La Paloma," because whenever I hear it I am overcome with love for my Mahapurusha, and in that outpouring of longing for Him somehow the work gets done. I could not bear living for even a moment in the world if it were not for Him supporting me. If you had ever lived the free life of a sadhu you would know what I mean. To have lived free and then to be caged up is enough to kill most wild animals; it would have killed me, had not my Mahapurusha had some work He wanted me to do. Let any other being in the universe come to me and I don't bother with them; for me, only my Mahapurusha exists.

# DEVOTION TO THE GURU

Do you know the story of Meera, the great devotee of Krishna? When Krishna stood before her in all his bewitching beauty, as a result of the method she had been taught by her guru Raidas, she composed a lovely Hindi couplet on the spot: "My guru and my beloved deity Govinda both stand before me; to whom shall I first prostrate myself? I must pay my first respects to my guru, because it was he who showed me Govinda." Such devotion always pays dividends. Meera understood how important it is to have a guru; how much the disciple owes the guru. Most knowledge you can pick up from somewhere, but until you put it into practice it remains as a mere intellectual understanding. The guru forces you to learn it, he rubs your face into the ground until you learn it, if he is a real guru. That is why I say that none of the people you have in America can be classified as gurus. They teach a little to the students who come to them, and they collect money for it.

If you are interested in making money out of someone you can't afford to offend them or else they'll immediately run away to someone else. A real guru doesn't care for money: he wants

a disciple he can be proud of. And he will tear that disciple to
pieces if necessary in order to make sure that certain lessons
get learned. Then when that disciple gets an opportunity to
meet a deity, or a Siddha, or some other Mahapurusha, there is
no question of the disciple making the wrong choice. The disciple's own personality has been so effaced by the guru, the
false e-y-e (eye) consciousness has been so thoroughly crushed,
that the disciple must make the right choice, and then he or
she is made; there is no question of a doubt.

Eknath Maharaj was one of the greatest saints Maharashtra
has ever produced. His guru's name was Janardan Swami, and
in fact today people only know the name of Janardan Swami
because he was Eknath's guru. This is the play of guru and
disciple.

*Eknath* literally means "one master," and that fit Eknath perfectly. He was totally devoted to Janardan Swami. While still
a boy Eknath had heard a voice from the sky telling him to go
to Janardan Swami, so he walked the 200 miles from his home-
town to Deogarh where Janardan Swami was the ruler of the
fort. For a number of years Eknath served Janardan Swami faithfully without being taught anything at all about spirituality.
He never objected, never complained.

After some time Janardan Swami put Eknath in charge of
the treasury. One night Eknath had some trouble balancing the
books. His accounts were off by a single pie (a fraction of a cent).
Late into the night he sat, trying his best to locate his error.
When he suddenly discovered the elusive pie his joy was so
great he shouted. This woke up Janardan Swami who came in
and demanded to know what the boy was doing up so late at
night. When he was told the story Janardan Swami said to
Eknath, "My son, if the discovery of a single pie which has
been lost can cause you such great joy, can you imagine what
your joy would be if you discovered God?"

Eknath replied humbly, "Maharaj, I don't know how to go
about looking for God. Will you teach me?"

A few days later Janardan Swami told Eknath to accompany
him on a trip outside Deogarh. The Swami was riding a horse,
and Eknath had to run along behind it for fifty-five miles, dur-

ing which time he did not get the opportunity to drink even a drop of water. Eknath did not complain.

Late that night as Janardan Swami and his disciple sat quietly together in a lonely place, an unkempt man trailed by a dog came up to them. Handing a bowl to Eknath he hold him to milk the bitch and bring him the milk to drink. Even though Eknath had had nothing to quench his thirst all day long he was not tempted and brought the bowl back to the man, who drank it down. He then made Eknath milk the bitch again, and this milk he gave to Janardan Swami. When the bowl was empty he told Eknath to go and wash it in a nearby stream.

Eknath had not been told anything, but he was convinced that the man was none other than Guru Dattatreya, the guru of the Naths, because Dattatreya is always accompanied by a dog and always affects a wild appearance, to scare away ordinary mortals. So Eknath poured a little water into the bowl to wash all the remaining drops of milk into the bottom and then drank down the mixture. Immediately he could see the man in his true form, and yes: it was Dattatreya himself. Dattatreya was pleased with Eknath's cleverness and blessed him. That was enough; Dattatreya's blessing was precious to Lord Shiva Himself, so what effect must it have had on Eknath? And this was all thanks to his unflinching devotion to his guru.

If you are out to locate a guru it is best to look for a real one instead of all the fakes that are around nowadays, but it is not essential. If your desire is strong enough and your heart is pure enough Nature will teach you Herself if need be. Remember the story of Ekalavya from the *Mahabharata* (the great Indian epic poem)? Dronacharya refused to teach him archery so Ekalavya went out and made a statue of Dronacharya and worshipped it as his guru. He worshipped it so hard and so well that the statue began to teach him, and he actually became a better archer than any of the direct pupils of Dronacharya. Dattatreya himself had twenty-four gurus: birds, animals, beings who didn't know they were teaching him. By observation alone he learned what they had to teach.

However, it is much easier to have a human guru. You must test your guru thoroughly to make sure he can teach you, but once you accept him as your teacher you must stick with him. There is no use in running from guru to guru; you will end up falling between two stools. Find one and stick to him. Don't be like the swan, who when her pond dries up flies off to find another one. Be like the moss, which dries up along with the stone which it covers. The moss sticks to the stone in good times and in bad times, without trying to calculate whether it is profitable or not.

Remember that when you love a guru you are not loving his external personality; you have to love his perennial personality, the Shiva-consciousness which he is trying to instill into you. That means that you are actually loving yourself; the Self is loving the Self. Instead of attempting to love the entire universe you try to learn to love one person properly, because the Atma is the same in every being. And remember that no matter how much you love, or think you love, your guru, he loves you much, much more because he has already learned how to love the Infinite. He is trying to make you into his own guru: the One.

Once a moth, circling around a lamp about to make the fatal plunge, spoke to the flame: "What do you know of love? All you do is stand there as I whirl about you until I can no longer bear to remain separated from you and I embrace you. And in the moment I embrace you I am consumed, burned into nothingness."

The flame smiled and replied, "You fool! Do you call that love? Look at me; I am burning. You burn only when you embrace me, but in my longing for you the pain of my separation from you has transmuted me into fire itself."

This is what should happen in real life. A disciple may think he really loves his guru and has done a lot for him, but the disciple is too stupid to realize that his guru is absolutely burning to give something to him, to give his essence to the disciple. At first a disciple is nothing better than a prostitute; he flits from object to object, teaching to teaching, guru to guru, like a fly who enjoys sweets and filth equally. Little by little the "child" loses his taste for other things and slowly develops devotion to his mentor. Only then does he realize that his guru is his all-in-one, one-in-all. Only then can the "child" merge with the mentor and receive what the mentor wants so intensely to give.

How many people can understand the play of guru and disciple? Almost no one. If the disciple himself can't understand it, how will some outsider be able to? And this is true of all disciples, even those who may be great saints on their own, like Ramakrishna Paramahamsa. The first time Ramakrishna Paramahamsa visited Benaras he exclaimed that he saw heaps of gold in the city. He did not mean metallic gold, of course; he meant the gold of minds filled with the power of discrimination. When he visited Telang Swami, Ramakrishna was overcome with spiritual bliss and said openly, "I see before me the incarnation of Shiva," meaning that Telang Swami had so perfected himself that there was no false personality remaining; all had become Shiva-consciousness.

Then he tried to speak with Telang Swami, but Telang Swami was observing complete silence, though he did deign to answer Ramakrishna's questions by means of gestures alone. Ramakrishna repeated, "I see before me the incarnation of Shiva, but this is a selfish Shiva," meaning that he was unwilling to part with any of his knowledge, to teach it to others. Ramakrishna was blind to say this. Can God ever be selfish? God is always magnanimous; if He isn't, he isn't God. That's all there is to it. Telang Swami did not bat an eyelid, but decided to teach Ramakrishna Paramahamsa a lesson. After Ramakrishna returned to his home in Dakshineshwar, a village near Calcutta, he began to become restless. Now, Ramakrishna was one of the greatest saints the world has ever produced. He achieved success at sadhanas of Jesus, of Mohammed, of so many forms of God, but his success started with sadhana of a form of Kali called *Bhavatarini*.

He became very restless, so he asked Bhavatarini Ma, "Ma, You have showed me so many sadhanas of God with form, and also of God without form, but You have never showed me anything of Tantra. I want to learn about Tantra. Send me someone to teach me about Tantra." And thereafter, one day, a woman called the Bhairavi Brahmani arrived in Dakshineshwar and proceeded to teach Ramakrishna a bit about Tantra. And who was she? A little disciple of Telang Swami.

When all of Ramakrishna's Tantric sadhanas were over he had occasion to go back to Benaras. Telang Swami dragged him without his knowing it. Ramakrishna had one of his devotees cook up an immense quantity of rice pudding, about ten gallons, and with his own hands Ramakrishna fed the entire amount to Telang Swami in thanksgiving. Telang Swami, who was a true Siddha, had no difficulty in consuming the whole cauldronful, but did not bother to look at Ramakrishna. And that was the last sadhana Ramakrishna Paramahamsa ever did; Tantra was the culmination of his sadhana. He did have to suffer for calling Telang Swami selfish, though; he developed cancer of the throat eventually, and died. It is never wise to insult Shiva, as that priest of Benaras learned about Telang Swami so many years before. So Telang Swami taught Ramakrishna a good lesson, didn't he? Just because he did not move his lips did not mean he was not teaching Ramakrishna; he did it with his fingers. Then he caused Ramakrishna to develop the desire to learn Tantra. There was no need for Ramakrishna to have such a desire otherwise. It was all the play of Telang Swami, who contacted him from a distance and disturbed his mind to demonstrate what child's play it was to direct his consciousness. It was all the magnanimity of Telang Swami; otherwise Ramakrishna would never have had the opportunity to learn Tantra.

# GURU AND DISCIPLE

You know, getting a good disciple is a real boon. To get a good guru is the best blessing, no doubt, but to get a good disciple is really rare. The Rishis of course bring their own with them when they come, just as Krishna and Ramakrishna Paramahamsa did.

Once Matsyendra Nath, the direct disciple of Adi Nath, who is Lord Shiva, wanted to test his pet disciple Gorakh. You know for a sadhu his dhuni (fire) is his TV. He looks into it and can know anything that is going on anywhere in the world. One night as Gorakh was sitting on his dhuni he saw his Guru Maharaj in Assam in the company of dancing girls and thought, "Oh my God! Guru Maharaj has become entangled in the samsara! He is in danger of losing everything that he has gained through his penances! I must go and save him. Matsyendra is mine, he belongs to our tribe of Naths. He is not meant for these things." Gorakh had intense possessive love for his Guru Maharaj.

So Gorakh journeyed to Assam, disguised as a minstrel. When he located his guru, Matsyendra, he was drinking wine and had two girls in his lap, one on each thigh, with a hand on one breast of each. Gorakh, still in disguise, began singing a song: "Look, Matsyendra, Gorakh has come; remember who you are and forget this Maya."

But Matsyendra did not want to leave. Gorakh literally had to force him to start the long journey back to Girnar. Along the way, Matsyendra went off for a bath, leaving his shoulder bag with Gorakh for safekeeping. Gorakh thought that it felt quite heavy, and when he opened it two gold bars fell out. He became wild and thought to himself, "What is wrong with my Guru Maharaj? He is a Nath; he can piss on a rock and turn it into gold. I will not allow him to become entangled in Maya," and he threw both bars as far as he could into the jungle.

Finally they arrived in Girnar and Gorakh said, "Now Guru Maharaj, do you remember who you are?" He was feeling very proud of having walked 3,000 miles to save his Guru Maharaj from the clutches of the world.

Suddenly Matsyendra Nath passed his hand over Gorakh's head, and Gorakh Nath realized that all that he thought had happened had been an illusion, and that in fact neither of them had even left Girnar. And then Gorakh Nath realized how foolish he had been to imagine that his Guru Maharaj could ever become enmeshed in Maya. But Matsyendra loved his disciple all the more, seeing that Gorakh loved his guru enough to search him out and force him back to his senses.

Of course you can't expect ordinary people to play about like Aghoris do. Only Aghoris really know how to play about — and Naths are Aghoris, nothing else. But to understand their play is extremely difficult. The ordinary seeker feels revulsion when he hears about using wine in rituals or seating a naked girl on the left thigh with a hand on her left breast and her hand on his penis. That is how Dattatreya got rid of all his so-called disciples except one, who became the Adi Nath. Dattatreya was the guru of Lord Shiva himself, the Lord of Aghoris.

Of course Dattatreya is too good, but other Indian gurus have learned from his example and have made use of it to test their own disciples. I know of a case which happened in Girnar. There was a Muslim fakir who had 1,000 disciples. When he was about to die, his disciples all began to pretend to love him a lot. So he said to himself, "Is that so? I'd better teach these buggers a lesson."

So, the next day he announced, "I have decided to leave this world, but before doing so I have a desire to have sex with a female donkey. Then I'll be ready to die."

Of the 1,000 disciples, 990 said, "Guruji has gone crack," and left him. Only ten remained, thinking it was some sort of joke. The next day the fakir said to them, "Now, please collect the money necessary to buy the donkey." Then those ten realized he was serious, and seven of them left saying, "What can this man know when he is entangled in such worldly desires?"

Three remained, and the next day the fakir said to the three, "By my astrological calculations I have determined a good day. Now, be prepared with the donkey." Another departed after this speech, leaving two. After the donkey was brought one of the two boys realized that the old fellow was going to go through with it, and he too got fed up and left. The fakir looked at the sole survivor and said, "What are you waiting for? Better go now."

The boy said, "Oh no, my Lord, I want to see how you do it with this donkey."

"All right," said the old man. "Bind her legs nicely so that she doesn't kick me." After this was done he said, "Now, lift her tail so that I can have a clear passage."

As soon as the boy touched her tail the donkey turned into a beautiful Shakti, a Yakshini, who went and sat on the fakir's left thigh. The old man said, "Now, take this Shakti, and she will teach you what you want to know." When the Shakti had passed from the fakir to the boy, the old man died.

There is also the story of the head of a Hindu monastery who was getting old and nearing his end. As usual, many of the sadhus in the monastery were anxious to become *mahant* (abbot) to get their hands on the lands and money that belonged to the monastery. So the old mahant was not sure who should succeed him.

Finally one day he stood up in the middle of his assembly hall and said, "How many of you would like to become mahant?" When almost all the sadhus there indicated that they would, he turned to his throne and said, "I curse this chair that whoever sits in it will be a pauper and will be eternally ill, but will achieve all the Riddhis and Siddhis (supernatural powers)."

Well, suddenly, none of the sadhus were willing to sit on that seat. Only one person in the whole hall, the young boy who swept the floors and who had become a disciple of the old man only a few days before said, "I will," because he said to himself, "If I need to I can use the Riddhis and the Siddhis to produce wealth." And when he sat on the throne he immediately received the old mahant's Shakti, which astounded all the old cronies of the monastery. So, the ways of these Indian gurus are not very straight.

You know, actually even though that disciple who was ready to help his guru have sex with a donkey achieved something, he was still not a really good disciple. If he had been a good disciple he would have told his teacher, "No, I won't let you go. Stay with me. If you've created one Shakti you can create more. I don't want to possess Shakti, I want to learn how to create Shaktis." But the guru was far more clever than the disciple. He didn't want the boy to know that he could produce these Shaktis and so he manifested one in the form of a Yakshini. Then the boy thought that the Guru had merely gained the Yakshini instead of having used his own Shakti to produce her.

At least this guru permitted his disciple to pass the test. Once there was a disciple who thought he could do anything his guru could do. So naturally his guru decided to teach him a lesson. They were traveling one day and the guru saw to it that they had nothing to eat all day long. The disciple started to forget the mantra he was supposed to be repeating and began to listen to the rumblings of his stomach instead.

At length they passed a fish seller's stall. The fish seller offered them some fish. The guru took some and swallowed them whole. The disciple did the same, even though he was supposed to be a vegetarian, and because of his hunger began to appreciate their taste. Then the guru calmly vomited up all the fish — alive. He turned to his disciple and said, "Can you do that? If not you have no right to eat. Get away from me, I have no use for fools like you."

Sometimes when a guru wants to test his disciple he can be very devious. Once there was a guru who had a disciple who had been with him for twelve years. The disciple felt that the guru was not teaching him anything, and the guru felt that the disciple was being taught nicely. One day the guru decided to teach the fellow a good lesson and make him permanently forget about complaining.

In the course of their wanderings the two came to a certain town and camped on the banks of the local river. The guru decided to have a bath before his midday meal and, accordingly sent his disciple into town to find some food. As the boy was walking about shouting, "Bhiksham dehi! Bhiksham dehi! Give alms!" he heard a parrot calling, "Come here, Maharaj, come here." The boy followed the parrot's voice to the place where he was caged and found a nice home. The lady of the house invited him in and insisted he eat while she prepared food for his guru. Of course a sincere disciple will never eat before his guru does, but this one was rather hungry, and he decided that it wouldn't matter much. When he had finished his meal and the lady had packed the guru's lunch in a box, the disciple started back for the riverbank. Suddenly the parrot called out to him: "So, you are a sadhu!"

"Yes," the disciple replied rather proudly, "I and my Guru

Maharaj are enjoying the hospitality of this town today. I am just taking food to my mentor."

"Please ask your Guru Maharaj one question," said the parrot. "When will I be free of this cage?"

"Since you are the reason that we obtained this delicious food," said the disciple, "I will certainly ask him." So saying, he returned to his guru. The guru was served his food and, on inquiring about his disciple's food and learning that he had eaten already, shook his head in a knowing way and finished his meal. Afterward while enjoying a pleasant smoke from his chillum, he asked his disciple what had happened in the town that morning.

"Well," said the boy, "as I was strolling about, shouting 'Give alms,' I heard a parrot calling, 'Come, Maharaj, come!' and when I went to investigate, the lady there gave me the wonderful food which Your Lordship has just consumed. And as I was leaving, the parrot called me over and asked me to ask you when he would be free of his cage."

As soon as the guru heard these last words his eyes rolled back in his head, he gasped for breath, he clutched at his chest, and he toppled over on the ground. The disciple thought to himself: "Now what is happening? Just when I asked that stupid parrot's question my Guru Maharaj collapsed. If I ever want to get any of his knowledge I'd better try to save him somehow." After several splashes of river water the guru regained consciousness and continued with his smoke.

Next day the boy was again sent to town to beg food, and as he passed along that certain lane he again heard the parrot's call: "Come, Maharaj, come." The disciple entered and collected the food after eating as he had done the previous day, and as he was leaving the parrot asked him, "What did your Guru Maharaj have to say in answer to my question?"

The disciple replied, "You fool! When I asked that idiotic question of yours to my Guru Maharaj he turned pale and fainted, and I thought I would never be able to revive him."

As soon as the parrot heard these words his tail feathers went limp, he paled, and he fell off his perch into the dust at the bottom of the cage with a loud squawk.

His mistress, hearing the commotion, rushed outside and with a little shriek opened the cage and took the prostrate parrot into her hands to try to gauge the seriousness of the disorder. Whereupon the wily bird flew from her hands onto the branch of a nearby tree and said to the bewildered student, "Dunce! You have been with your guru for twelve years and learned nothing, while it took only one lesson for me."

Puzzled, chagrined, and insulted, the disciple returned to his master, only then wondering how the parrot could have known how long he had been with his guru. After the Guru Maharaj had eaten his dinner, the disciple related the whole story to him while the master was having his smoke. At the end the Guru Maharaj retorted, "Stupid donkey! Don't you understand yet? I have been teaching you for the past twelve years, and you haven't even been aware of my teaching, much less tried to learn anything. And that parrot, who was my disciple in a previous birth, got the idea right away. Do you think that you deserve to be taught anything further?"

That disciple who had become a parrot must have made some mistake in order to be reborn as a parrot, right? He must have failed some exam his guru had set for him in their previous encounter. The guru had no choice but to locate him and save him, though he took his own sweet time about it, to let the disciple stew and realize the gravity of his failure so that he would not fail again.

That progression is always there. A "child" may truly love his guru, serve him faithfully in so many ways, and generally endear himself to the old man, but when the time for examination comes around the guru will forget all the "child" has done for him. You may call him ungrateful, or hard-hearted, or whatever, but that will not make any difference to him. He wants to make his disciple firm and for that there can be no wavering. Does a surgeon waver when he operates?

Let us take the simplest possible example so that you will understand what I am trying to get at. Suppose we are sitting quietly together after lunch and I say to you, "Come along, let's go see my Guru Maharaj."

Now, if you say, "No, not today, today I am rather busy with some other work, I will meet him later," what have I learned about you? I learn that you are not too interested in progressing. If you wanted to make progress you would have said, "Yes, come on, get dressed, let my other work go to hell, I want to meet your mentor."

Whatever your answer may be I will keep quiet because I will have what I want: the result of my test. Actually, as I said before, there is no such thing as a test. This is a simple measure of the causal body. If there are still too many karmas stored in the causal body then a "child" will not get the desire to achieve, or will only get that desire off and on, not continuously. In either case more sadhana is necessary to wean the "child" from desire completely. Other gurus may work in different ways. Namdev thought that he was quite somebody, because Lord Vishnu in the form of Vitthala ("He who stands on the brick") came in person to eat lunch with him every day. One day an assembly of all the great saints of Maharashtra took place. Tukaram, Jnaneshvara and many others were there, and so was Gora Kumbhar, the potter-saint. When everyone was seated, Jnaneshvara's sister Muktabai said, "Gora, why don't you use your stick and test all of us to see if we're well-done?" She was referring to the stick which a potter uses to determine whether or not the pots are fully fired. Gora Kumbhar smiled and began to test. He pronounced everyone passed except Namdev, about whom he said, "This one will have to go back into the oven for some time more."

Naturally Namdev was angry, because he had been considering himself God's greatest devotee, and he went to Vitthala to complain. But Vitthala told him, "Namdev, Gora was right, and if you don't believe him I will also test you. I will come to you before sunset today, and you must recognize me; otherwise, you fail." Namdev agreed.

In the evening, as Namdev was out walking he saw a Chandala (scavenger) and his wife — who were really Vitthala and his wife Rukmini, in disguise — cooking their evening meal. Namdev was feeling tired and sat down to rest nearby, where he could watch what was going on. The Chandala said to his wife, "The pot is not full. Cut up the chickens and put them in." There were twenty-five chickens, representing the twenty-five Tattvas, or essential principles of the universe. But Namdev did not realize this, and he thought to himself, "Oh, my heavens, how violent. However, it must be God's will."

After some time, the Chandala said to his wife, "Still the pot is not full. Cut up the dogs and put them in." There were four dogs — the four Vedas. Namdev should have realized this, but didn't. He thought, "Well, the Chandalas will have to endure the burden of their karmas eventually." What Vishnu was trying to teach Namdev is that when all the Tattvas and the Vedas have been killed, butchered and cooked, only the absolute, undifferentiated reality remains. That was the last lesson that Namdev had to learn. He had achieved success in worshipping Vitthala, but such worship is limited by duality, and now he would have to go beyond duality. Because of the play of Vishnu, though, he didn't realize any of this at that moment.

Suddenly, the Chandala said to his wife, "Still the pot is not full. Now let's cut up that man over there and put him in!" Namdev jumped up and forgot all about God and everything else and, remembering only self-preservation, ran as fast as his legs could carry him. Vitthala wanted to initiate him into the undifferentiated reality, by killing, butchering, and cooking: Sadguru, Karnaguru, and Upaguru.

Have you ever heard of the Sadguru, Karnaguru, and Upaguru? The *Sadguru* kills the aspirant — separating him from his mundane existence. The *Karnaguru* flays the carcass: the ego. All the accretions of untold births, the false personality, is chopped into tiny pieces. When my Mahapurusha cut Haranath Thakur, my parents' guru, into tiny pieces and removed Sattva, Rajas, and Tamas from the pile of sixty-four, this is what He was doing. The *Upaguru* cooks the ego in the fire of Shakti, and the result is a tasty dish: an enlightened being.

The best guru, of course, combines the Sadguru, Karnaguru, and Upaguru into one, like my Mahapurusha. This is what Vishnu wanted to do for Namdev — but Namdev was still not ready. Namdev stopped running after reaching the nearby village, and seeing a Shiva temple decided to go there to rest. When he went inside he saw an old man with his feet resting on top of the Shiva Linga. Namdev said to him very sententiously, "Do you know, my good man, that you are defiling the sanctity of this temple?"

The old man looked at him and said, "My son, I am very old and infirm and cannot move my legs. Will you help me so that I can avoid angering Shiva?"

At first Namdev felt revulsion because he would have to dirty himself by taking hold of the old man's feet. But finally he overcame the revulsion, picked up the offending feet, and laid them down a short distance away.

"Nam," said the old man, "I still feel there is something under my feet. Would you just look and see?" The old man called him "Nam." He didn't call him Namdev because Namdev literally means "name of God," and the old man was insinuating that Namdev had not yet reached that state, but was still only a common name. In fact, being addressed as "Nam" irritated Namdev, but he forgot then there was no way the old man could have possibly known what his name was. It was all part of Vishnu's play.

Again Namdev unwillingly lifted the old man's legs, and saw another Shiva Linga. When he placed them down again, another Shiva Linga spring up from where the feet touched the ground. Then Namdev realized there was something more to the old man than met the eye. "Nam," he said, "tell me where Lord Shiva isn't, and there I will put my feet." Namdev embraced his feet and took him as his guru, and the old man, whose name was Vishoba Kechar, taught Namdev that though he had known one limited aspect of God he had still to learn of the universality of God.

After Namdev finished his lesson, and Vishoba Kechar sent him back to the assembly, Gora Kumbhar hit him with his stick and said, "Now this one is done, too."

No matter how your guru works, if he is a real guru he will push you to the limits of your endurance and then further. He will test you until you think you can no longer bear it, but it will be worth it because once he is finished with you, you will be ready for real sadhanas — like Aghora, for instance.

# CHAPTER SIX

# AGHORA

*When I look at someone I don't see them as they are now; I see them as they will be. Then I can try to change them if there is something in them I think I can change. If I love skin and bones how will I be able to help them! Skin and bones will only decay, but the individual will continue to exist even after death. That is why I can say that I love people not for their present value but for their future value; not for what they are but for what they will become, or for what they have the potential to become. This is an Aghori's love.*

## THE TRUE AND THE REAL

I have never believed in religion. Religions are all limited because they concentrate only on one aspect of truth. That is why they are always fighting amongst one another, because they all think they are in sole possession of the truth. But I say there is no end to knowledge, so there is no use of trying to confine it to one scripture or one holy book or one experience. This is why I say when people ask what religion I follow, "I don't believe in *Sampradaya* (sect), I believe in *Sampradaha* (incineration)." Burn down everything which is getting in the way of your perception of truth.

I also often say that I belong to the Vedic religion. But there are problems in that also. For example, the Vedantins. *Vedanta* means the end of the Veda, and the Vedantins try to distill the essence of the Veda away from the minute rituals. But sometimes they make a mess of it.

For example, the philosophers of *Advaita* (absolute nondual) Vedanta say, "Brahman sat, jagan mithya," meaning that the Universal Soul or Atma exists in reality but that the world, the manifested universe, does not. An Aghori believes, "Brahman sat, jagan sat": Both the Atma and the Samsara (the world of manifestation) are real and existent because the Samsara manifests itself directly from the Supreme Soul. If the product is impure and the process is efficient then must not the raw material be impure? But we know the Atma is pure. If all is part of a harmonious whole then all must be accepted as real. The world may not be true, no doubt. The world is in fact full of falsehood. But it is real, at least as real as you and I are. And you cannot deny your own reality, because when you do you enter a logical paradox: If you are unreal then you cannot comment on the reality or lack of it in your existence. This is all such a waste, a labyrinth of words, which does no good to anyone, and will not get you to where you want to go: to God.

Advaita Vedanta suggests in fact that nothing exists except the individual; that each of us has our own individual realities which are real only for us. That being the case, how can you communicate your experiences? It is impossible. That is why the Vedic religion, which is one of the two eternal religions, gives the same advice to everyone: "Carve out your own niche." There is no such thing as sin; we have invented sin, along with heaven and hell. You must work at your own rate of speed toward your own goal; no one is required to do anything else. You will achieve, after some time. There is nothing to worry about.

The scriptures talk about enlightenment, not because when you are enlightened you are supposed to see some clear white light, but because you have been "lightened" of your heavy burden of karmas and rnanubandhanas thanks to your own penances and to the grace of your guru. And, because you have developed the "light" of perception so that you can "see" truth directly, without any interpreters. Vedic religion is the religion of light, the light of lights, the light of the sun, and modern scientists put the lifetime of the sun at about 10 billion years. Isn't that almost eternal, as far as you and I are concerned? So, if you are in no hurry you can afford to wait.

Very few can worship according to the rules of the other eternal religion; Aghora is too rigorous for almost everyone. Is there any limit to darkness? None. In Aghora, you embrace darkness and make it work for you. Does it sound easy? Only the seniormost Rishis can master both the Veda and Aghora.

The Upanishads have a nice little prayer: "Lead me from untruth into truth; lead me from darkness into light; lead me from mortality into immortality." What is untruth? The world, which is composed of an aggregate of limited forms. Whatever is limited cannot be true. The true is that which is beyond every limit. What is darkness? The darkness of a mind clouded by ignorance. The light is your own inner light, which is your true self. The Veda teaches you to achieve immortality without renouncing the world, but the procedures of its rituals must be rigorously adhered to. We do things differently in Aghora.

Aghora teaches you to embrace the world, embrace impurity, embrace darkness, and push through forcibly into light. You must catch Shakti by the hair and drag Her to you.

There is no life without Shakti. But everyone is afraid of Shakti: "Beware of Maya, my son" is what our present-day religions teach us. Do they realize that every individual creates his or her own Maya? It has to be this way. Maya is just the projection of Shakti into the outside world. Because you get yourself entangled in your own Shakti, you scuttle yourself. And that is why everyone fears Maya, simply because they know they can't control Her.

But an Aghori never gets entangled in his Maya. He self-identifies himself so perfectly with Shiva that he pulls the Shakti forcibly back to him. Shiva is unborn and undying, and therefore, permanent. He is also that which is to be known, the permanent reality. From the untruth of limitations the Aghori goes to the truth of Shiva; from the mortality of earthly existence he propitiates the Destroyer and becomes immortal; and by harnessing his Shakti he floods his consciousness with light. Doesn't a lamp give light to all? The oil burns, but the lamp is not consumed. This is the Aghori: illuminating everyone with the light of his own incineration, fueled by his Shakti.

Nothing is inauspicious to an Aghori. He can do Sattvic sadhana very easily, because he develops obsessive love for his deity. But Sattvic people have a hard time with Aghora sadhanas because they find Tamas very difficult to control. That is why everyone says "Aghora is extremely dangerous; you may fall and ruin yourself." It's all wrong. If you're naked you possess nothing, which means you have nothing to lose. Let any thief come; what can he take? All other paths to knowledge have traps: Once you learn a little it goes to your head, and you remain just on the outside of the truth, never making the final renunciation. The ego of knowledge is the worst trap of all. But there is no such danger in Aghora because you throw everything away in the beginning. Then there is no impediment to your perfect enlightenment. There is only one requirement: Your mind must be absolutely firm.

There, of course, lies the problem. To maintain a firm mind while a beautiful female spirit dances lasciviously on top of your body is the test of a real man. You have to die while still alive; then you can succeed at Aghora. Then let the ghouls throw live coals onto your flesh, and watch your skin char without flinching: You've given up your body as well, you have nothing to lose. As long as you hold onto that determination you are perfectly safe.

To die while still alive means to relinquish all attachments to your possessions, including especially your body. Everyone can do it to some extent. An Aghori goes all out to do it. Every morning when I wake up the first thing I do is look at my body I see skin, muscle, and bone, and then I think to myself, "This will go. This will all go and only my consciousness will remain." In this way I inoculate myself against being attached to my own existence.

# RESTRICTIONS

If you want to die while you are still alive you have to restrict the three things which most bind us down to the body: food, sleep, and sex. The Naths (a tribe of immortal Aghoris) have a prescription for spiritual advancement: "Break up your sleep, and cut down your food." No matter how far your mind may soar into the astral regions while you are awake, once you go to sleep you erase all the benefit. Sleep is very much like death, just less permanent. It is the overcoming of the mind by a blanket of dullness.

Food makes you sleepy by filling you up; sex exhausts you, it makes you sleepy by draining you. Aghoris cannot afford the luxury of relaxation; they have to be sharp at all times. They work all night long in the smashan, where drowsiness makes them much more susceptible to attack from spirits.

Food and sex also both make you more conscious of your bodily processes. In fact, in the case of all three — food, sleep, and sex — the more you get of them the more you want. Other desires can be eliminated by gratifying them, but these three desires have to be carefully regulated. If you eat an entire chicken today does that mean you won't be hungry tomorrow? No, you'll be hungrier. If you sleep nine hours today you're likely to sleep ten hours tomorrow. And it is the same way with sex: The more you get of it, the more you want of it. Until you begin to at least curb these desires you will never make any permanent spiritual progress. Write it down; it is impossible. All your gains will be continuously wiped out by your indulgences. And worse, if you ever permit yourself to be tempted in the smashan, you've had it.

Consider this indulgence: Sadhus and other spiritual aspirants are forbidden to drink alcohol; some are not even allowed to take medicine which contains alcohol. Aghoris, however, drink; but only because they can master the intoxication. You must drink the drink; you must not let the drink drink you, lest you become its slave and be lost. You must always retain your control.

What is the use of drinking and becoming drunk? You slobber all over yourself while you run off at the mouth to whoever will listen, buying them drinks if necessary so they'll listen. Then you gorge yourself on a big meal, and probably vomit it back up. Eventually you get into a fight, make a pass at somebody else's wife, or pass out.

Alcohol makes you extroverted, but this extroversion must be firmly controlled. Most people permit the drink to drink them: They allow their conscious minds to be overcome by all the little yeast cells crushed after the fermentation process is completed. Yeast cells undergo such agony during the crushing operations that a great current of Tamas is created by their unvoiced screams in the resultant alcohol.

When I want to drink I always allow a drop of the drink to fall on the ground before I begin, as an offering to Mother Earth. I am asking Her to redeem all the wretched little yeast cells. When She does, each cell becomes filled with the transcendental wisdom and blessing of the Mother, and by my consuming them, I do too! When I offer that drop I repeat a certain mantra and then say "Prajvalita!" because both the yeast cells and I should have our intellects become *prajvalita* (enkindled). By doing this the alcohol enkindles my Bhuta Agni and enables me to soar into the astral regions. Anyone else who drinks will enkindle his Jathara Agni which will increase his appetite and drag him further and further down into physical consciousness. *Jathara Agni* is the fire which digests our food; it is the body's power of digestion. *Bhuta Agni* is associated with the subtle body; it enkindles and inflames Jathara Agni. When the mind is disturbed the Bhuta Agni is weakened, which weakens the Jathara Agni. This results in indigestion, which causes disease.

The Bhuta Agni acts as the digestive fire for the subtle body, except that the subtle body does not live on food; its food is *Japa* (recitation of mantras). If you want to become spiritual you must preserve and protect the power of Bhuta Agni so your spiritual practices will be properly digested by your mind. So many Western seekers have ruined themselves physically or mentally by overdoing mantras or pranayama or whatever before they were strong enough to digest, to properly make use of, the energy they were creating. Because the Bhuta Agni gives energy to the Jathara Agni, when one is strong the other must necessarily be weak.

If you want to enjoy mundane life to its fullest you will need a strong, well-nourished body, for which you must keep your Jathara Agni well inflamed. And, the best way to increase the power of your Bhuta Agni, your "spiritual digestion," is to do exactly the opposite: eat less. As your physical hunger decreases you will find an increased mental hunger for knowledge, and as you find you can only digest smaller quantities of food you will find that you can digest many more new things mentally, and vice versa. Sleep and sex will generally dull both Jathara Agni and Bhuta Agni. No, there is no escape, to make permanent spiritual progress you must make your Bhuta Agni predominant.

# INTOXICANTS

In an ordinary person the consumption of alcohol will lead to an enkindling of the Jathara Agni. Ayurveda recognizes this and prescribes medicinal wines when there is a need to increase the appetite and promote digestion.

An Aghori, though, is not an ordinary person. Aghoris do not live to eat. An Aghori who drinks must drink not to lose his consciousness and become more enmeshed in the world's Maya, but rather to dilate certain brain cells to increase, not decrease, the awareness. Alcohol should sharpen your mind so much that a problem which might take hours to think out in the normal state can be done instantaneously. It's the same with every other type of intoxication also: if you can't control it, don't do it; you're sure to scuttle yourself.

When an Aghori takes a lot of intoxicants he feels like going to the smashan and being alone with his thoughts. He becomes more introverted; he feels like telling everyone he meets "Leave me alone!" And if he covers himself with ashes and remains naked and shouts obscenities, no one is likely to come near, and he can be in his mood all day long. This is one of the reasons why Aghoris act the way they do. I used to do it myself.

Aghoris are thrill seekers; that's it in a nutshell. When I went to the U.S.A. in 1981, what was the thing I most enjoyed? The roller coasters! Especially "Space Mountain" at Disneyworld and the old wooden roller coaster at Circusworld. I could stay on a roller coaster all day! That rush of speed, that excitement! Most people just scream and forget it, just as most people who drink get drunk and pass out, and most people who indulge in sex have an orgasm and go to sleep. But what is the use in that? That is mere bodily indulgence. To be an Aghori you must go beyond all limitations, and the biggest limitation is the limitation of the body. When we Aghoris use thrills, intoxicants, and sex we use them to go beyond the body. It is the same way with music. Maybe if I use music as an example you'll understand what I mean about intoxicants and sex. Music is vibration, just like mantra. You can use it to benefit your sadhana. Any music will work, if it has a nice melody and a good rhythm. I love Jim Reeves because he has both melody and a good rhythm, and also pathos. I enjoy Spanish and Caribbean tunes, and I will even listen to some rock music, though much of it is too violent for my purposes. Some of our bigoted Indians say, "Only Indian music can make your mind more meditative," but that is all bull. It is true that our Indian rhythms are far more advanced in complexity than are the Western ones, and our tunes are much more intricate, but there is something about Western music which makes it particularly useful for getting into certain frames of mind.

Meat is also an intoxicant, by the way. It is just as intoxicating as music, alcohol, marijuana, or sex. But it involves killing a sentient being, which I don't like; I am fond of animals. Besides, when you eat meat you must be in a position to ensure that the animal gets a higher rebirth, if you don't want to be stained by karma. So it is better to avoid it.

There are three important reasons why Aghoris love to take intoxicants. First, it is a question of challenge and response. It is a contest between the Aghori and the drug: Who is stronger? Will the drug be able to overcome the Aghori's will and drown his consciousness or will the Aghori be able to control the drug's effect and bend it to his will? The exhilaration of such a duel is a sublime intoxication in itself.

Second, if the Aghori is able to master the intoxication, the force of the intoxicant magnifies the force of his concentration, since the mind is a chemical phenomenon. As the concentration is strengthened, the image of the deity which is being continually formed in the subtle body is made firmer and clearer, and this brings success at worship all the closer.

Third, Aghoris always worship Shiva, Who loves intoxicants. This has a dual-purpose effect. Not only does the Aghori please Shiva by offering Him the intoxicant, but the very act of taking the intoxicant helps the Aghori self-identify with Shiva, since permanent intoxication is one facet of Shiva's personality. Shiva is intoxicated with Samadhi-consciousness: We have to work up to His level gradually.

Most people never realize that the purpose of intoxication is to sharpen the mind. They take marijuana, then eat heavily, then enjoy sex. They will enjoy penetration for one minute and think that they are copulating for years because of the drug's distortion of the sense of time. It's all such a waste.

Aghoris take all sorts of intoxicants, some much worse than these. It is a part of the sadhana. I used to keep a cobra and let him bite me on the tongue every hour, just for that peculiar thrill. To feed him I had to put a small hole in an egg and then forcibly pour the contents down his throat. The idea that cobras drink milk is ridiculous. I had several cobras, including one albino who had three lines on his hood: the symbol of Shiva. I kept a king cobra also. Its poison is much deadlier than that of other cobras because its diet is nothing but other cobras. I used to keep white arsenic also, and lick one of the crystals every hour or two. For my marijuana and hashish I had a special pipe made from a particular type of clay into which I had mixed arsenic, aconite, Datura seeds, opium, and whatnot. It was a chillum, about a foot long. Beautiful! I used to drink twenty-four hours a day sometimes, and go through cases and cases of Scotch. I drank it neat, straight from the bottle. But after a while I began to think "What is the use?" I have stopped most of my intoxicants, though I sometimes still drink alcohol or use bhang.

One of the big disadvantages of intoxicants is their side effects. Smoke chillum after chillum of marijuana or hashish and you are bound to develop a terrible cough, and probably chronic bronchitis. Drink bottle after bottle of whisky and your liver must suffer. Drink bhang and become chronically constipated. And long-term use of arsenic or mercury? Don't even *ask* about it. But all these substances have their own special advantages, which is why Aghoris put up with all the disadvantages.

Most people think tobacco has nothing but disadvantages. They are so wrong. Tobacco is really a marvelous plant. Nowadays it is being misused by everyone because very few know how to use it properly, and that is why there are so many side effects. Poor tobacco is blamed, instead of the stupidity of the user. If it is properly employed it can work wonders. It has 100 important uses in Ayurveda. Do you think that the American Indians were fools to worship it? Never! They knew what it could do.

But there are even better intoxicants. The Rishis used to take *soma*, which is a type of leafless creeper. Some people today think soma was the poisonous mushroom *Amanita muscaria*, but that was also merely a substitute for the real thing. Only the Rishis know what the true soma is, because only they can see it. It is invisible to everyone else. Before taking the plant the Rishis would first worship it on an auspicious day and take its permission. If the plant refused its permission it was left alone. If it said "Yes," if it was willing, then they would make sure the plant would take birth as an animal after its demise. Then they would gather it with the appropriate mantras.

If you want to use an intoxicating plant and can't collect it yourself with mantras, you have to add a mantra afterward if you want it to have the proper effect on you, and if you want to avoid the karma involved. Taking an intoxicant without its appropriate mantra is certain to ruin your Bhuta Agni, and your mind.

Sometimes some of my "children" have started using alcohol or marijuana, thinking they could imitate me. But they have all landed in trouble, because without knowing the method you just can't fool around with these things. Even those of my "children" who I allow the occasional use of intoxicants have gone beyond their limits sometimes, and I have had to be strict with them.

One boy I am very fond of started thinking he was a great Aghori because I would permit him to take intoxicants with me. I decided he should be taught a lesson for his own good to prevent him from going overboard before he was able to gain complete control.

Someone had given me some charas, and this boy was anxious to try it out. You know, charas is not the same thing as hashish. Hashish is the pollen and resin of the cannabis plant. Charas is prepared by taking the fresh fleece from a slaughtered sheep, stuffing it full of this resin, and burying it in the ground for a month. The fat from the sheep and the lanolin from the fleece mix with the resin and liquify it, and the liquid drips into a little pot. After a month the pot is removed, and there you have charas.

I prepared this charas for the boy personally, mixing it with tobacco and rubbing it with my hand in a little water, and I warned him; "Don't inhale too hard. This sort of charas gets a firm grip on your head very easily. I know you've taken plenty of intoxicants in your life, but this one is different. Beware!" But he ignored my advice, as I knew he would, and he and I started puffing away.

Within five minutes — only five — he realized he had taken too much; but it was too late. He began to lose all his body consciousness. His *prana* (vital force) collected in his throat, which prevented him from wagging his tongue. He was game for it, though, I must admit. He started to try to make the prana go up to the *Ajna Chakra* (the energy center between the eyebrows) and then out through the *Sahasrara* (the energy center at the crown of the head) — gone for good! Had he succeeded he would have gone into *Nirvikalpa Samadhi*, a state in which he would have been permanently unable to self-identify with his body.

But I could not permit that to happen. After all, he still has plenty of rnanubandhanas to clear off yet, and if I prevent him from doing that, I become responsible for clearing them off myself. No thank you. So I told someone to give him some water. Drinking that glass of water kept his prana right there in his throat, unable to go up any farther. Of course the charas was still pushing from below. Now he was in the *Trishanku* state: unable either to go up or to come down. He was neither in the world nor out of it; he lay suspended between the world — the lower five Chakras — and the true *Shunya* (state of "spiritual vacuum") of the Ajna Chakra. So that he would not forget his lesson I permitted him to remain like that for several hours, while I went to the stables to see my race horses. When I got back there he was, still hovering somewhere in between. When he was finally able to talk again I asked him what he had experienced. He told me, "I felt as if I was on the threshold of forgetting everything; as if just a little farther and it would have been only Thee and Me, and from there onward only Thee — or maybe only Me."

"Wait, wait," I told him laughing, "there is still time. Don't be in a hurry. To go up fast is fine, but to come down too fast is fatal." And since that day he has always taken his intoxicants according to his capacity without permitting them to overcome his conscious mind, even by Shunya. You must work very gradually with this intoxication business; Rome wasn't built in a day, you know.

Now, obviously, when I prepared that charas for him I added a mantra to it. Otherwise do you think the charas would have sent him into Shunya? If that were so, all the charas addicts in the world should be enlightened by now.

One thing I always make sure to do is to take the antidote for whatever intoxicant I use. Ayurveda, our ancient Indian medical science, has provided us with methods to limit or eliminate the side effects on the body which these intoxicants cause, so that you get only the intoxication and none of the evil repercussions on your body, or almost none anyway.

Even with all these precautions, however, your body will deteriorate when you take intoxicants, because your mind becomes partially free of the constraints of the body: That is the whole purpose of becoming intoxicated. Your mind works so fast that your body can't keep up with it, and it becomes flaccid, loose. The less the mind self-identifies with the body the better for your sadhana, but the worse for your body; your physical health will give way to improved mental health. Or at the very least you will remain healthy but you will lose weight and fitness, because you are sitting all day long without exercise or food. But then you don't care two hoots for your body because you find your mental play much more satisfactory.

Of course it is very good to possess a body when you take intoxicants; it acts as something like a sheet anchor when you want to retain your awareness. When you are ethereal you have nothing to hold onto, and other ethereal beings can play havoc with you if they catch you unaware; the possibilities are really frightening. But when you become really firm in your subtle body there is nothing to fear.

Until then, though, you need to have a strong, healthy body to withstand everything you will be going through. Don't get me wrong; I was a wrestler myself, and I appreciate the benefits of a good physique. And this is another reason I discourage people from taking intoxicants: You have to be very healthy first and have done a lot of physical and mental cultivation before you can afford to get involved in this intoxicant business. Otherwise you'll just make yourself toxic. And remember, the brain is a chemical matter, and each toxin produces a certain state of mind. So if you are not intrinsically healthy the intoxicant will not only not make your mind soar into the astral regions but it will create new brain toxins, which will overwhelm your mind with disturbing emotions, which will ruin your sadhana. So it is usually better to leave such things alone.

Aghoris believe in reducing sleep to the absolute minimum, because during sleep there is a possibility the mind may slip out of your control. All your careful precautions during waking will come to naught if you get caught up in a dream. Either you must suppress sleep absolutely or you must learn to control your dreams. There exists a plant for this purpose. Make a paste of it and apply it nightly to the soles of your feet. If you do it for thirty nights, or even forty nights, every night you'll get the same dream. It is a type of intoxication; the toxins from the plant are affecting the same brains cells each time in the same way. This is necessary for the sadhana of *Svapneshvari* (Goddess of Dreams). Once you get Siddhi of Svapneshvari you can control your dreams or stop dreaming altogether. You can also control the dreams of other people, which can be very useful.

Once one of my friends had taken Aghori Baba's stick for some work. When I asked him for it he refused to return it. I sent Svapneshvari to him. When she comes to someone she comes in a dream; her face can't be seen. She warned him to return the stick or face the consequences; he ignored the warning. This was repeated three or four nights in a row. Then Svapneshvari came to him and told him, "This is your last warning. If you don't return it, you're heading for big trouble." When he woke up in the morning, he found a handprint in blood on his pillow. He obstinately refused to return the stick even then. The next night Svapneshvari came to him and said, "Now you have gone too far; take your punishment." The next morning he and everyone in his household woke up with high fevers, which would not go down; no medicine could cure them. He returned the stick, and then the fevers subsided.

There are plenty of other uses of Svapneshvari, but any way you look at it wakefulness is better than sleep. Intoxicants can be extremely useful in sadhanas, or they can ruin your consciousness. It all depends on how you use them, and to use them correctly you have to die first.

# TO DIE WHILE STILL ALIVE

To die while still alive means to eliminate all involuntary stimulation of your senses. You cannot salivate when you see a nice roast. Do dead men feel hunger? You cannot become aroused, even mentally, when a stunning woman walks by. Can a dead man get an erection? And remember, once you get involved in this there is no limit to the amount of testing which will be performed on you. You will be tested to your limit.

To die while still alive means you must melt your bones. Why are some spirits depicted as skeletons? Because when the body dies and decomposes the bones still remain for them to self-ioentify with. To melt your bones means to lose the ability to perform any action with your own individual will as opposed to the cosmic or divine will of Nature.

Do you remember the story of Sagal Shah? The Aghori who was brought to Sagal Shah's home had to be carried in a basket; he had so thoroughly given up action on his own that he was, in effect, boneless.

They say that three creatures have no bones: the earthworm, the madman, and the God-intoxicated man. To be an Aghori you must become just like an earthworm, completely boneless, so that you can be tied in knots and still not suffer. When a cyclone comes through, trees are uprooted, but the grass bends down and escapes.

To die while still alive means to dry up, to become desiccated. Dry herbs are usually more useful than are fresh ones; they gain in potency as they dry. It is the same with an Aghori. He or she dries up and loses all the juices which are necessary to maintain life. Physically it means your digestive juices dry up, your reproductive fluids diminish, your skin may even become harder and wrinkled, especially if you live in a smashan for months at a time.

But the mental effects are more important. Remember, the entire world is a smashan for an Aghori: Everyone is born with their death fixed, which means to an Aghori that they are all dead already; they are all already skeletons. The juices which must be dried up are all the juicy thoughts which keep you bound down to the world by perpetually producing desires. If you can dry these up mentally you can do whatever you please physically; if you can't you will have to observe some preliminary discipline and restrictions. But only when these juices of desire have dried up can the *real* juice of life — the *Amrita* (nectar of immortality) — be obtained.

To die while still alive means to extinguish all thought of dualities. The Universal Soul is single, not dual, so you must eliminate all perceptions of duality: desirable and nondesirable,

pleasant and painful, interesting and boring, and so on. Does a
corpse care about anything? No, not a thing — and you must
become a corpse, in the eyes of the world, if you want to succeed at Aghora.

# THE LEFT-HAND PATH

Why do they call Aghora the Left-Hand Path? Look at the difference between the right and left hands, at least in Indian culture. The right hand takes the food and drink to the mouth,
performs religious ceremonies, makes offerings, and does everything else auspicious. The left hand must perform all the inauspicious activities: cleaning the excretory orifices, even killing
animals. And almost all the people in the world are naturally
right-handed. Aghora is the mastery of all actions, inauspicious
as well as auspicious. Left is always more intense than right,
because the left side of the body is controlled by Shakti. This
is why a man's wife must sit at his left side when they perform rituals together. Left-handed people are really good in their
chosen fields, especially music.

An Aghori forgets the meaning of "inauspicious." Orthodox
people think that corpses, skulls, and menstrual blood are filthy,
and that anyone who would use them for worship is insane or
worse. The very thought of eating human flesh nauseates them.
But an Aghori finds these things extremely useful to him.

To become an Aghori is to accept everything in the universe
as part of the Atma, but you don't just jump to that stage directly, because you could never cope with it without a satisfactory preparatory period. You must do things stepwise, just as a
child does his schooling. You don't ask the child to take an
examination in algebra on the day he learns addition, and in
Aghora you always start with the basics and work up very slowly, unless, as in my case, you start at the top. But this is exceedingly rare.

An Aghori is awarded his diploma only after he becomes fear
less. What should he fear? Not only spirits, ghouls, and whatnot, but the entire working of the Samsara. Do you have any

idea how many murders occur every minute on the face of the globe? How many rapes, how many robberies, lootings, tortures, and other heinous crimes? How many times each second people are cheated, misled, duped, and made fools of? When you try to put it all into perspective, it's too much; it will frighten you, when you think of the tremendous load of karmas. Once you have Jnana, and you know the consequences of each action, you will be so scared of karma you will think a thousand times before doing anything at all; so deep will be your fear.

But you must go beyond this fear and realize that it is all part of the whole, all moving according to Nature's sublime plan. Every murder, every cruelty has its significance. You must love everything taking place in the Samsara. That doesn't mean you should go out and murder, but you will realize that even murder is just part of the play of the Three Gunas, all due to the Law of Karma, and therefore a part of Nature.

A good test for an Aghori is this: When you can eat your own feces with real love for it, you have achieved a tiny bit. I don't mean perversion; I am talking about true oneness with all existence. You have produced the feces; it is a part of you; you enjoyed eating the food which produced it, and the only thing between the food and the feces is you. Why should you find it so repugnant? Feces is just as much a part of the Atma as your body and your consciousness are; who is feeding what to whom? The Atma is feeding the Atma to the Atma: It is all the play of the Atma. When an Aghori reaches this stage, he eats whatever he finds: dead dogs, offal, slops from the gutter, his own flesh. He finds whatever he eats equivalent to the tastiest dishes, all because he does not falsely discriminate. He sees everything as One; no attraction or repulsion. When the body demands food, he eats whatever is available.

Aghoris eat human flesh, but not because they have become cannibals. There is a ritual involved. I have eaten human flesh many times; even my son has eaten human flesh. I used to wait at a funeral pyre until the skull would burst — it bursts with a fine "pop" — and then I would rapidly, to avoid burning my fingers, pull out parts of the brain, which would be a gooey mass, partially roasted by then, and would eat it. It was nauseating, but at that moment you must forget your nausea and everything else: This is sadhana, not dinner at the Ritz. There was an Aghori in Girnar named Sevadas who had specialized in eating the human brain. But after some time he left it and became absolutely Sattvic, the sweetest, softest possible sadhu. That is the true test of an Aghori: From full-blown Tamas he must graduate to pure Sattva, love for all.

When you see One in All and All in One, there can be no fear; fear of what — of yourself? "Everywhere I see, everything is Me": a little saying I once thought up. "Me" is capital "I," the Atma, which conveys the whole sense of the experience. If a Zen Buddhist heard it I think he would experience satori. Can you fear yourself? No, you fear only the unknown; once anything is known, the fear drops away. Once you know yourself to be part and parcel of the Atma, what is there to fear?

The worst fear of all is the fear of death; once you go beyond the fear of death, you go beyond all fears because you go beyond expectation and anticipation, which are the causes of most karmas: "I must experience this enjoyment before I die," or, "I must prevent that person from interfering with my enjoyments." When death has no value for you, time loses its value, and then you don't bother about anything. Then you say, "If I am meant to experience this enjoyment, I will experience it; why bother about it?"

Once you drop fear, the whole world is open to you, because you have nothing to take from anyone; you know only how to give because you have nothing to hold on to. What can you possess when "everything is You"? You already possess everything; it is really a superb feeling.

From your high school diploma, you go on to the first two years of college: temptation. All sorts of temptations will come your way: spirits offering you fame or riches, ghouls offering to slaughter or maim your enemies, Yakshinis offering you sexual favors, any possible whim you might want fulfilled. If you take any of them up on their offers you are finished. There is only one way to avoid it: refuse. If you are really sure you are part of the Universal Soul then how can they give you anything or do anything for you? You are being taken care of by Nature, you need not bother to accept any of these baits.

The college degree is awarded in Aghora only after the next examination: attack. When the hordes of ethereal beings find they can't tempt you, they will try to drive you mad with their power of fright. But don't bother; how can they harm you? You are part of the totality of existence, and your Mother is looking after you; what more do you want?

After your graduation, you are awarded your degree: clair-audience and clairvoyance. Then you go anywhere, eat anything, and you are carefree, because something is directing your every move. You become just like a Yantra. The cosmic Shakti plays through you, and you enjoy the bliss. But this is the final stage. You must start at the bottom and go through the grind.

I hope you can understand by now that it takes a special temperament to become an Aghori; not everyone will be able to do it.

And doing it is just part of it; getting out of what you are doing is even more difficult than doing it in the first place. Suppose you get involved in strenuous penances with the use of intoxicants. You can't just quit them once you feel you've had enough because your body won't be able to take it. You have to reduce them gradually. And so many Aghoris forget why they have been taking the intoxicants, and even after years they may become simple addicts, unable to give them up, ruining their consciousness in the bargain.

You know the reason I quit using intoxicants? I used to use them all day long, twenty-four hours; but then I realized that the greatest intoxicant there is exists within me at all times. It is free, easy to use, harmless, and never gives me a hang-over. It is the name of God. It gives the best concentration of mind. The effects of alcohol or marijuana or whatever will wear off by the next day, but the intoxication caused by God's name just goes on increasing; there is no end to it. I use it all the time, and it always works for me. No matter what has been my problem, the holy name of God has always been my solution. This is true Aghora. Forget all the externals; only when your heart melts and is consumed in the flames of your desire for your Beloved will you ever come close to qualifying to learn the true Aghora.

# CHAPTER SEVEN

# SPIRITS

*If a four-year-old boy were to sit on top of his dead grandmother, pick up his father's japamala and begin to do japa, what sort of boy would you say he is? You would have to say he was born to do Smashan Sadhana. I have seen a boy who did that. Why, even I, when I was a child, used to build toy funeral pyres out of twigs and matchsticks; it's an inborn tendency in someone who is meant to be an Aghori.*

## SPIRITS

The true nature of Aghora sadhanas has always been a closely guarded secret, given by a guru only to his most trusted disciples. They have to be secret, because they are not in the realm of the written or spoken word. They deal with planes of existence which are unbelievably alien to our everyday lives. And ethereal beings are jealous; they don't like just anybody to find out about them. If you go around telling everyone what you have achieved you will definitely suffer.

You should always eat in private, you should always go on pilgrimage alone, when you make love there should only be the two of you present, and when you perform a ritual you must never permit anyone else to be present if you don't want it to go wrong. This is the sensible way of doing things. One of the most basic of Aghora sadhanas is Munda Sadhana. *Munda* means skull, and this sadhana involves the use of both human and animal skulls. You prepare them in a certain pattern, cover them nicely, sit on top of them, and then do your japa. Very simple.

After you have been doing japa for awhile some doubts will probably arise in your mind: "Can there really be any use in such things?" or "Do spirits really exist?" or some such. You'll forget all about your doubt when one of the spirits whose skull you are making use of loses his temper over your persistence in disturbing his repose and throws a live coal or a heavy rock on you. You will be burned or bruised, and the pain will remind you that, yes, there is indeed some truth in the whole thing.

This is the time when you need to know how to protect yourself. Before you sit for japa you must do Kilana by drawing an ethereal ring around the spot on which you'll be sitting. As long as you stay inside that ring, nothing can harm you; no spirit can throw anything on you or harm you in any way. But the moment you step outside you are at the mercy of the spirits, and compared to what they will do to you, being flayed alive is pleasurable. Don't step outside; sit and watch the fun in safety. Slowly your confidence will develop, and you will be able to move up to more difficult sadhanas.

Sadhana of a spirit means enticing it with things it likes and then maintaining it with mantras. You must perform Kilana and Stambhana. Both mean "to fix something in one place." *Stambhana* is the first, temporary fixation, and *Kilana* (literally, "nailing") is the permanent attachment. If you want to hang something on the wall, first you decide where to put the nail, you put the nail in the appropriate spot, and then you hammer it in. Here, the spirit remains with you as long as you follow all the rules appropriate for the particular sadhana. One mistake and all your work is undone.

And remember one thing: No one likes to be chained up. And no one likes to do work for anyone without being paid for it. So unless you know exactly what you are doing, you will someday make a mistake, and then all the chickens will come home to roost. Some people think they are very clever to do sadhana of Yakshas and Mokuls to force them to do work, but I think they are the biggest fools, because they become dependent on these spirits, who are really our servants and must be treated appropriately.

If I ask my servant Dhondu for five rupees he will give it to me. But even after I pay him back, when I try to dismiss him he will tell me, "I'll go, Saheb, but to think there was a time you needed to borrow five rupees from me and I lent it to you. Now you're telling me to get out. What sort of man are you?" Then I am completely lost; my honor is smashed beyond repair. The only way out is to commit suicide. I may ask my friends the highest deities for help, but not my Dhondu.

I draw a distinction between spirits and deities because a spirit is bound in one way or another; otherwise, why would they live in the smashan? They would locate a deity, or take rebirth, or otherwise find their own way to a better existence. But for various reasons they are obliged to remain in this intermediate state, wandering about. A deity or a Siddha visits the smashan or lives there with a specific purpose in mind but without any necessity to remain there unwillingly. I've told you the smashan is known as "Shahr-e-Khamosh," the City of Silence. Why city? Because it is not empty, as you might think: It is filled with spirits.

Of course not everyone can see these spirits. Nowadays most people's minds are so enmeshed in the slush of the Samsara that they have no subtlety of perception whatsoever. Only when your mind becomes subtle can it soar into the astral regions and begin to perceive all that is waiting to be perceived.

Matter and energy are never destroyed. Just as the astronomers can take measurements and tell us what happened billions of years ago, thanks to dim light being emitted from distant stars, all the events which happened in our universe millions of years ago are still present as subtle vibrations, which are available to anyone who is subtle enough to become receptive to them.

It is the same way with ethereal beings: Only when one has an extremely subtle mind can one perceive them. But even with a fine mind you can't just stroll into a smashan and expect to be entertained. You have to awaken the smashan. Spirits have a different sense of time, space, and causation than we mortals do. To "awaken" a smashan means to bring it into a state where you can eavesdrop on what is going on and where you can communicate with the inhabitants if you like.

Finally, even if you have perception and you know how to awaken the smashan you should never, never, under any circumstances, venture to attempt any sadhana you might read or hear about unless you have a guru to save you if something goes wrong. Even then your guru may also make a mistake and then both of you will be sunk, but at least you have tried to provide for a safety net. Many rituals exist which can give you amazing results, and you can succeed at them very quickly, but most of them are so dangerous that 99 out of 100 who attempt them go insane or die. Spirits are not to be trifled with.

When I say *spirit* I mean ethereal beings in general, excepting deities. There are so many categories of spirits, such as those who were once human, those who were never human and can never become human, and those who might get the opportunity to become human. There are less in this last category, however, because animals don't self-identify with their individual personalities to any great extent which makes rebirth easier for them. Humans self-identify with their past lives so strongly that it takes time for them to forget sufficiently so they can be reborn, unless someone drags them forcibly into a womb.

One of the useful things you can do in the smashan is to arrange for spirits to obtain wombs, with the help of Lord Shiva, of course. You know, in the South there is a temple whose Shiva Linga is actually in the form of a human penis, made of eight different metals. When a girl is about to be married she is taken to the temple and made to sit on the Linga so that her maidenhead is broken. In that way Lord Shiva is her first husband.

It seems paradoxical, doesn't it; the God of Death being the ideal husband? There is an esoteric significance: Shiva being the God of Death is lord of all the spirits, and it is only through His grace that a spirit can be reborn on the earth. What this means, practically, to an Aghori, is that with the blessings of

Shiva you can give a child to a childless couple. It is not all that difficult if you know what you're doing. First you must go to the smashan and find a spirit. He has to have at least a little rnanubandhana with the parents, and you should try to get one that does not have such bad karmas that he will immediately be the ruin of the family.

Then you must ask Shiva for His blessing to allow the spirit to take birth. Once the blessing is there nothing can stand in the way. The spirit waits until intercourse takes place, and after ejaculation picks a sperm and actually drags it to meet the egg. After fertilization occurs the spirit ensures that the zygote is firmly implanted into the wall of the uterus. Then there is absolutely nothing to worry about. The spirit will sit at the mouth of the cervix and make sure that the baby grows to full term and that the delivery is smooth and without complications.

Now, there is a *Jiva* (an individual soul) in every sperm. But in this case the Jivas are very weak, unable to grow on their own. So the child will have most of the attributes of the spirit and very few of the Jiva, because the spirit's tendencies will be so strong as to overpower those of the Jiva. And of course the child will have less of the father's traits, because they were represented in the Jiva who is eclipsed. In this way the future personality of the child can be predicted, because the spirit is a known quantity. The spirit has little affinity for the mother and father, since most of the rnanubandhanas with them were in the Jivas in the sperms, which means the child will leave the family earlier because his rnanubandhanas are with other people.

Not only that, but you can know other things about the child because he has had the blessings of Shiva, for instance, *Dirghayuh* — long life. How can Shiva allow him to die young? Also, he will be full of intelligence, have no birth defects, and so forth.

Isn't this a fine way to do things? The parents get what they wanted: a child. The spirit gets what he wanted: a womb. Shiva is happy to see one of His spirits get a womb, and a human one at that. And by doing this you finish your rnanubandhanas with the parents and with the spirit, and yet you perform no karma. You are just a bystander. Isn't it wonderful?

It *is* wonderful. Unfortunately most of the people who go to the smashan to do sadhana don't look at it in this way. They go to try to capture a spirit and make it do work for them, which as I've told you does not pay in the long run. I know; I have made mistakes, but thanks to the boundless compassion of my mentors I have escaped the worst consequences. For example, once I became fed up with having to worry about how to make money. I went to the smashan, and when I got home in the evening my cupboard was filled with piles of banknotes: 10,000-rupee notes, 5,000-rupee notes, 1,000-rupee notes. "That's right," I said to myself. "Nothing to worry about now."

The next day I forgot the key to my cupboard when I left the house. My son found it and opened the cupboard and was astounded. He ran to his mother and told her. They both felt I was hiding it from them because I had been complaining for months about the pitiable condition of my finances. Unfortunately, they succumbed to temptation and they took out one-quarter of the amount and locked it into a chest. Then they relocked the cupboard.

Meanwhile an ethereal being had told me, "Your Lordship, this is the situation. Don't lose your temper." I decided I should go home to see for myself. Once I was home I had tea, and while I was sitting with my wife and son I said offhandedly, "Oh, you know, I forgot the key to my cupboard today. Have either of you seen it?"

They both denied it, but they both darted a little glance in the other's direction, which confirmed the information I had been told by the spirit.

Then I asked for the key to the cupboard. My wife became very defensive and said, "What makes you so suspicious? Why should we touch your precious cupboard?" A guilty conscience biting. I replied, "Who said anything about your touching it? I just want to show you something." I located the key, opened the cupboard — and it was empty. I told them, "And if you open your trunk you'll find it empty also." These things are just too dangerous to play around with; they ruin your mind without expert guidance.

I once knew one Narayan Das who had gained control of a small spirit. When I say small, I mean in power; a spirit is ethereal, so there is no question of dimension. Narayan Das used his achievement to enrich himself. I suppose it's logical: Both of us studied with Jina Chandra Suri, and Narayan Das took the old man's advice about making a pile of dough out of his knowledge.

Narayan Das would make you hold a currency note between your index finger and thumb. He would tell you, "Grip it tightly, even tighter . . . ," and suddenly it would disappear into thin air. Or, he would take a banknote, make you sign it, and then say, "Go out and buy us some snacks with this." You would, and on returning you would be asked for the change. Then he would say, "You thief! Here is the original banknote in your pocket!" And there it would be, signed in your own handwriting, with the same serial number.

Narayan Das could also remove roses from cabinets, sweets from tables, and more of such tricks. But when he made a very minor mistake, the spirit, who was furious at being overworked, took hold of his only son and was about to squeeze the life out of him until Narayan Das came to me and begged me to save him. I did, since we had been fellow students, but Narayan Das died shortly afterward; a miserable death.

I could go on and on. There is a lady near Bombay who can make red powder appear out of thin air, but her daughter is crippled, and mad as well. And no one on earth can cure her, except someone who knows about this sort of thing, someone who can understand the spirits. A spirit is of the same form as the mind, so it can enter your brain and do plenty of damage: create temptations, pervert your intellect, and so on. Only if your acuity is as subtle as theirs will you be able to control them absolutely.

And remember, most spirits are miserable. They don't want to harm you, but if you come along and tease them they have every right to hit out. This is how most spirit possessions occur. Someone just sleeps under a tree or urinates in the wrong place,

and he or she gets possessed. It seems unfair, doesn't it? But if
there is a spirit in the tree you sleep under, it may suspect you
of ill will. We all know attack is the best form of defense, so
the spirit may strike. And as for urinating, spirits have some
rights: You can't just do anything to them. They don't like urine
any more than anyone else does. They like it even less because
they have no mouths and so cannot eat physically; they eat
through their sense of smell. This is why they love incense
and scent so much, and why these are so important in the
sadhanas. Deities are even more refined: In addition to the sense
of smell they eat with their gaze, their sweet glance. But none
of them likes the smell of excrements, except the lowest possible spirits, who possess the forms of skeletons. But you definitely don't want to attract *them*, because they are 100 percent
sure to ruin your mind; they are far worse than mad dogs. The
spirits you want to attract hate filthy odors, and if you offer
such to them, you had better be prepared for punishment. You
may chain up a dog, but if you venture too near you are going
to get bitten without fail if he is vicious. Always remember:
Most spirits are not evil, they are just miserable, but they will
attack if provoked, like a dog or a snake, and, of course, they
can only take possession of you if some rnanubandhana is present. And what sort of possession occurs will depend on the type
of spirit.

I can't begin to explain all the types of spirits; I'll just tell
you about a few so you'll get the idea. There are *Pretas*, people
who died without any relative to perform the appropriate ceremonies for them and who are doomed eventually to take the
form of a cobra; and *Bhutas*, spirits of the newly dead who are
still quite attached to embodied life. There are *Dakinis*, the
spirits of women who died in childbirth and who frequently
have such morbid possessive love for the child that they cause
it harm or kill it so they can be with it again.

There are headless spirits, who were decapitated during life.
There are the spirits of those who were murdered: hacked to
pieces, buried alive, poisoned, you name it. Almost everyone
who dies a sudden death becomes a spirit because there is no
time to select a new life; this is why a peaceful death is so

important. There are also tiny children: those who were born dead or who died of disease or accident or some more terrible fate. There is the *Karna Pishachini*. *Karna* means ear, and when you have succeeded at the sadhana for this type of spirit, it will come and sit on your shoulder and whisper things into your ear. It knows a lot about the past, a little about the present, but very little about the future. This knowledge can come in handy when you are testing someone to learn the source of his knowledge: If he can't predict the future, he may have a Karna Pishachini.

Besides telling you events, a Karna Pishachini can protect you, and see that you get enough to eat and drink, and help out with your sadhana. But they are possessive and jealous. You try to get into a romance with someone of the opposite sex, and you and your partner will have a hard time of it. But they are very useful. Arjuna started out with a Karna Pishachini; so did Veda Vyasa. Once you have learned all you can from yours, your guru can remove it from you, and you can go on to something higher.

Higher than a Karna Pishachini is a *Yakshini*, the female form of the *Yaksha*, a male spirit almost at the level of a minor deity. Yakshas and Yakshinis were once human and were good sadhakas at that time; otherwise they could not possess such powers. Yakshas and Yakshinis were Hindus during their lifetimes, Mokuls were Muslims, Angels were Christians, but their condition and level are roughly the same. Since they were once humans, they still retain some human traits: A Mokul is most likely to speak to you in Urdu, a Yaksha will like the sort of things Hindus like, and so on. For instance, hibiscus flowers play an important part in the sadhana of a Yaksha. During the sadhana of a Mokul, a lamp filled with the pure essence of *hina*, a Muslim's favorite perfume, must be kept continuously burning. There is a type of spirit who comes to a woman and makes her fall into a stupor, what we call the state of *Tandra* in Sanskrit, and then enjoys sex with her. If you were to watch it, and I have watched it, you would see her lying on the bed, twisting and turning, oozing, enjoying orgasms, and what-have-you. In fact, she will find it much more satisfying than physical sex, because he has no body to tire out, and he makes her enjoy much more than any man could. If the spirit is of a really high caliber, a child may even be conceived out of this kind of intercourse. It may sound unbelievable; don't believe it if you don't want to, I don't care. But it's true.

A man can also be entertained by a female spirit, and he will have more or less the same kind of experience. He will also find it more satisfying than ordinary sex. But, and here's the rub, by indulging in this you can never again be satisfied by a physical partner. You will long for your ethereal lover, and, when you die, you will also become a spirit.

This is one of the things a Yakshini can do for you. When she is satisfied with your sadhana, she will come to you in whatever form you desire: Marilyn Monroe, Jayne Mansfield, anyone you want. Have you ever heard of performing sex with a corpse? It can be done. I don't mean in the perverted sense of necrophilia, of course; I am talking about a ritual. You can call a Yakshini into a corpse and then enjoy sex with her. And believe me, a Yakshini can make you enjoy sex. If you do this five or six times the Yakshini will come to you on her own and force you to copulate with her and extract all your energy. And you can't get free of her; it's next to impossible. When you die, you become one of the fraternity of spirits, of an order lower than even the Yakshini, and you will have to work your way up from there, roaming about. You don't even have to copulate with her; just kiss her — once only — and you are finished, done for.

Our scriptures mention all the various hells, like Raurava and Maharaurava, and each of them can be identified. *Raurava*, which means "terrible" or "terrifying," is an ethereal hell. This is terrifying because anyone who is sent to such a hell is born into an ethereal womb as a spirit. Spirits have no physical bodies, and therefore they cannot die. They have no choice but to exist, no matter how painful and miserable may be their plight.

There is no time limit. They might have to wait millions or even billions of years, until a higher being takes compassion on them and makes them enter wombs. They have no hope whatsoever of escaping otherwise. Isn't this terrifying? It terrifies me. It is a great blessing, perhaps the greatest, to be born human, so that you can die and move on to new things. But I would never want to perform such karmas that I would have to go to an ethereal hell after my death.

Can you guess who would go to this type of hell? Someone who had fooled about with spirits during his lifetime. Take that fellow who had spent some time with me some years back. All my friends saw how he could help gamblers by correctly predicting what would turn up, and he has helped many people become rich. He does it with spirits. He failed with me, though, and ever since his career has been in a tailspin.

As for his sadhana, his specialty was to take women who had died in pregnancy or in childbirth — Dakinis — and force their spirits to do work for him. He and his guru also unearthed the corpses of over 200 babies — most Hindus don't cremate their babies — and made them work also. Those babies; so innocent! When I think of it I go into a blind rage. They don't deserve to be used like that, to have their rest disturbed. Shouldn't they get their revenge on this man? They must, and it has already started. His guru made a mistake one day. The guru went blind, his family business was ruined, all his brothers and sisters died, his wife and children died, and he, too, died after watching them all go. His disciple made a mistake one day, and now his younger son is raving mad, worse than an animal. All his family members are cursing this fellow for getting involved in this; he is penniless. The babies are harassing him, and as soon as he dies, I can promise you, he will become a spirit, and they will have him in their power for good or until someone pardons him and helps him find a womb. Sadhanas can be dangerous.

I say it over and over again, just so you'll remember it: Playing with spirits is fun, and boosts your ego, and so on, but it is very, very dangerous; so dangerous, you cannot even imagine all the possible dangers, all the nuances of danger involved. For example, suppose a *Pishacha*, a low sort of spirit, becomes pleased with you and blesses you. You may not have asked for the blessing and yet you get it. And the only blessing a Pishacha can give you is that you will receive everything you ask for, and that can be so dangerous. Naturally if you are a saint or a sadhu you may be able to take it. But even good sadhus have had to suffer, even when they had not done any sort of sadhana for the spirit, never asked it to come. Once I was in Bombay, and I started to get a mental request from someone to come to visit him in Bhopal, because he wanted to take *Agni Samadhi*, to end his life by consuming his body in flames he would create from within. He had some things which he had collected during his life, and he wanted me to be their custodian. I resisted for a few days, because I was very busy in Bombay, but finally I agreed to go.

When I got to Bhopal, he greeted me as his spiritual "heir" — and then I found out the problem. Some time before a man who was possessed by a spirit had been brought to him, and just to help the man out, he exorcised the spirit. The spirit, who had been removed by satisfying him, not by force or violence, was pleased with this sadhu and asked what he desired. I suppose the sadhu's mind must have been elsewhere because he said, "Be with me always."

Thereafter, the poor sadhu had not been able to get a single night's sleep. Every time he would drop off to sleep, the spirit would prod him awake and say, "Here I am; what do you want?" The sadhu was so exasperated he decided to end his life, which is why he had called me. I removed the spirit, the sadhu took Agni Samadhi anyway, and I took a truckload of herbs, Yantras, and what-have-you back to Bombay.

And when the spirit asked me what I wanted, what did I say? "Come when I call you." For a higher class of spirit, "Be happy with me always as you are now" is a good formula, but not "Be with me always." To escape from a spirit is next to impossible once you have taken work from him.

You are probably thinking by now, "Then what is the possible use of all these sadhanas if you are in danger of ruining yourself for untold aeons?" There are plenty of uses, and once again I tell you it all depends on your presence of mind and strength of will as to what you do with your success. I did these sadhanas because I wanted to know if they really worked, and I have always believed that whatever anyone else can do in the smashan, I can do better. You may call it egotism or whatever, but that's the way it is.

Another reason I did these things was to help out the spirits. If you were to develop a sense of perception and you could hear them talk, your heart could not help but be smitten by the pathetic lamentations they make. Once I was in Hyderabad, and as I was walking down a certain street I heard such a noisy wailing I felt I must find out from where it was coming. It turned out there was a female spirit in a tamarind tree nearby. She had been a Muslim — spoke beautiful Urdu. It seems her husband had murdered her, and all she could do was wander about and try to find some way to get even with him.

I asked her if she would come with me, and she agreed. I put her into a small cemetery and had her repeat a certain mantra for some time, and after a few months she was able to leave, go into a womb, and be born again. She forgot all about her revenge, too. Of course, she will get her revenge eventually. Nature's wheels grind very slowly, but there is no escaping from them. They do a thorough job. By the time she takes her revenge she will have forgotten why she was entitled to it, and her self-identification with her actions then will act as a new karma to bind her further to limited existence. That's the way things are in this world.

And, of course, if you know about spirits you can help people who are being troubled by them. Once someone brought home a picture called *The Shining* and we watched it on the video. The people who made that film made some good guesses about spirits, but that's all they were: guesses. The reality is entirely different, though the picture did come close in some respects. But when I think of all the fake exorcists and all the damage they do when they really have no idea of what they are doing, I really lose my temper.

When I had my dairy in Borivali, North Bombay, the man who was chairman of the Bombay Milk Producers Association was named Magan Seth. His wife was possessed by a very low sort of spirit. Ordinarily she was a very meek and mild woman, but whenever the spirit entered her she would develop immense strength and would attack her husband. He found this very embarrassing, and also painful, and was on the look-out for someone who could exorcise the spirit. I could have done it, but the spirit was not harming her, and her husband deserved a beating for some of the things he did. So I did not let Magan Seth know what I could do. I have never advertised myself. Not only is it beneath my dignity, but I would never have any peace if I did things openly.

Anyway, one day Magan Seth came to me excitedly and said, "I've located someone who can cure my wife!" I doubted it, but I decided to play along. A few days later we all met at my flat in South Bombay: Magan Seth, his wife, myself, my foster daughter, and the exorcist. The exorcist was a sweetmeat merchant; can you imagine it? He had offered *attar* (concentrated floral essence) by the pound to Bhairava (a terrifying form of Shiva) and thought he was quite something. I decided it would be wise to teach him a lesson. Not only would it prick the bloated balloon of his ego, it would also make him turn away from such things before he would fool around with something he couldn't handle and *really* got himself into trouble.

He was explaining, "When I pronounce the sacred syllable "Om" in the correct way the spirit will be forced to obey me and leave this woman." The sacred syllable "Om"! Who did he think he was, some Rishi? Suddenly the spirit came into the woman's body. I contacted the spirit, though not through vocal speech of course; that is useless with spirits. There is a different method. I explained my plan to him, and he was only too willing to cooperate. So as soon as this sugar butcher opened his mouth and began to warble the "sacred syllable," the woman rose from her chair, walked over to him, and gave him such a tremendous slap that he was floored. Yes, actually laid out flat on the ground.

I made a show of concern for him, helped pick him up, dust him off, and so on. Then I picked up a few incense sticks to show the spirit I was friendly. Spirits eat through their sense of smell, of course, so I was feeding him. If you throw a steak to a vicious watchdog chances are he'll let you pass, right? So I asked the spirit, "Now look, what is it you want that you are harassing this poor woman for?" He told me what he wanted done. I said, "If I promise to ensure that it gets done will you leave her?" He said yes. I shook the incense sticks a couple of times, and he left — and she was suddenly normal again. And she has not been troubled again. It is not always so simple, of course. Sometimes the spirit refuses to leave, and then you have to resort to other measures. At least you can always control such spirits, even if you can't make them exit immediately. Then, gradually, you can usually make them see reason, unless the spirit involved is of the lowest possible category; then it is a real job to make them see reason.

One of my friends is possessed by a spirit. It was not his fault at all. He had gone to Chowpatty, Bombay's downtown beach, and decided to relieve himself under a tree. Unfortunately for him — it is all a matter of rnanubandhana anyway — there was a spirit in that tree who resented it and immediately he was possessed. He fell down in an epileptic-type fit. But it wasn't epilepsy; there was no tongue-biting and so on.

Eventually someone brought him to me. I was in Poona, and this fellow was chatting with us all very nicely when suddenly the spirit entered him. I told a boy standing nearby to hold our friend so that he wouldn't fall and hurt himself, but the spirit tossed that boy aside like a stuffed animal. The eight or ten men in the room then grabbed hold of him, but they also could not hold him down; he threw them off one by one.

I decided that things were going too far, so I sent a girl with some ash to throw on this fellow. It was special ash; I knew it would probably calm him down. But as soon as she threw it he slapped her, and she came running back to me, crying.

This was too much to be borne. Attacking an innocent girl! I decided it was time to teach this spirit a thing or two. I was a wrestler in my heyday, you know. I walked up to him and hit him so hard that he fell to the floor in a heap and slept like a dead man for several hours. When he got up we found that his shoulder had been dislocated. In fact, he had to have it operated on later.

That sounds cruel, doesn't it? But after that the frequency of possession by the spirit is much less, and our friend can lead an almost normal life. His shoulder is healed also. And even when the possession is there it is much reduced. One day it happened at my place in Bombay, and I just told Ravi to sit on him and the problem was controlled in just a few minutes — although the sight of the spirit contorting our friend's features scared everyone else in the room into speechlessness. That spirit is now learning how to behave. It is not an ideal situation, but it is the best that can be arranged under the circumstances.

You can learn a lot from spirits. A *Brahma Rakshasa* is the spirit of a teacher or guru who while he was on Earth was negligent about passing all his knowledge on to his pupils. After he dies, he must station himself somewhere and wait for a suitable individual to come by to whom he can give his knowledge. If you take the knowledge from him, you should be aware of the strings which are attached to it. One is if you ever sell the knowledge, if you commercialize it, you will become a Brahma Rakshasa when you die. But you don't have to commercialize it. You can use it to help out other suffering beings.

Yakshinis can teach you as well. But if you really want to learn, you should go to *Gandharvas, Kinnaras,* and *Vidyadharas:* the celestial musicians, dancers, and pundits. These are much higher than ordinary spirits, and they can teach you their arts if they become pleased with you. Once I took my son into the jungle to a particular spot and made him listen to ethereal music; it scared him a little, hearing the music but being unable to see what was going on. Many of my friends have heard disembodied recitations of the Vedas. But to see one of these beings is more difficult.

You can see them after they take birth, though; all of them eventually make some error, however minor, which forces them to take birth in the physical world. Once a Gandharva or Kinnara comes to Earth, he or she becomes entangled in the samsara and then for thousands or millions of births it is impossible to regain that former state. Once back there, the Gandharva realizes the limitations of being a Gandharva, and then he or she goes higher. But to be a Gandharva — marvelous! What joy!

Unfortunately, whenever a Gandharva comes down to Earth he lives a life of misery, even though he makes beautiful music.

Look at Beethoven: a typical Gandharva. He achieved unheard-of heights as a musician, but he was thoroughly syphilitic, his body was full of pus, and when he died he was in misery. Very rarely, though, a Gandharva will come down to Earth and not ruin himself completely. I am thinking of the last Nawab of Oudh, Wajid Ali Shah. From his childhood he had been quite a different type, and though he was a Muslim he used to dance with such intensity that Lord Krishna himself used to come and take possession of his body.

He had two musicians who were brothers: Kalika Prasad, who was a singer, and Bindadin, a percussionist. One day the Nawab told Bindadin, "If you are such an excellent musician, you should be able to make Krishna come and dance before me. If you fail, you will have to suffer." What was Bindadin to do? And the Nawab made the conditions even harder by saying, "You must sit in your own house and play, and Krishna should come before me." His house was about 100 yards from the palace.

Bindadin composed a new song, and told Kalika Prasad, "You go before Nawab Saheb and sing this song as loudly as you can. When I hear you singing I will start to play my drums, and then we shall see the result."

What was the result? Wajid Ali Shah forgot his identity entirely and imagined he was one of the Gopis, the milkmaids who loved Krishna. He began to crave for Krishna so intensely that he started to dance. He danced for three hours, unaware of his earthly existence; he went into *Bhava Samadhi* (a state of emotional ecstasy) and did not return to earthly consciousness for three days. When he finally came to his senses again, he asked what had happened. Bindadin told him, "I did as Your Highness commanded. I played, and Krishna came." Then the Nawab realized what sort of musicians he had.

What happened to the poor Nawab? All during his reign he encouraged music, dancing, perfumery, all the high arts. And the British, who disliked him for his extravagance with money, overthrew him. And what did they do with him? They incarcerated him in a small house surrounded by a sewer. The Nawab said bitterly, "What do these pork-eaters understand of me? I have lived my life surrounded by the finest of fragrances, and they give me this." He died after a very short time.

I am sure Wajid Ali Shah and Beethoven were originally Gandharvas because they were born musicians; they began singing or playing instruments as soon as possible after birth. Whenever a higher spirit is born on Earth, some of the impressions of that celestial existence will be retained. A Kinnara, when he is on Earth, will have an innate ability to dance; right from his birth he will be light on his feet. A Vidyadhara will have an innate love for Jnana. That doesn't mean every spirit who is fond of music is a Gandharva, however. You must know how to distinguish. Once I was in Berhampur, Orissa, and I was told about an old palace which had been converted into a school. During the day there was no difficulty, but no one dared stay there at night. I immediately said I would; I had to find out what it was. And besides, I needed a place to stay.

I became wonderfully intoxicated and sat in the main hall waiting for the circus to begin. Eleven o'clock — midnight — one o'clock. I was beginning to feel it was just a case of the fertile imaginations of the local inhabitants and was thinking of going off to sleep when suddenly a young dancing girl came in to me, bowing low, and saying, "I am indeed sorry, my lord, for having been late tonight. Now we are ready to begin." Let me tell you, I have never seen such dancing nor heard such singing as I did that night: superb! About dawn, the little girl came to me again and said, "My lord, we must take leave of you; please do come back tomorrow night." I did, and for several nights thereafter; I enjoyed myself thoroughly before I left town. And no one ever found out what I had seen there.

They were all spirits, of course. The palace had belonged to a Nawab, and one night his enemies had come under cover of night and slaughtered every living being within. Now they were all spirits, trying to maintain the standards of the court as they had while alive. They were deathly afraid that I would try to remove them, which explains why they were being so nice to me. But they weren't harming anyone, and school was going on uneventfully during the day, so I left them alone.

One of the females there was a princess, and she and I took

to each other from the start. She told me, "Why don't you keep me with you?" I said, "How can I? I'll be going away before too long." Then she indicated to me the place where her skull was buried, and I unearthed it, cleaned it, and kept it with me. She was with me for quite some time; her dancing was something superb. Spirits are infinitely more faithful than humans. Once a spirit loves you he or she will never desert you no matter what. Can you say that about any human you've ever met?

I don't know why, but I have always had good relations with spirits. Even the most vicious spirits try to harm me only very rarely. Once I was in Bihar, and at night I saw an unusual procession: several naked women carrying torches and charcoal braziers. They were *Chudails*, a very low type of spirit, and it is said that after seeing them you cannot survive. But nothing happened to me. Last year in Bombay I was driving along when I saw a group of people carrying a corpse and running. The corpse's head had slumped to one side, and there was a sickening fixed grin on it. Again, Chudails. No one else in the car could see it besides me, but again, nothing happened. Maybe it has something to do with my years of sadhana in the smashan.

My suggestion is, if you ever happen to propitiate a spirit, accidentally or intentionally, don't use it to make ash fall from your hands or any other such tricks. Take a lesson from the story of Tulsidas. He found his deity, Ramachandra, with the help of an ordinary spirit.

Tulsidas was in the habit, after relieving himself in the early morning and washing up, of pouring any leftover water on a nearby pipal tree. After forty days of this, the spirit in the tree said to him, "Now I am pleased with you; what can I do for you?"

Tulsidas said, "I wasn't pouring water here to please you; in fact, I never knew you were here. I was only doing it out of love for the tree."

The spirit replied, "That's all right, still I'm happy. What do you want?"

Tulsidas told him, "All I want is to see Lord Rama."

The spirit said, "If I knew the location of Lord Rama, I would go there myself. But I can do one thing for you. I can send you to Anjaneya, and he can take you to Rama. In a certain place a recitation of the Ramayana is going on, and a group of lepers comes daily to hear it. Anjaneya is always the first of the group of lepers to arrive and always the last to leave. Catch him, and he will show you Rama. That's the best I can do for you."

Tulsidas did as he was told and watched a few days to make sure the same leper came first and went last. When he was satisfied, finally, one day he waited until the recitation was over and grabbed the leper.

The leper, struggling to get free, asked him, "What are you doing, you fool? Do you want to catch my disease?"

Tulsidas said, "Yes, I want to catch the disease of devotion. Take me to Lord Rama or kill me if you can't; I don't want to live."

At the mention of the word *Rama*, Anjaneya immediately understood. And, it was not long before Tulsidas located Rama, all thanks to an ordinary spirit in a pipal tree.

You should treat a Yakshini in the same way. Don't look at her with eyes of lust; treat her as your own mother, and she will treat you as her son and love you maternally. When the Yakshini accepts you as her child, then you can ask her, "Ma, won't you show me where I can find Anjaneya," or a Yogini, or a Siddha, or whatever. She probably won't know — if she did, she would be there herself — but she may know where to tell you to look, like Tulsidas's little spirit did.

One of my old pals pestered me for years to teach him some rituals. Eventually I initiated him into a mantra which allowed him to handle the most venomous snakes with ease and even to cure snakebite, but that was not enough for this fellow; he demanded more.

I knew there was a rnanubandhana between him and me regarding transfer of knowledge so I did try to oblige him. I made him go out one day and sit on a rock at the seashore with a vessel full of water next to him. I told him, "All you have to do is offer water to whomsoever comes to you."

He said, "Ha! Don't worry! It is all over now, but I will go through with this just as a formality." He was so sure of his success. All I could do was shake my head in disbelief. I went off to sit nearby to watch over him.

After some time an old woman walked up to him and asked for water. He could do nothing but look at her with his mouth agape and his arms and legs shivering. He couldn't move a muscle. Again she asked him, "Please, my son, do give me just a sip of water." No response. A third time she asked, and a third time she remained unanswered, and then sadly she walked away, while this fellow remained as insensate as before.

I went over to him and said, "Well, what about the formalities?" Unfortunately, he couldn't answer me; he was still speechless with terror. I tried a second time to make him do it, but the same drama was repeated, and then I just told him, "You can't do it, it's just not in your destiny; why don't you realize that?" And since then I have never tried this with anyone else, because I know what the result would be. For your information the old woman was not an old woman at all but a Yakshini. I told her to come as an old woman, because if she had come as a young girl this fellow would have run amok and tried to climb on top of her, and then he would have really ruined himself. And who would have gotten all the karma? Me! So I washed my hands of the whole affair and said, "Nevermore!"

I had felt like there was a good chance my friend would have been able to relate to the Yakshini as a mother, and she would have taught him so many useful things. This fellow was not an ordinary individual, by the way: He had already done several million japas of a mantra for Ma, so I was just trying to accelerate his spiritual progress, but it was not meant to be. Even though she was in an old woman's form my friend could still sense her tremendous power, and he simply was not strong enough to endure it. Not that there was any real danger: That's why I was present, to watch over him. And besides, I had put the Yakshini up to it so she would not have ruined him.

I can't repeat it often enough: Don't fool around with spirits. When this fellow could not endure a Yakshini in spite of his years of penance, what will you be able to do if even a small spirit comes up to you? And spirits are really the least significant of ethereal beings.

Of course if you have a competent guru, the matter is different. And that is why I will always salute my own mentors;
they were wonderful, really amazing. They taught me everything very systematically. For example, sadhana for deities is
hundreds of times more difficult than is sadhana for spirits.
Deities are higher, no doubt, but what is the use of knowing
about them if they are too difficult to reach?

You have to use your brain. If you can first succeed at the
sadhana of a spirit, that spirit can help you with your sadhana
of a deity. Both you and the spirit will be benefited; isn't that
better?

Or, if you like, you can do sadhana of a Yogini. There are
sixty-four Yoginis, who act as companions or handmaidens to
the Great Goddesses; Smashan Tara is one of the Great Goddesses. The Yogini can teach you a lot herself; she can make
you immortal, take you to the Himalayas and bring you back
in the twinkling of an eye, and make you succeed at other
sadhanas. And with her introduction a productive audience with
one of the Great Goddesses is certain.

I have always preferred female spirits and deities to males,
for the simple reason that I always look at every female, ethereal or human, as if she were my mother. All females are facets of the Divine Mother, after all, and you can't go wrong this
way. When your mother is pleased with you there is no end to
what she would do to promote your prosperity, physical or spiritual. That is the sublime nature of maternal love. I think this
is the best way to do sadhana, especially in Aghora.

Can you understand now why Smashan Sadhana is the best
of all sadhanas? The longer you sit in the smashan the more
you learn about death, which will teach you about life. Some
of the things you see there are heartbreaking, but you must go
beyond them. There is a sadhana done in the smashan, only
on one certain night in a year. You repeat a particular mantra,
and hundreds of dead children will flock to you. Hundreds; some
murdered, some crushed in accidents, some who fell to disease. They will crowd around you and cry, "Give us! Give us!"

Then you must cut your finger and throw blood to them, just a bit, to satisfy them. You should have made preparations for forty to forty-five kilograms of sweets, and when you throw them to the children, they will catch them; it's a sight to see! After they've all eaten you ask them, "Have you had enough?" They will say yes and ask you what you want.

Here comes the dangerous part. If you ask for anything, eventually they'll come back and extract work from you, and you'll never be able to take it. Don't even ask for knowledge or for help in finding deities. If they volunteer information, OK, but not otherwise. If you ask even one question, you are bound to repeat this procedure each year on the same night; if you don't you'll never know what hit you. And if you take work from them, be it stock market fluctuations, races, or whatever, you'll get it in the neck.

So never ask anything. On the contrary, try to help them out. They are only children! Can any parent take anything from his or her children? Of course, nowadays parents expect their children to slave away for their whims and fancies, but they are not real parents. Treat these children as your own children. Suppose you saw your own child in such a predicament; could your heart bear it? Wouldn't you forget any danger to your life and try to rescue the child? You would if you were a real parent. You can help these children out by doing sadhana for them. Everyone will be benefited by it. Your own sadhana will be made firm by the effort, your rnanubandhana with the kids will be snapped, and when they are able to locate wombs and be reborn to continue their evolution the blessing they'll give you is something unique. You cannot purchase such a blessing or the satisfaction you will derive from seeing a child smiling, even with billions. And you will come closer and closer to the deity who hates to take children, the Lord of the Smashan: Mahakala.

# CHAPTER EIGHT

# AVISHKARA

*One of my friends once asked me, "Is there ever one moment of the day when you are not doing Avishkara?" What could I tell him? Does he know the wonderful joy of Avishkara? He can't imagine it because he does not really know how to love.*

## AVISHKARA

When I say that spirits can be helpful, I am sure you cannot imagine all the ramifications of such a statement. Let me explain it in this way. Why do we Hindus worship stone or metal or wooden images of our deities? We are not worshipping the image; we are requesting the deity to come in His or Her ethereal form and take possession of the image, where we then concentrate our worship. We treat the image as a living being, because a ritual called *Prana Pratishtha* is performed in which *prana*, the life force, is actually transmitted into the image.

You don't just take any image and try to add prana to it. The first thing you must do when you want to perform a Prana Pratishtha is *Bhuta Shuddhi*. That is, you must clear out all the filthy, troublesome spirits. I don't say "evil" spirits because no spirit is really evil. But some are so miserable they will try

211

to harm you without any reason just as a mad dog bites whoever crosses its path. After Bhuta Shuddhi is done, then *Bhu
Shuddhi*, purification of the ground where the image is to be
located, is indicated. Only when everything is purified should
the Prana Pratishtha be performed. However, it will take years
and years for a stone image to respond to you, because even
after prana is added the deity must be called repeatedly, and
only if the worship is continuous for some time will He or She
become fixed there. True, if an image has been worshipped
before by a Siddha or a Mahapurusha or some other high-ranking
immortal being you will get all the benefit of that previous worship; but where will you locate such an image?

To avoid this problem, you can worship mentally with your
subtle body. By long worship your subtle body will actually
take the form of the deity you are worshipping, and you can
achieve. This is much better because there are no external
images to be broken or defiled; there is only your inner self
which is impervious to all exterior pollution.

So, you can worship an image which has been made to live
or you can use your subtle body, which is already living. And
there is a third way also, which I am sure you have never even
imagined. The deity can enter into someone's body, and you
can worship Him or Her in that way. Your sadhana is very easily accomplished; the deity is pleased; and the person into whose
body the deity enters plays with his Beloved and is purified in
the bargain. Besides deities, you can call the spirit of some saint
or fakir, who can do many mundane works for you. Isn't this
useful? We call this *Avishkara* in Sanskrit, and *baithak* or *hazri*
in Hindi or Urdu.

It is handy if the body into which the deity or spirit enters is
well prepared for it through long sadhanas, but it is certainly
not essential. In Brindavan, the Ras-Lila, the story of Krishna's
dalliance with the milkmaids, is performed by many troupes
of players. Krishna is played by the most beautiful ten- or
twelve-year-old boy who can be found. Daily he self-identifies
with Krishna. If you were to worship him ritually as if he were
Krishna, before long he would start to get Krishna within his
body, and then you would be worshipping Krishna directly.

Unfortunately, no one ever thinks of doing this; they are all too busy worshipping stones. And besides, these troupes have to play for big merchants in order to survive. While the play is going on the merchant worships the boy as if he were Krishna; after the performance is over, he goes to the manager of the troupe and says, "Take this money and give me the boy who played Krishna. I want to fire his ass." How can such a thought enter anyone's mind?

You don't even need a human for Avishkara. On the day when Ganesha is to be worshipped, I go to the zoo and feed the elephants with my own hand. I give them the things they like, especially sugarcane. By reciting a certain mantra I cause Ganesha to enter the body of the elephant, and by worshipping the elephant I worship Ganesha. Isn't this better than worshipping a rock? Not only will Ganesha be pleased, the elephant will appreciate being fed and will bless me himself in his own way. I am doubly fortunate. Roshni learned to do this from me. She even climbs the fence to get inside the elephant pens to feed them if necessary!

If you want to do Avishkara yourself, you have to create a spiritual vacuum within; otherwise how will the other personality be able to come in and take control? You must "get lost" in order to get the result, because the spirit or the deity can enter you only if you are empty. The superpowers are busy creating political vacuums that they can fill; you must do the same thing on the spiritual level.

Next, you must self-identify with the spirit or deity who is being called. In the beginning when you do Avishkara, you must put on all the outer garments and accessories characteristic of the desired personality. If your imagination is not strong, these props are necessary. For instance, when someone I know wants to do Avishkara of Kalaji Rathod, one of the Rajput generals, he dresses just like a Hindu prince of 400 years ago and carries a cavalry saber. He wears a Rajput-style turban and offers everyone present opium diluted in water, the warrior's favorite drink.

This is the lowest form of Avishkara. The intermediate stage is when you can self-identify mentally, directly, with no thought for the physical details. If you are really sensitive, the right music should be sufficient to induce Avishkara. The ultimate is to be so attuned that the spirit or deity comes at the merest thought.

At first you have no control over who comes or when; they come and go as they please. As you get better at it, you request certain ones to enter you at certain times. When you are really expert, the ethereal beings themselves will beg you to permit them to enter, because they love to play about. That's the beauty of it. Finally, you enter the state in which there is no need of even the formality of Avishkara: The spirits and deities are always with you, coming in and going out as required.

During the Avishkara the subject has no idea of his earthly existence. Afterward, his body feels terrible because Avishkara is a tremendous strain on the nerves, but he doesn't care. If he does Avishkara of a deity, he is in a state of total bliss; no iota of ego separates him from his beloved deity. After the Avishkara is over he feels blank, empty for several hours, until the old personality becomes firmly fixed in the body again. Ramakrishna Paramahamsa loved to go into *Mahabhava Samadhi*, emotional highlights, and play about with the Divine Mother Bhavatarini, but at the end of his life his disciples actually prevented him from doing so as much as they could to save his body. He never cared for his body, though.

You can't afford to care for your body if you really want to do a good Avishkara. When the Avishkara is going on, the subject's body can do and endure things it would never be able to do otherwise. There is a certain fellow many of my "children" know. We call him Das Bapa. When he does Avishkara of Mahakali he slashes his arms, neck, and tongue, and blood pours from the wounds, but he doesn't feel a thing, until afterward. Even then there is no problem, because the wounds close automatically and heal quickly. When Anjaneya enters him, he can drink a bucket full of mustard oil with a pound of oxide of mercury stirred into it, and nothing will happen to him. *That* is the power of Anjaneya.

Once some townspeople tried to test Das Bapa. They told him they were going to build a bonfire into which he would have to jump. If Anjaneya really entered his body he would remain unburned, and only then would everyone believe his claims. The fire was built, and as soon as Anjaneya entered him, Das Bapa jumped directly into the flames and stayed in there about an hour. And who got burned? The people who forced him to jump in and stood there to watch. They got their demonstration, all right.

When this Das Bapa does Avishkara of a certain spirit named Bhima Bapa, his body is tied into a shroud, just like a corpse. When the Avishkara begins, the body jumps into the air, despite the fact that the arms and legs are tied. This particular spirit likes cigarettes and smokes fifteen at a time, in a big bunch. Once a fellow watching this demonstration tried to be funny and challenged Bhima Bapa to do some of the work immediately. The spirit said, "OK, if you think I can't do anything, try to get up from where you are sitting." He couldn't.

Three or four people were unable to lift him. After some time the spirit told this fellow, "Well, now we are all going to leave. If you are interested, why don't you come along with us?" Tears came into the man's eyes, and he was finally allowed to get up. But this was a good sign that Bhima Bapa was able to do work. You must always test these things thoroughly. If you are requesting a deity to come, you must make sure that it is really a deity which has come and not a tiny spirit of a lower order who may masquerade as a deity and fool you.

Take the example of Das Bapa again. When he wanted to do Avishkara of Gorakh Nath he had to dress up just like a Nath: black handkerchief, ash on the forehead, strings wound round the waist, jingle bells on his feet, and a fire tongs with bells on it. He smoked quite a lot of ganja and then started to shout, "Aa-o, aa-o, aa-lek, aa-lek," just as a Nath would, waving the fire tongs over his head and bashing himself with it over his shoulders, neck, and head. All this was necessary for him to self-identify with Gorakh Nath sufficiently to permit Gorakh to enter him.

During the Avishkara he had to cross a water channel in the floor of the cave in which we were seated. Some people got up to help him over it, thinking that he might trip, but I told them to sit down. If Gorakh was there, he would never lose his footing — he is a Nath, after all — but if there was only a spirit there he would have a nice fall. In this case, Gorakh was there, but only for a few minutes. Then a little spirit came and started playing about. I knew about it because I knew the signs. For instance, he gave his fire tongs to someone else to shake while he was talking: Would Gorakh ever give his fire tongs to a human being? Never! Then he was talking about himself (Das Bapa). Would Gorakh Nath ever bother about anyone as mediocre as that? And there were some subtle changes in the eyes also. Besides, he was answering so many questions wrong. Gorakh could never be wrong.

I love to do Avishkara, because I get an opportunity to play with my beloved deities: Anjaneya, Ma, Gorakh Nath. But I never bother about the external formalities; I don't believe in using crutches when you can walk on your own two feet. Still, if there is music I appreciate it, and incense is essential since deities "eat" through the sense of smell. The music can be anything appropriate; for Anjaneya I prefer devotional chantings, but for Ma there is a song from a certain Hindi film which always sends me into an Avishkara unless I am careful. It is dangerous to go into Avishkara when you're driving down the road at top speed listening to the radio.

Unfortunately, I can't do Avishkara of deities too frequently because it is too great a strain on the nerves, and it makes me want to leave this miserable existence and get on to greater things; do you think this is the only place I have to play in? But I want to finish up certain projects before I die, so I have to restrict my Avishkara. Instead, I often do Avishkara of sadhus or fakirs long since dead. It's interesting.

Suppose I want to do Avishkara of the Mughal Emperor Akbar. Now, Akbar must already have taken birth in so many wombs and probably is embodied even now. What will happen is that when I call for the spirit of Akbar the body in which he now resides will lose consciousness. Without a personality to self-identify with how can it express itself? As long as the Avishkara goes on, that body will be inert, and as soon as Akbar leaves me he will return to the other body, which will awake without any knowledge of what has happened. Akbar in his present condition may not know he was once Akbar; that's not necessary. But all the old records are still stored in the causal body, and that's what I'm interested in. So I don't bother about Akbar's present personality; it has its own job to do.

I'm very fond of Kinaram Aghori; he's so sweet and gentle, the ideal Aghori. But for mundane benefits, Muslim spirits are always better. Muslims live for emotion, and they are always more playful after death. Hindus, on the contrary, become steadier, and if they want to make you rich they will take their time about it so you will be able to digest your new riches before going overboard. But if a Muslim decides to make you rich he says, "At least once I'll make you exuberant like I am, no matter what the consequences may be." I don't have to request them for their exuberance; it is natural to them. I often do Avishkara of Nizamuddin Aulia from Delhi, and also of Abdul Qadr Gelani, one of the most famous saints of Iraq. But I guess my favorite is Akbar; there must be some rnanubandhana there somewhere.

When I do Avishkara of Akbar I always wear a turban. I tie it myself; none of these modern pre-tied turbans for me, thank you. I don't require the turban for my concentration, to be sure, but Akbar *was* Emperor of India, and if I want to play about with him I have to respect him in that way. So I am actually offering him what one offers an emperor. Those who come to witness the Avishkara must also behave as if they are actually in the presence of Shahanshah Mohammed Jalal-ud-din Akbar, Jahanpanah, Alamparah, Khudavan, Mere Dil-e-subahni, Mahabali.

Pretend you had come to visit me, and we decided to have an Avishkara. Once Akbar came, you would first know it by my eyes: They change color slightly and become fixed, staring directly ahead into yours. As long as Akbar is within my body they will never blink. Also, my foot will begin to shake as long as Akbar is there. Then you must play your part. Imagine yourself as a courtier in the hall of audience of His Majesty; how would you act? Reverently. You have to, because insolence in front of a king is equivalent to inviting death to approach you. Remember, my body is still present, but I, Vimalananda, am not; I have gone elsewhere, to play about in another way. Your work is with Akbar, so you forget my body and concentrate on him.

First, bend low to salute him. If he is pleased he will offer you his hand; kiss it. Then, to please him all the more, apply *attar* to his hand. Hina attar is the best; all Muslims love hina. When you speak to him, use Urdu if at all possible; it was his court language. I also love to speak in Urdu, but you'll notice that when Akbar is within me, my vocabulary and style of speech change drastically. He was an emperor, after all, and emperors are always fond of flowery speech.

They are also fond of flattery, if it is not too obsequious, so when the Emperor asks you to admire his turban describe its beauty to him in glowing terms. Offer him a cigarette if you like. Hookahs were in vogue at that time, but he has no choice if he wants to play about in today's world, does he? Hookahs are outdated according to so-called modern people. Akbar loved wine, so you can offer him drinks also. His wine was much different than is ours, much sweeter and tastier, but if you offer it with respect he'll accept it.

Offer him music. Don't make the mistake of expecting him to appreciate modern music; it is just so much noise to him. Offer him classical Hindustani music, especially Raga Darbari or Raga Miya ke Malhar. These two Ragas were specially composed just for Akbar by his court musician, the famous Tansen. If you can't sing or play an instrument yourself, a recording will do just as well.

Once he is feeling intoxicated from the attar, the tobacco, the alcohol, and the music he will begin to talk about any subject which seems fit to him. Keep quiet and listen to him, speaking when he expects you to. Don't be argumentative; it will just sour his mood and he won't be willing to do any work for you. Roshni used to wrangle with him, and for so long he would never come when she was around. Can an emperor permit any insubordination? Never!

He may speak about anything; he may even tell jokes. Here's a sample: Do you know the main difference between the days of the Mughals and these days? Back then, before you started on a journey, you would take your horse or elephant aside and permit it to remove the liquid element from its bladder. Today, before you start you must take your mount (motor vehicle) and put the liquid element into its bladder. Whether you think his jokes are funny or not, though they usually are, you must laugh a little to be polite.

When he is finally satisfied and feeling expansive, he will ask you what you want. Don't hesitate; he is an emperor, and emperors know only how to give. They are famous for giving, because it builds up their reputation. Does anyone dare to give a better present than the Emperor? So be bold. Tell him what you want, preferably material, from life. You can ask him about the spiritual also, because he became very spiritual in his later days, but he is better with the mundane, because he was Shahanshah, the King of Kings, and Jahanpanah, the Refuge of the World.

There is no use for me to speak: Dozens of people have attended Akbar's Avishkaras, and they have had their work done. Any sort of work: passing exams, getting new jobs, removing thorns in the office, finding a runaway child, curing diseases, anything. He will ask each person present in the room what he or she desires and will spend time with each discussing it before he moves on to the next, just as if he were still seated on his throne, dispensing favors. That is why he is valuable, because he was installed on the throne: It is the throne which gives him his authority. "Takht ki tasir" is the Hindi phrase: The authority or power lies in the throne itself. Even his son Salim, who got away with murder otherwise, had to tremble once in his august presence. So as long as you play along with the situation, your work will be done along with everyone else's.

Finally, when everyone has been attended to and all problems have been dealt with, he will ask again two or three times, "Is there anyone left to ask anything?" When no one replies, then he'll say, "Now I'm going to return to Sikandra," which is where he was buried, and he may say something like, "When I was alive I had authority over the whole of India, but now I am reduced to an ethereal form; all my worldly authority has disappeared. That is the way it always is with the world; seek that which is beyond the world." Then you should salute him in the Mughal way: head bent low from the neck, palm raised to the lips. He will then return to his own place.

Each personality has his or her own peculiarity, of course; you don't treat Ganesha the same way you would Akbar. You have to be clever enough to know how to satisfy each personality and what sort of work to take from each. Asking about money to Smashan Tara is useless, but She might be willing to cure disease. It takes experience to know all about it, but some of my "children" have sufficient experience and get all their work done this way. I'm very happy, since it's that much less for me to do.

Someone once asked me, "Why should these people who lived so long ago bother to come back and play with you? What do they get out of it?" I can't tell you what they get out of it, but they must get something; otherwise they wouldn't do it. Here in the world, no one does anything without some self-interest, not even spirits. But then that's between them and me.

The best kind of Avishkara is the one in which no one has any idea of what is going on. Once I decided to teach a lesson to a friend of mine who refused to believe in such things. I never told him what I intended to do; I just suggested that there was no limit to the power of the human mind. When he challenged me to prove the truth of my statement, I told him I would perform a keratoplasty operation with my own hands. He was an eye surgeon, and he knew I had never been trained in surgery, though I had qualified in Ayurveda.

He thought I was just gasbagging, so I outlined the operation in detail. He was taken aback, but to test me he took a tray of instruments and asked me to pick out the trephine I would use. When I immediately selected the right instrument he was impressed, and he agreed to permit me to perform the operation. A suitable patient was located, and I operated a few days later. It was all over in a matter of minutes, and the patient recovered much sooner than expected. My poor friend could never understand how it might be possible.

It was not me, of course, doing the operation; it was an expert surgeon. I had been able to locate one, and he was willing to perform the surgery using my body in return for a certain favor which I was happy to do for him. A fair exchange is no robbery.

Maybe the ultimate in this sort of thing is to cause Avishkara in someone else, without either that individual or those around him having any suspicion that something is unusual. I recall a very sad case which fortunately turned out happily. There was an Australian lady who had come to India with her small son in hopes of procuring enlightenment from one of the local "holy" men in Poona. She and the boy, who must have been five or six, had been reduced to living in a small hut in a smashan, of all places, because she had donated all her money to her guru and there had been nothing left to live on.

A smashan is a fine place for an Aghori, his home in fact, but it is no place for the unwary, like this tiny Western tot. He developed typhoid, and after it seemed he might recover, suddenly he turned up with all the signs and symptoms of acute peritonitis. One of the typhoid ulcers in his intestine must have perforated.

The mother went to her guru for help, but she might as well have approached a stone for all the good it did her. One of the disciples told her, "We can't help it if your child is sick. All humans have to die sometime; be prepared." A fine attitude from a guru! None of her fellow foreigners were inclined to help her; the only person who was in the least interested in her plight was Dr. Lad, the chief medical officer in the hospital into which her son was admitted. He provided him free medicines and donated a pint of his own blood for the operation. But the surgeon who was to operate was convinced of the likelihood of failure and was leaning in favor of cancelling the operation.

Dr. Lad, who has known me for some time, came to me and explained the entire situation. I sat and smoked over it for a short while, when suddenly I heard the tinkling of bells outside: an elephant! The sight of an elephant is always auspicious, or so we Indians believe, and I rushed outside and fed it some apples, the only fruit we had handy. "Well," I said to myself, "this is a good sign! It seems that what I have planned will succeed!" And I turned to Dr. Lad and told him, "Go and tell your surgeon to operate without any fear; the child will pull through."

I had to return to Bombay that day, so it was only the next day that I learned over the telephone the outcome of the operation. First, it had been almost bloodless; there had been no need of administering any blood. Second, well, let the surgeon speak for himself: "Until now my hands always used to shake when I would operate," he told Dr. Lad after emerging from the operating theater, "but I don't know what happened this time. It seemed to me as if something had taken over my hands, that they had a life of their own, and they moved so quickly and accurately that I was myself surprised."

"Not only that," he continued, "but as soon as I opened the abdomen the intestine leapt out at me, and it was child's play to repair it. I have never operated like this before; I just can't understand it, but I think God must have been helping me."

He can never know what was helping him; but why should he bother about it? The little boy made an uneventful recovery, and after he was strong enough his mother's sister sent them plane tickets from Australia and they returned there. I am sorry to say, however, that after leaving her son in the care of her sister, the lady came right back to India and resumed her place at the feet of her guru. I don't care for her at all. If she is so heartless and cruel as to expose her son to such dangers in the first place, then desert him, and run back to her playmates, she is no mother. But I am glad the little boy could be saved; Mahakala always likes to avoid taking children. And I was happy to see the honor of India preserved. Supposing he had died here; forever afterward the mother, her relatives, and their friends would have cursed India for killing him, forgetting their own complicity in it. So, everyone's work was done, and no one was stained by karma.

I have never hesitated to do anything when I thought someone could be helped by it. A good illustration of the use of a long-term Avishkara comes from my own family.

I have never scolded my children. I've always tried to understand their problems and sympathize with them. When my son said he wanted to marry a certain girl, I said, "Go ahead." When he told me he wanted 50,000 rupees to celebrate the wedding on a grand scale, he didn't bother to ask whether I had that kind of money or not. Anyway, I got it from somewhere and gave it to him. A few days later I was sitting early in the morning, as is my habit, checking on what was going on with the people I love, when I saw my mother dying. My visions have a habit of proving true unless something is done about them. The first thing I did was call my son and tell him to get married as soon as possible; otherwise, according to the customs of our community, he would have to wait a year. I don't bother about such things, but all my relatives would. I told him not to bother about the lavish ceremony but just to go to the marriage registry and tie the knot without further delay.

While we were busy with that procedure a message came: My mother had suffered a severe heart attack, massive. All the doctors, including my brother-in-law, advised us to put her into intensive cardiac care immediately, but they, with my son who is also a physician, were of the opinion that she was going.

How compassionate she was! In the ambulance on the way to the hospital she told me, "I hope I don't die. Not because I'm afraid of death, but my poor daughter-in-law will be blamed for it. All the gossips in our family will say, 'Ha, look what sort of luck she has brought us! On the day of her marriage her mother-in-law passed away.' "

Isn't that unusual, at least nowadays, for a person to be more concerned about someone else's welfare rather than their own when they are near death?

"Kuputro'bhijayate kvacidapi, kumata na bhavati." (A bad son is sometimes born; there is no such thing as a bad mother.) Unfortunately, Shankaracharya, the author, was wrong when he composed that line. In Kali Yuga most physical mothers are bad mothers, especially in the West. Here at least we still have strong family ties, but in America when the child comes of age the parents tell him, "Now go out and take care of yourself. We are finished supporting you." How could any child not become bad with parents like that?

And in the case of boys like my Ravi who have good parents but have gone astray, it is only because of the loving kindness and forgiveness of the parents that they have been saved at critical moments. Had it not been for parental teachings protecting the mind from complete degradation, where would such prodigal children end up?

A good mother can make all the difference in a person's life. Motherly love is the finest, highest form of love. Our Vedas say that the mother is the first guru. The Muslims say that paradise lies at the feet of the mother. A bad mother, though, is the gate to hell. Why? What sort of mother will tell her child, "Get out, earn money, enjoy your life, and forget about everything else," if not one who is uninterested in the child's ultimate fate? This is not motherhood, it is mere rnanubandhana. Very rarely do you find a saint who had a bad mother, and he or she could become a saint only by guru's grace. Today a real mother, *Sumata*, is very rare, so the lack of love in the world is not surprising. Motherhood is inherent in a woman's body, but it must become conscious for the emotion to manifest itself. There is a big difference in physical and emotional motherhood.

I have been lucky in so many ways, but I was really lucky in having a mother such as I had. She was a *Jnani*, a woman of true knowledge. She was worshipped by half a million people as a goddess. She never claimed to be a goddess, of course, but people treated her that way. She had ashrams in Secunderabad and in twenty-two other cities. But besides that, what a wonderful woman she was. When she was dying she was fingering her rosary, repeating her mantra, in spite of being in great pain. The day she died she fixed food for my father. They lived together for sixty-seven years, and he never took any food not prepared by her hand.

Just as she was dying my father was sobbing. She asked him to come over to where she was lying and told him, "What are you doing? Haven't you always told me that suffering is only elimination of karmas? So what is there to cry about? You should be happy instead." Imagine, remembering that at the moment of death, when most people can't remember anything.

My mother always had good advice for me. Once I was feeling low because a friend had let me down quite badly. I went to see my mother and told her, "Give me some paan." I always loved to take paan from her hands.

She said to me, "Why are you so miserable?"

I told her, "Please put down your rosary for a few minutes and listen to what I have to say. Once a man found a little doll in the street. It was very dirty and broken in several places. He took it home and washed and mended it, put nice clothes on it, and kept it with him. He and the doll enjoyed each other's company for several years. But one day the doll found some other man and ran away, and now the first man, the one who retrieved and took care of the doll, is very sad."

My mother just smiled at me and said, "That man should realize that a doll from the street belongs to the street; it is not possible to change its nature. That man should forget all about external dolls. Instead, he should seek and play with the little doll that is here in everyone's heart, because that doll will never fail him or be untrue to him as long as he lives. Other dolls will break or run away, but this one is always there." How beautifully she put it! She was right. There are two words to describe the world: wretched and thankless. That's all there is.

Anyway, at the hospital, the doctors were telling me she couldn't last long. I lost my temper. Fortunately, a friend was with me, and he cooperated; everyone else was busy otherwise. I made him go down and buy me a bottle of whisky. I broke the bottle open at the neck by smashing it against a table and drank it down neat. Then my mind became a little clearer.

Suddenly, I started hearing music. I realized when I went over to the window that it was a *qawali* (a variety of popular song), sung by Shankar and Shambhu. "*Ohhh*," I said to myself, "now there is nothing to worry about." I located my friend and told him to drive me to the cemetery. My elder sister looked at me strangely and said, "But we'll all be going there within a few hours after Mummy dies. Why should you go there now?" "You keep quiet," I told her, "I'm going."

When I got to the cemetery, I told my friend to drive off, but he suggested I might need the car later on, so he slept in the car while I did my work. It was the burning ground at Banganga, where all the members of my family, including my son Ranu, have been cremated. After I was finished and I knew my work would be done, I woke up my friend and we went home. When I got there my foster daughter, Roshni, inquired as to my where-abouts: "Don't you know Ma must be dead by now? Twice, people have called from the hospital to get in touch with you, but you were out somewhere."

I told her, "Don't be ridiculous, Ma is perfectly fine." After a cup of tea and a brief rest, we went to the hospital. There was my mother, sitting up, talking with everyone. The oscil-loscope, on which her heartbeats were being displayed, showed perfectly normal. The first thing she told me was, "What is this thing in my arm?" She meant the pacemaker they had implanted the day before. "Take it out immediately." She was OK, so they removed it. "Now, I'm hungry. Give me tea and biscuits." They gave her tea and biscuits, and they even allowed her to go home. Can you believe it? One day on the threshold of death; the next day fit as a fiddle.

There was one small problem: She had been in the habit of speaking Gujarati all throughout her life; and now suddenly she was speaking in Hindi and Urdu, which she had never known fluently before. What you can understand from this, assuming your mind is subtle enough, is that my mother was no longer in her body. She had died at the time appointed by Mahakala; and someone else had been forcibly placed inside. That someone else, who happened to be a male, a spirit of a very high caliber, was made to self-identify with her so per-fectly that she continued to live.

When we reached our house, my father came to the door and greeted her in Gujarati. She replied in Hindi. He asked her in Gujarati, "Vimu" — that was his pet name for her — "Vimu, when have you started speaking Hindi?" She replied to him in Hindi, "I know Hindi perfectly. Why shouldn't I speak it?" I took her, or rather, him, aside and said, "Look, talk in Gujarati if you don't want to cause a big brouhaha."

After that, she was absolutely fine for four to five months. My son had his glittering reception; everyone was happy. Only my elder sister, who has always been a troublemaker, tried to ruin things by insisting that a pacemaker be implanted in my mother's chest. "To forestall any further deterioration" was the explanation or some stupidity like that. When she is fine, why torture her with an operation? But they operated, and she died on the table. The surgeon was saying, "Oh, please don't die, it'll be a stigma for me." He began to massage the heart. Fortunately I was there. I rushed into the operating theater and gave the heart a good solid blow from my fist, and it started beating again. This was not a medical procedure, really; it was a way to remind my friend to do his work properly.

Many of my friends met my mother during this period, and they were most amazed at the conversations she would have with them. She would discuss how metals are formed deep down within the earth or how the conditions are on other planets, things she couldn't possibly have known. Of course, *she* wasn't talking, don't forget that.

Finally, the spirit that was within her came to me one day and said, "Now look, enough is enough. I've done your work for you; what is your idea? You think you can make me stay here permanently?" Strictly speaking I could have, but it would have ruined our friendship, so I agreed. I selected a good day for my mother's death: the day on which Kapila Muni gave Jnana to his mother. As the auspicious moment approached, the spirit left the body of mother, and my mother returned to her body. She had been kept in a safe place during those months, reviewing her life, removing all delusions. That is why, when she was gasping out her last few breaths, she could remember the name of her guru, Haranath Thakur, and repeat it: "Hara, Hara, Hara." Now, as I've told you before, Hara is one of the names of Mahakala. How many people have ever died with the name of the Destroyer on their lips? Too few to mention. So I think she was very lucky.

Interestingly enough, when we took her for cremation the next day, she was looking rosy, absolutely healthy, and rigor mortis had not set in. My son, who is a doctor, became bewildered about the whole thing and asked me, "Papa, is she really dead?" I told him, "Yes, this time she's really dead." And we burned her.

I had warned her long before she would have to suffer at the time of death; that's just the way things were written in her destiny. But as her son I felt my duty to my mother was to help her with all means available to ensure a higher rebirth, and, God willing, I think it may succeed. If she has given me good teachings I must pay her back adequately.

Very few Aghoris are really terrible. Most are soft as foam, because they know all about suffering. Take Kinaram Aghori, for instance. He used to live on Asi Ghat in Benaras, and his sect of Aghoris can still be found there. People used to say about him, "What Rama can't do, Kinaram can do," so he must have been quite something.

Once there was a dancer in the court of the King of Benaras. One day when she stretched her leg up higher than usual, everyone noticed a white patch on her thigh. At that time leprosy was the disease most feared by all, so she was immediately driven from the palace. She had decided to drown herself in the Ganges when Kinaram came across her and heard her sad story. He told her, "Go to my well in the middle of the night every night for seven nights. Bathe, then change your clothes, and throw the old ones away." She did so, and by the sixth night she was completely cured and was in fact much better than she had been before: more beautiful, more talented, and healthier.

Kinaram invited everyone in Benaras for a dance program. He was very fond of music himself and played the sitar. When the girl danced at this program, everyone was enraptured by her performance and wanted to know who she was. The king was especially interested. Kinaram told the king, "Don't you know who she is? You should. Look closely; she is the dancer you threw out of your palace." And Kinaram got the two of them married also. That was Kinaram — unique.

Don't be deluded by the ease with which Kinaram cured the girl. He knew exactly the burden of her karma he would have to bear, and he was willing to bear it. You can get yourself into a lot of trouble if you perform penances, develop good spiritual powers, and then use them without any regard for the consequences.

You have to be just like a snail walking on a razor blade if you want to do Aghora sadhanas. Any other beast than the snail would be cut, but the snail moves very slowly and never deviates from its path. If it ever veers, well, that's it for the snail. If you want an example, here's a story:

Once upon a time there was a guru who was traveling about with one of his disciples. Having reached a certain town, the guru stopped beneath a shady tree and sent his disciple to beg the day's dinner.

As the boy cried, "Give alms! Give alms!" here and there, he was invited into the house of a certain lady, who prepared food and served it to him. The boy said, "I can't eat food before my Guru Maharaj does." But the woman replied, "Don't worry about it. I am packing his lunch, and as soon as you have finished yours it will be ready for you to take to him." The boy gobbled down a delicious dinner and then said, "Well, I am satisfied. Now, is there anything I can do for you?"

"There is just one little thing that you might do for me," said the woman.

"Speak it and it shall be done," said the boy.

"I have no child to rear and love. Give me a child."

"Saubhagyavati bhava! Have a child! Your wish is granted."

Having dispensed this royal favor, the disciple picked up his guru's lunch and set out to deliver it. When he arrived his guru asked him about his adventures in town. The boy said, "Oh Maharaj, a beautiful lady called to me and provided us food. I ate my portion there and have brought the rest for you."

"All right," said the guru, "and although you forgot that you are to eat after I do, it's all right, I forgive you. What else happened?"

"The lady, after giving me my food, asked one little boon, which I granted. She wanted a child."

"Mm-hmm!" said the guru, "so you have developed the Siddhi of having all that you say come true, I suppose. Did you grant her this on the strength of your own power?"

"No, no, of course not, Maharaj. I guaranteed it on the strength of *your* power, so that she could know what a great guru you are," said the boy, who was really more interested in his own fame than in anything else. "Well, well, well," said the guru, who had understood the boy's intentions, "you leave me no choice. Someone has to be found to go into that woman's womb. You will die and be reborn as her son."

And that is the way it happened. Watch out! Don't fool around with things you can't handle. The boy in this story was a fool. He couldn't spot a dangerous situation and avoid it. Of course, there are times when even if you see the danger coming, you can't avoid it and you shouldn't try, because you have to endure some privations because of your past karmas. Listen to the story of Shams al-Tabriz.

Shams al-Tabriz ("sun" of Tabriz) was a fakir who received that name because of his great spiritual power. He became known in Tabriz as a man who could work miracles, and naturally he developed some enemies, who were jealous of his position. To test him, the chief religious magistrate called him one day and said, "We hear that you are able to do many impossible things. Will you please bring this man back to life?" pointing to a nearby corpse, that of the king's only son.

Shams agreed to do so, and asked the boy to rise in the name of Allah. He requested him thus twice or thrice, and then he got wild and shouted, "All right, then, in my name get up!" The boy was restored to life.

Naturally everyone thought Shams al-Tabriz would be rewarded for bringing the king's son back to life, but the magistrate said, "No, because he has raised the boy in his own name, he is an infidel and must be skinned alive."

Shams had to raise the boy in his own name because it was his own Shakti that was doing the job. He was skinned alive, but as they did it he remarked, "It doesn't matter. Do they think they are injuring me when they torture this body?"

Now there was a good reason that Shams had to be skinned alive. Years before, when he had been wandering about near what is now Abbottabad in Pakistan, he had become intoxicated with his own power. When he came to a certain river one day he was hungry and said to the fish in the river, "Get up here!" and they jumped out onto the bank. Then he looked up to the sun and said, "Shams (sun), cook these!" and the sun cooked the fish for him. But he didn't bother about the other creatures and plants in the area, which were roasted by the sun. For exceeding his limits he had to pay, later in his life. Even today, Abbottabad is the hottest place in Asia.

Most sadhus become proud of their achievements, and that makes them miserly; they aren't willing to use the fruits of their austerities to help out anyone else. But then what is the use in doing the austerities at all if you mean to use them only for yourself? You will get the results, no doubt, but that is all. Compassionate love, which God's devotees have, you will never get, because for that you must forget all penances, all karmas, everything, except your beloved. And that intoxication of love is worth all the penances you can do in your lifetime.

One day King Janaka was taken to heaven by a messenger of the gods. While there, he asked to see hell, which he had not seen before. A demon was summoned, and Janaka was taken to hell.

When they arrived Janaka was surprised to see that everyone there was happy and smiling, but the demon was even more surprised, because everyone in hell is supposed to be in agony, miserable. When the demon asked for an explanation one of the inhabitants of hell replied, "When we look at him (meaning Janaka), we feel that he is bearing our karmas for us, so that soon all our evil karmas will be finished and we will also be able to go to heaven."

The demon was stunned and asked Janaka to return to heaven. The spirits of the dead said, "No, don't go, please stay with us." Janaka said to the demon, "No, I don't want to go. I would rather stay here, for tens of millions of years if necessary, until all these people are freed from their bondages."

When Vishnu heard this, he was amazed and said to himself, "Even though I am the preserver of the worlds, still I haven't done as this man has." Then Brahma, Vishnu, and Shiva performed Abhisheka on Janaka and blessed him, and one of the results of the blessing was the birth of Sita (Rama's wife).

This is the way a real Aghori feels. Because he has endured so much suffering himself he knows how miserable other people are who don't have the spiritual advantages he has, and because of his compassion he tries to help them face their problems fearlessly whether or not he does anything else concrete to relieve their sufferings. To overcome fear is a great thing, because Maya is not really dangerous; She has no teeth. She tries to scare everyone, and usually She succeeds. But if you refuse to be scared then She has no power over you.

An Aghori always seems a little ghoulish to the ordinary observer, but inside he is never ghoulish; he is simply acting according to his inherent nature, without hindering it in any way. Besides, since his friends and colleagues are spirits and other ethereal beings, shouldn't he seem ghoulish?

The whole idea of Tantra and Aghora is transmutation. Whether you make use of the Shaktis of spirits or deities or magical plants or whatever, transmutation is the goal. That is why some Tantrikas practice alchemy and learn to transmute one metal into another, in preparation for transforming themselves.

Aghoris don't bother about such piffles. If they want gold, they'll piss on a rock and it will become gold. Tantra is limited by time, space, and causation, but Aghora is beyond all triads, all dualities, beyond all limitations. Tantra is just the preliminary finger exercises a musician performs to train his hands; Aghora is the full flowering of the musical talent.

For example, remember Telang Swami. By the force of his austerities he had developed the ability to transmute his own excreta into purified substances. That is why he could worship in the temple with his own urine and feces. When the Veda calls for Ganges water there is no alternative but to go to the Ganges and get the water. Telang Swami did not need to bother; he could create Ganges water within himself at any time.

Telang Swami was the pride of Benaras. He was originally a Brahmin from Kanyakubja and was devoted to his mother, who always despaired of her son's queer behavior. Finally she decided he should get married and located a good girl for him. He told his mother, "Why do you want me to bother with all these worldly formalities? Anyway, the girl is destined to die." The wedding took place — and the bride died before the honeymoon could even begin. When his mother finally died Telang Swami sat for twelve years right there in the smashan in which she was cremated. Eventually a Brahmin guru came to him from Telengana (in what is now the state of Andhra Pradesh), which is why he came to be called Telang Swami. After meeting his guru, Telang Swami spent another twenty-five years sitting in the smashan, twenty-five years sitting *inside* a blazing fire, fifty years on the bottom of the river Ganges at Benaras, and finally about a century on the shore of the Ganges in Benaras, observing absolute silence.

He made it a habit to worship at the temple of Annapurna (the goddess of food), using his urine and feces as offerings. You know what happened the day he decided to do it at Kashi Vishveshvara. After the king's dream of Shiva the king sought out Telang Swami and asked to be taught something. Telang Swami agreed to come out with the king in his boat, and as they floated down the river Telang Swami sat quietly listening until the king started to talk something out of his wits about what belonged to him.

Suddenly Telang Swami grabbed the king's sword and threw it into the river. The king was flabbergasted and asked, "What have you done? That was my symbol of authority, and besides, it was an old family heirloom, priceless."

Telang Swami reached into the river and pulled out two swords, one exactly like the other, and said to the king, "Pick out your sword." Then the king understood that he could not even recognize that which he claimed as his own. Wasn't that a good way to teach?

Telang Swami was a Siddha, after all. Ramakrishna Paramahamsa met him; then Ramakrishna's disciple Vivekananda met him both before going to America and also after returning. Even after Vivekananda's death Telang Swami went right on living. That's how I was able to meet him.

Finally he did decide to take samadhi. His devotees nailed his body into a coffin and cast the coffin into the Triveni Sangam, the meeting of the Ganges, Yamuna, and Saraswati Rivers at Allahabad. As soon as the coffin entered the water someone looked up and saw Telang Swami standing unconcernedly on the opposite bank of the river. Then he disappeared, and no one has seen him since.

Yes, Telang Swami knew how to transmute; if he didn't who would? How else could he have dared to worship Shiva with his own excreta? I remember another story about him. One day he was standing naked, minding his own business, when some English official came by and was scandalized by the sight of this nude behemoth of a holy man and ordered him to be brought to his office for questioning.

Back then when the English were ruling our country they enjoyed ridiculing our customs and sporting with us because we couldn't fight back. This official decided to have some fun with Telang Swami, in the privacy of his office, and said to him, "Will you eat what I eat?" Telang Swami did not bother to speak, but merely nodded his head in the affirmative.

The official then uncovered a plate of roast beef and offered it to Telang Swami. Now you know that Hindus never eat beef; some would fly into a murderous rage if they were even offered beef. But Telang Swami did not bat an eyelid. He ate the beef and then he said to the official, "Now, will you eat what I eat?" When the official agreed, Telang Swami shat on the salver on which the beef had been served and covered it with the lid.

The Englishman flew into a frenzy — forgetting he was just being offered a taste of his own medicine — and shouted, "I'll have you thrown in jail!" He turned to call a guard. As he turned around again Telang Swami told him, "Look a little more closely at that salver." And when he did he saw there was not any shit on it at all; instead, he saw a well-roasted chicken, dripping with gravy and ready to eat.

The Englishman was quite naturally astonished and became the greatest devotee of Telang Swami. I just mention this story to give you some idea of how an Aghori can transmute. Telang Swami once pulled this trick in court also: he shat and transformed his feces into roses. He was too good.

Why Telang Swami? I can give you an example from my own life. One day I wanted to drive from Bombay to Poona but I had no money, and there was no petrol (gasoline) in my car; I had a Humber Super Snipe at that time. A naked Aghori by the name of Mangalgiriji happened to be with me, and when I explained my problem to him he said, "What, you are worried about such a trifle? Don't worry!" Then he stuck his penis into the petrol tank and pissed into it. I was aghast: I thought the engine would be ruined. When I told him so he replied, "Don't be silly, let's go." We got inside, and when I pressed the starter the car started! We drove all the way to Poona and back, almost 300 miles, without ever adding a drop of petrol. Hard to believe, isn't it? I would never have believed it had it not happened to me.

All these external transmutations are mere trinkets, of course; it is the internal transmutation which is important. And that is where Avishkara is important; the more you bring your deity into your body, the more He or She will transform you from a limited personality, the one you possess now, into an unlimited personality — the personality of the deity you are worshipping, and, ultimately, into the Absolute personality: His personality, with a capital H.

# CHAPTER NINE

# SEX

*I have always maintained that there are two parts of the body which move even though they have no bone to support them: the tongue and the penis (or clitoris). These organs are made to move by the ego alone. They can take you to the heights of success if they are controlled, and if they are misused — if you make just a single mistake in your sadhana — down you go, divebombing like a Stuka.*

## MAN AND WOMAN

I am afraid that nowadays most people don't understand the natural differences between the sexes as well as they should. This is why there is so much misunderstanding between men and women, and why men have become so passive and women so aggressive.

Ultimately, no doubt, there is no such thing as gender. In fact I always had the desire to fill a room full of skeletons. One would be lying one atop another as if copulating; one would be holding a skull as if contemplating it, and so on. When anyone came to me to ask about spiritual knowledge I would show them this room. Then I would say, "Do you see those two skeletons over there? That is what you look like when you are making love. There is no gender! Gender was created by Nature for Her own purposes. Copulation is due to rnanubandhana, the bondage of karmic debt."

As long as we exist in the world we are enmeshed in duality. For worldly purposes we have to consider gender. Until you can go beyond your body completely your gender will exert its effect on you. So I don't think there is any use in trying to avoid gender differences or pretending they don't exist. You have to know a thing before you can go beyond it.

Men are creatures of ambition, and women are creatures of emotion. Yes, women can have ambition, and yes, men can have emotion. But only a woman can be overwhelmed by emotion, which is why she can succeed at achieving emotional ecstasies fairly easily. A man must encounter plenty of obstacles before he can enter emotional highlights. He has to work hard to develop such extreme emotion. Of course men are better than women on the path of Jnana, or knowledge. Rarely can a woman develop good Jnana. Why? Because she is the very embodiment of Shakti.

Now I know you can argue that men are also the embodiment of Shakti because the entire manifested universe is nothing but Shakti. But then the entire universe is all the creation of Shiva as well. Both men and women possess attributes of both Shiva and Shakti, but in different measure. The chief characteristic of Shakti is that She is kinetic, She moves. And this is the chief characteristic of a woman, that she is changeable. Some call her fickle. Shiva's chief characteristic is His immobility. Likewise, a man is, or should be, firm. Often, he is unyielding. Women have to learn firmness; men have to learn emotion. The universe cannot exist if either the male or female principle ceases to exist. There is no way to determine whether men are greater or women are greater. Both of them *are*, that's all.

Once the Adya Shakti said to Lord Shiva, "Ha! Who do you think you are? Without me you are nothing!" Shiva smiled his deep, secret smile and said in reply, "Be calm, my dear. Remember, I gave you birth. Your very existence is due to me."

Consider something else. Women are meant to be more closely bound to the world than are men. Only women can give birth. What is birth? It is the process of taking a spirit and enmeshing it in physical existence. A woman's job is to clothe spirit in matter. This is why traditionally in Vedic times women were supposed to look after the home and the mundane side of existence while their men went out and did rituals and provided for the family's spiritual advancement. The man never had to worry about providing for his physical necessities so he would be free to spiritualize himself to the maximum. The woman never had to worry about tough penances and other spiritual practices because whatever penance her man did automatically came in some measure to her. Now things have changed. It is hard for a woman to find a good man, I don't deny it, and if she can't find a good man then she has to try to do sadhana on her own; it's only reasonable. But it is not the ideal situation.

Even physically we can find evidence of this truth. Consider the vagina, a hollow organ. Hollow means empty. A woman has a very basic emptiness which she is always trying to fill and which can best be filled by a man. A man has a solid, firm penis which is always on the lookout for emptiness which can be filled. The vagina is an expansile organ; it can change size to fit any penis. The penis does not change size to fit the vagina, remember; it is the vagina that makes the adjustment and clutches the penis tightly. Just as the proton is enveloped by the "cloud" of electrons which whirl about it, just as Shiva is encompassed by Shakti, even so is a man surrounded by his woman, physically and mentally.

This fact makes women more superficial than men. I know that this statement will offend many self-professed feminists. But look at the vagina again. Is it not superficial to the penis? Does it not cover, as its function? Is not the penis central, the thing covered? Shiva is impulse, Shakti is that which limits the impulse. Is not the limit superficial to the thing limited?

There is nothing wrong per se with being superficial. It has its benefits and drawbacks, like everything else in the universe. If Shakti was not superficial, then Maya, Shakti's skin, would not exist, and the universe could not hold together. And then none of us would exist. Which is why I worship Ma. But it is necessary to call a spade a spade.

Our Vedic religion made a thorough study of this whole business of male-female duality. Remember, the Vedas never discriminated against women; the discrimination came much later. Many of our great sages were women, like Lopamudra and Gargi. All of our Rishis were married householders. As I said before, in an ideal Vedic marriage the husband exists to provide stability and direction while the wife sees to the details. In music the rhythm (Shiva) provides the stability, and the tune (Shakti) provides the ornamentation. It is a partnership, a mutual thing: You can't have one without the other.

Our scriptures describe in detail the qualities of a good wife. When her husband is troubled or tired or fed up with life or needs advice, she is friend, companion, and advisor. In his work she shoulders part of his load, as a servant would; she shares his karmas with him. When she feeds him and cares for him when he is ill, a wife must mother her husband. And finally, "Shayaneshu Rambha": in bed she should be as passionate as Rambha, the most sensuous of the dancing girls in the court of Indra (king of the gods). In fact she has the right to demand that her husband satisfy her sexually.

Most important, a good wife will always encourage her man to do his sadhana, since he is doing it for her also: They have become two parts of the same being. Never forget that sadhana is possible only when your domestic life is stable. As the great saint Tukaram said, "Pahile Pothoba, nantar Vithoba," meaning that you should first make sure that your belly has been satisfied and only then think about going out to search for God.

If a man and a woman can cooperate like this then the sky is the limit for what they can achieve together. I once told this to an American couple whom I treat as my spiritual children. The lady told me, "This is all about a good wife. Didn't anyone in India ever bother to consider what makes a good husband?"

She was right, of course; she had every right to demand to know. I told her, "A good husband does all he can to satisfy his wife's desires, beginning with sex. He must not fail to satiate her with sex. Our ancient scriptures even mention this." In

one of them, Parvati, Shiva's wife, says, "Among all the pleasures of women the greatest pleasure is to unite with a good
man in private, and the misery which arises from its interruption is not equalled by any other."

A man's enjoyment in sex and in family life in general is
meant to consist of the satisfaction he obtains from being able
to satisfy his family's desires. If his woman is a good wife all
her desires will benefit him directly or indirectly anyway, so
he is not losing anything. It is a mutual benefit, an attempt on
the part of both to do the best they can for each other.

Of course, nowadays such well-balanced couples are so rare
as to be almost nonexistent, and this is all because men and
women no longer know who they are and what they are supposed to do. Every woman has within her a measure of the original Shakti but very few women know their own capabilities,
all because of the heavy overlay of karmas which obscures their
perception. A woman who learns her capabilities as an embodied Shakti, well, she becomes someone. And this goes for men,
too. Deep down inside they have a spark of the divine Shiva.
Unfortunately most humans perceive things so dimly that wom-
en interpret the Shakti they feel as a need to smother their men,
and men feel just sufficient force of Shiva to make them think
they need to dominate women without knowing how to control them. Control of a woman can never be by force, which
produces too many deleterious effects. Control must always
be by love alone if it is to be effective. How many men know
how to control a woman today? Even a handful? Ha!

Remember, always remember, that just because Nature wants
men to control women that no one should ever think that wom-
en are in any way inferior to men. Never! They are just different, and it is not enough for a man to say to himself, "Men are
supposed to control women," and then proceed to beat his wife,
physically or mentally, if she refuses to indulge his whimsi-
calness. Women are different from men emotionally, and they
have their own advantages which men cannot claim. For example, once a woman decides to do something and sets her mind
to it no force can dissuade her. Once an object is electrified
the electricity never leaves on its own; it must be drawn away.

This explains why women are more passionate than men: They abandon themselves to their passion, they lose themselves in it.

This is why I am never bothered when I find a spiritual aspirant who is obsessed with sex. It is a good sign. Once you can transfer that obsession to a deity it will always pay dividends. After all, sex is just an attempt to return to the state of primordial unity; it is just misdirected. Once such aspirants are given the proper direction they can achieve very quickly, in a blitzkrieg.

I have told you stories about Tulsidas. Did you know that sex made him renounce the world? It happened this way. When he was a young man he married a young beauty named Ratnavali, and he went mad with lust for her. He couldn't sleep at night unless he had slaked his lust with her at least once. She enjoyed this in the beginning, of course, but eventually she became tired of it and one day decided to take a break. She told him that she had to consider her obligations to her family and so needed to make a social call on her mother and sister for a day and a night. She left.

That night Tulsidas found himself unable to sleep without his usual sexual release. It did not take him long to become frantic with desire, and in the course of the night he determined that he must have Ratnavali or he would surely die.

The night was dark. Rain cascaded down onto the insatiable Tulsidas as he careened through the town's muddied streets. Ratnavali's family lived across the river from Tulsidas, and the swollen torrent of the stream temporarily stopped his progress as he feverishly considered ways to cross over.

It so happened that a corpse lay there on the riverbank waiting to be cremated. The rain had set in before its pyre could be built, and the mourners had had to run to shelter to await a drier moment to perform their duty to the deceased. Tulsidas's desperate brain saw the corpse as a suitable raft on which to cross the river, failing to register that it was indeed a dead body. Overjoyed at his good fortune Tulsidas dragged his "raft" into the water and begin wild paddling for the opposite shore.

Once on the bank he leapt ashore and flew toward Ratnavali's house. It was lightless with midnight. Knowing Ratnavali's room to be on the top floor, he grabbed a handy rope, knotted one end into a lasso, and looped it over an obliging tree branch, entirely oblivious to the fact that the rope was not a rope but rather a large, very venomous, and thoroughly astonished snake.

Into Ratnavali's room Tulsidas catapulted. Embracing her out of her sleep he had his way with her over her shame-filled protests that her mother and sister would hear. Spent, he lay back exhausted, soaking her bed.

She spat at him disgustedly, "Tulsidas, you came to me only to satisfy your lust. You crave my flesh and bones. If you had put as much emotion into worshipping Lord Rama as you have in longing for this impermanent body of mine, just think of what heights you could have reached by now."

This barb embedded itself deeply in poor Tulsidas. All his sweet intoxication of passion and satiation evaporated instantly, and he replied, "Oh, is that so? Well, I'll show you!" He left, noting in passing the corpse and the snake, amazed at the blindness which sex had engendered in him. He left his own home and wandered the world as a sadhu. He searched and searched and eventually found Rama.

And Ratnavali? She was as good as a widow after that. She helped her husband attain God and ruined her marriage in the bargain. She did not meet Tulsidas for several years. Once she finally located him he told her, "You are my first guru. I must always respect you for pushing me onto the path that led to Rama. But now I have greater happiness with my Rama than I had with you. So please go back to your mother and sister."

Here is a wonderful example of a lost opportunity. If Ratnavali had had subtle intelligence she would have converted her husband's sexual energy into love for God by always seeing him as Shiva and always imagining herself to be Parvati. She would still have been his guru, fulfilling that rnanubandhana, and he would still have achieved, perhaps after a longer time, but then both would have achieved, and what love they would have had for each other! But by being insulting she lost everything. That's why I always say that the tongue and the penis can lift you to the heights or drag you down to the depths. It all depends on how you use them.

# THE NATURE OF SEX

Why do people enjoy sex so much? It's such a filthy activity, putting flesh into flesh, lying in a pool of sweat, oozings, and discharges. Modern people explain it by saying this is the way Nature ensures the survival of the species, but that is not an explanation. It is merely a restatement of the problem: How does Nature overcome individuals with the desire to mate?

Consider this: The ultimate foundation of all interpersonal relationships is cuddling and fondling. When a child is born its parents cuddle and fondle it, creating in it the feeling that it is loved. When the child is older it develops an attachment for a member of the opposite sex, which progresses from cuddling to fondling and culminates in the sex act.

After marriage some of the mystique of the romance between the two partners disappears. The solution? Produce a child which the couple can cuddle and fondle. Once the child is grown and married the couple will have their grandchildren to cuddle and fondle. All throughout life there is nothing but this.

When a man and a woman love each other they always try to get closer and closer to one another. Separation is always painful, and they try to avoid it by spending all their free time together. This is why the word "couple" is singular in English even though it means two. This feeling of separation is possible only because there is duality; the misery of separation is the misery of being unable to make the two, which were originally one, into one again. In the primal condition there was no male and no female.

When a man and a woman are really deeply in love, when the emotion is so strong that they are always mentally close, daydreaming about each other, imagining the next rendezvous, there comes a time when they can no longer resist the urge to be physically close, to unite sexually. The tension builds up to the point where release is inevitable. It is a question of possession: "I want to become you, and I want you to become me." This is impossible; the bodies get in the way. The next best thing is, "I should be in you and you should be in me." When the couple is overwhelmed by the imperative to unite, they have sex. Actually only the penis and vagina unite, but for the duration of the sex act the man feels, "Yes, I have penetrated her, I have possessed her," and the woman feels, "Yes, I have accepted him into me, I have possessed him."

I have always said that women are more possessive than are men, and that 99.99 percent of women are possessive. And whenever I say this some woman objects. But look at physiology again! The vagina accepts the penis, not vice versa. The female is meant to possess, and the male is meant to feel that he is being possessed. Nowadays, of course, when everything is so topsy-turvy many men have become possessive, but this is pathological; it only happens because they are unsure of their own masculinity. Men are very worried about their sexual performance, their ability to make a woman feel that she is "full." This fear of inadequacy makes them fear that their partners will have to go to other men to become satisfied, and they defend themselves by becoming possessive.

But that is abnormal. It is normal for a woman to be somewhat possessive, and only the greatest women can go beyond it, just as only the greatest men can go beyond their image of themselves as great stud bulls who women are supposed to want to possess. Then of course you have Freud, who claimed that everything was due to penis envy, but that is another matter. Right now let us consider the sex act.

When the penis and the vagina unite there is a great satisfaction in both partners; possession, partial unity, has taken place. This partial unity overwhelms them with the desire to attain to perfect unity, and they attempt to move their bodies even closer together until their nervous systems overload and orgasm occurs. During the moment of orgasm the two forget entirely their earthly existence, and for a brief moment — a very brief moment — they are again one. But only for the time the orgasm lasts. Afterward they are again separate.

Most people try to convince themselves that they are satisfied with orgasmic sex, but they cannot. Even if you enjoy sex with real concentration, with real cooperation between the partners, the satiation will last for a week or two at the most, and then the desire will again arise. Of course if you are chasing sex for the orgasm alone and not for the love, you will not be satiated even by copulating ten times a day. You will end up a pervert; there is no escape. Orgasm is just a physical reflex; it causes no satisfaction on its own, just "tension release." To really enjoy an orgasm you must enjoy your partner. You must love your partner sincerely, and you must be more interested in his or her gratification than in your own.

With ordinary sex between two partners who are fully receptive to each other's needs, satiation can't last more than two weeks. But with Vajroli (see p. 279) a couple can enjoy themselves so fully in one sexual experience that for three months or more the sexual urge never rears its head. They feel so close to one another that there is just no need for the temporary closeness provided by an orgasm. There is real beauty in such a relationship. This is what the West has yet to learn: Sex is something which deserves a lot of time and effort to perfect, to make the effect unique and lasting.

How many people in the world really know about sex? Oh I know, there are Masters and Johnson and so many other sexologists and dozens of books on the subject, but how many people have really become experts at sex? We Indians, only a few of us, are the only ones in the world who really know the spiritual erotic art. Westerners are doing plenty of research but they have a long, long way to go. If they were to learn our techniques they would be able to perform them very well, because they are willing to try anything new. They have very few inhibitions left, in contrast to today's Indians who have plenty.

But there is such a difference in the mentality of a Westerner and an Easterner! And sex is all in the mind, no matter what anyone tells you. Take prostitution as an example. A Western whore watches the clock very closely. Once your time is up you must emit and depart. But here in India suppose you try to climb on the lady too early. She will tell you, "No, my lord, wait, the night is yet young, we have until morning to enjoy our play." If you fart in the bed of a Western whore she will say, "Oh, you bloody stinking fellow!" But an Indian girl would tell you, "What a man you are! Even the gas you pass is melodious!" Of course this is the way things used to be; Indians are gradually becoming clock-watchers under the influence of the West.

Don't you think a man is more likely to perform well in response to a supportive and caring attitude rather than one which is strictly businesslike? I don't mean to say that Indian prostitutes have hearts of gold; far from it. They put on this act because they know it will help generate more revenue from the customer. Here in India both get what they want: The man thinks he is being treated like a lord, and the lady gets paid for having a good time. And in the West? Only business. We Indians are very emotional and to trick us you have only to play on our emotions.

Westerners have become very clinical on the subject of sex. I read in *Time* the review of a book written about the clitoris. Very nice, but inexact. Very few people in the world understand women's orgasms, and in the East only about 1/10 of 1 percent of women have any idea of what an orgasm is. In the West at least 10 percent do because they all read the sex manuals and try out what they read, but they are still groping, they don't have a complete grasp of the subject. To begin with they should forget all about quantity and should concentrate on quality; one good orgasm satisfying to both partners is worth a hundred ordinary physical responses. For this they must try to understand the true nature of sex.

# THE RNANUBANDHANA OF SEX

In reality there is nothing to sex but rnanubandhana. Freud was right to argue that the sex instinct is inherent in all creatures, inborn in each one. But did he know why? Did he know that the sex instinct actually begins with the union of the sperm and ovum, because that is a sex act all its own, a union of male and female? Sexuality begins with conception, and as soon as

the child is born it is aware of its sexuality. Doesn't the penis
of a tiny infant become erect? Since erection occurs only when
the ego self-identifies with the penis, ego awareness of sexuality must be present even in infancy.

Two people can be mutually attracted to one another only if
there was some relationship between them in a previous life.
They may have been animals or insects or humans, but if they
copulated then they will be overwhelmed by the urge to copulate when they meet in this life. And just because they were
mates or husband and wife in a previous existence it does not
always happen that they must be husband and wife in this life.
They may come back as mother and son, father and daughter,
or brother and sister; and then the result will be incest. In the
past these instincts were rigidly controlled by the rules of society, and those cases of incest which did occur were hidden deep.
Today everything is out in the open.

Now, the person of subtle intelligence will be able to discover so many things about two people who copulate. For one,
suppose it is a mother and her son who unite sexually. Does
the mother make the son climb on her or is it the son who
initiates the activity? By knowing this you can know who was
the male in the last encounter, in the last birth. Normally, the
male is dominant. He first indicates his desire for sex, and then
the female acquiesces. She will acquiesce only if there was a
relationship between them in the past. She will be overcome
by the urge developed during that previous liaison. If the female
in this birth takes the initiative, she must have been the male
previously.

Even the posture taken during coitus is determined by that
previous relationship. You know, I suppose, that camels and
rhinos mate hindways; the penis points backward in these species. Each species has its own peculiarities of mating, and if
you know all the possible wombs, like a Rishi does, the sex
posture alone is sufficient to pinpoint the species involved in
the previous relationship.

This knowledge can be beneficial. Suppose I have knowledge
of my previous births. I meet a girl I like and we go to bed together. Since I know the form we shared previously — fish, bird,

mammal, or whatever — I will refer to my mental files and locate the sex techniques appropriate to that species and then deliberately initiate that technique. She and I will then instinctively enjoy that sex much more than we would have, had we used any other posture, because subconsciously we go back to our previous state, which makes the conscious mind drop away, which increases the passion. That sex will be so satisfying that the rnanubandhana is fulfilled completely by one session. My work is done; another rna is crossed off my list. The girl enjoys herself better than she has ever enjoyed before. No one is a loser. This is especially important because, as a male, I have the obligation to satiate my partner.

To know the rnanubandhana is to be able to decide how and when to fulfill it. If I know *Shiva Svarodaya*, the science of breath, I can deliberately inhale certain of my partner's breaths during a deep embrace, and she will never be able to leave me. When I know the rnanubandhana is finished and it is time for our relationship to end, I will inhale certain other breaths and she will develop an aversion for me and we will split; it's as simple as that. She never knows what has happened. She thinks it is all her own volition that she came to me and that she left. She forgets that there is no such thing as free will.

There comes a point, though, when sex becomes tiresome. How much can you perform the sex act, anyway? You have to tire of it eventually. Suppose that a certain couple had enjoyed sex so much in a past birth that they were fully satiated. When they meet in this birth they will have a desire for sex but they will never be impelled to follow through on that desire. They must have a desire for sex together because they were related sexually in the past; it is axiomatic. But if they avoid sex in this birth their relationship will become much more intense.

Physical sex makes you more aware of your body, which weakens your mind. This makes you more interested in gratifying your body and makes it less likely that you'll remain faithful to one partner. When your relationship is purely or predominantly mental though, there comes a point when you will be unable to do without your partner, the ties will be so strong. You'll never be tempted to look at anyone else because you know you'll never find anyone else to understand you so well. A peculiar sort of Maya will bond the two of you together. Whenever you are apart you will always long for the day when you will be reunited; you yearn for each other, to share your professions, your hobbies, your pastimes, and, most of all, your sadhana. There is such a beautiful lingering memory that you can't bear separation, but there is almost no desire for sex because just a kiss or a hug or the touch of a hand is enough to satisfy. Isn't this better than repetitively going through the moanings and groanings of physical sex? Isn't this more refined?

Like music sex is an art, and you must be artistic if you hope to become good at sex. Everything in life should be artistic, in my opinion; otherwise, what is the use of living? This is the main grudge I have against Westerners: They are so crude and rough. It is because they are slaves to time, always in such a hurry to get things done that they rarely have time to do anything right, with art, grace, and culture. And now the Westerners are spreading this disease all around the world.

There has never been any other lover in the world like Lord Krishna, and there will never again be another like Him. He had more than 16,000 wives, and every woman who saw Him immediately fell in love with Him and melted into Him. When He lived among the cowherds of Brindavan He used to dance with the women of the village — the dance known as the *Ras-Lila*. There is an esoteric meaning for this and every other event in Krishna's life, of course, but besides that, an imitation of the Ras-Lila has been performed as a folk dance for millennia here in India. A boy and a girl stand opposite one another, each holding a pair of slim sticks. They wheel and whirl, tapping their sticks together to the rhythm of the dance. Most intricate; fascinating to watch. But now the vulgar have made the music disco, and the children beat their sticks together violently. The last time I encouraged Ravi to join in I thought he would be beaten soundly by the girl he was dancing with! She was that rough.

Our society is regressing into barbarism; it's sad. Is it any wonder that people have no time or interest for mere kissing and holding hands or lying together quietly side by side? Such development in a couple occurs only after many lives lived together. Today, people will not settle for anything less than sex, usually rough and violent sex, and even that fails to satisfy them.

# MARRIAGE

Most people cannot get out of the rnanubandhana of sex, which is why society developed the institution of marriage. Originally, there was no such system as marriage here in India. People were more primitive, something like cavemen. If I wanted some woman I would just go and take her, and no one could say anything about it. Swetaketu changed all that.

One day Swetaketu, his father, Uddalaka Rishi, and his mother were all sitting peacefully near their hut. A Brahmana walked up to his mother, said "Come with me!" and carried her away. Swetaketu wanted to follow him and bring his mother back, but his father dissuaded him gently, saying, "Someday you will steal someone's wife yourself." Then Swetaketu's young heart was so hurt that he vowed he would change society so that no children would ever again be so cavalierly deprived of their mothers. And so marriage came into being.

Still, the ancient sacrament of marriage was nothing like what we have today. Back then if a boy and girl decided to marry they would go out alone together to a secluded place and would take the sun, or the fire, the water or another of the Great Elements as a witness, and that was it. From that time forth they were man and wife. Plenty of rituals were added later by the priestly class to prolong the ceremony for the priests' benefit, but the essence of the rite is still the same. Every Vedic wedding today takes fire as a witness, because no marriage is regarded as irrevocably solemnized until the couple takes seven steps around the sacred fire.

The true Vedics never consummated a marriage the day it took place no matter how auspicious the wedding day might be. The bride would return home with her parents to wait for another auspicious day, so chosen that by copulating on that day the couple would achieve such satisfaction that they would never think of leaving each other. Another advantage to the wait between the ceremony and the consummation was that both parties had time to prepare themselves mentally. The days they spent apart served to heighten their desire for each other, from anticipation of the sex they would enjoy together. I have always said that 50 percent of the enjoyment of a romance lies in the waiting period, when you don't know whether the opposite party will fall in love with you or not. You can't be sure, you can't take anything for granted, you are on tenterhooks continuously. After you both know you love each other, part of the joy is lost, but part still remains: "If I make a mistake he (or she) might leave me." This keeps you always on your best behavior.

But after marriage you know you always have each other, you have ready sex whenever you want it, and your partner dare not leave you since society will point a finger if he or she does. The result? All the magic, the mystery, the danger disappears from the relationship; it becomes devitalized. And then there is nothing to do but endure it, or if you are an American, divorce.

In India we have known about human psychology for a long time, and this wait before the bride is taken to her husband's house is one means of making the marriage a success. Each day the longing would increase until both bride and groom would be half-mad with desire by the time the auspicious day rolled around. Then the bride would be decked out in a beautiful sari and whatnot and would travel by stages to her husband's house. With her she would carry a big silver glass filled with milk: two liters boiled down into one, mixed with almonds, pistachios, saffron, and so on. She would also bring five paans. Each paan would have extra ingredients added to it, and each would be folded into a particular shape.

After all the greetings and other formalities, which would be suitably prolonged to drive the newlyweds to distraction, the bride and groom would enter their nuptial chamber, and no one would disturb them until they emerged.

The first paan would be square-folded. Both would eat it

together so their lips would meet in a kiss. That kiss, the first kiss of passion in their lives, would be prolonged, and when the young man would then look at his wife's lips he would see them blood-red because of the paan juice. And you know what red is to a bull: it intoxicates, excites him.

People talk about kissing but they don't have any idea about how many types of kisses there are. Let me tell you about just three of them. The kiss of entanglement is a kiss on the lips, which is practiced by lovers or by husband and wife. It entangles you further and further in the Maya of sex. The satanic kiss is a kiss on the eyes by a Dakini or a Pishacha. This kiss makes you see the ethereal world, which will in all probability drive you insane; that is why it is satanic. When Ma kisses you, though, She will kiss you on your forehead at the location of your third eye, which She causes to open. This is the kiss of enlightenment, the kiss of true Motherhood, and the day Ma gives you this kiss you become filled with Her Divine Intelligence. I think this is the best type of kiss, and after enjoying it I never feel like enjoying any other type of kiss. I want only Her sweet lips.

But most human beings insist on fleshly lips. Most human beings, unfortunately, have become so obsessed with sex that they have forgotten the beauty of a kiss. Forget coitus; once you have kissed someone, once you have come so close to another being as to unite your mouths together, how can you forget that person? Isn't sex just the uniting of the lower mouths together? When someone has so totally surrendered to you as to open his or her body to you, shouldn't you always remember that surrender? Most people don't, though; they enjoy and forget. It just goes to show that all sex today is directed solely by rnanubandhana. Traditionally, though, a couple would experience a romantic kiss first on that night of consummation, and it would be the experience of a lifetime for them.

The second paan was to be placed between the girl's breasts. The boy would take it with his mouth, using his tongue to clean and excite the area, thus igniting the erotic centers of the upper body. Remember how the ancient Romans in their orgies used to pour wine over the women's breasts and then lick it up? This is the same sort of thing.

The third paan was to be folded flat and placed at the navel, a very important erotic center. Here the boy was not to use his tongue, only his lips. The erotic centers ignited above should now be truly inflamed.

The fourth paan was to be folded conically and placed in the vagina. As the young man bit it the conical tip would pierce the hymen. By this time the bride should be experiencing uncontrollable spasms. The boy would then mount her and discharge. If they knew Vajroli, of course, there would be no discharge; he would make her have so many orgasms that she would be satiated for a full three months. In any event after coitus they would both share the fifth paan, kissing again, and then they would drink the milk. Ayurveda says, "After food drink buttermilk, and after sex drink hot milk." The milk strengthened and invigorated them for further play.

At Indian marriage ceremonies a round fruit which looks something like a walnut and is called a *Madanaphala* is tied around the groom's wrist. Most people today don't bother to search for the real thing and tie any convenient root or fruit instead, and even the people who tie the real Madanaphala don't know what it is meant for. Madana is one of the names of the god of love, and Madanaphala is one of the best of aphrodisiacs. It is tied around the groom's wrist for the bride's benefit. Should he ever become impotent she would take that fruit which he had worn at the wedding, to which a small ritual had been done, and would administer it to him after preparing it in the prescribed way. Then he would again be able to perform his sexual duty to her. This was another of the customs propounded by our Rishis for the preservation of family and society, but as our society declines this knowledge is being lost.

Circumstances today just don't permit most people ever to have satisfactory sex. In the West no one allows themselves the time; as I've said, they are all clock-watchers. In India we have plenty of time but no privacy. The Indian couple is always afraid that auntie or little brother may be watching, spying on them. This destroys the mood. Sex being all in the mind, what is the use in indulging in it without the proper mood? Another reason I am not in favor of today's sort of marriage is that it ruins sex. Marriage has become licensed prostitution. Neither the man nor his wife is legally permitted to enjoy with anyone else, so there is no incentive to gratify the partner. Everything regresses to self-gratification.

For years and years the priests burned widows alive on their husbands' funeral pyres, claiming that by doing so the women would become Sati. Nothing could be more ridiculous. If a man and a woman are deeply in love the one will not be able to last once the other dies; the longing is just too strong. My own father lived only a couple of years after the death of my mother; and during that period we would often find him sitting apart, wiping the tears from his eyes. A woman who finds herself bereft of her husband who she truly loved as her god incarnate will not find any further interest in life and will die. She may not throw herself on the pyre; she may starve herself or just waste away, but she will quit living. She is Sati; she has gone beyond rna and will meet her man again in future births. As long as you are restricted by rna you have no free will; only when the limitation of rna is broken can you become Sati.

A woman who is not so attached to her husband will not bother too much about his death. She will continue living; she might marry again. The rnanubandhana between her and her former husband is broken. They will no longer be born together but will go their separate ways. The same goes for a man whose wife dies and who then forgets her. These are not true marriages, only arrangements for the fulfillment of rnanubandhana. I say, why bother with marriage at all? It is no longer necessary to marry to enjoy sex; people enjoy more or less as they please nowadays. The only other use of marriage is to make the children you produce legitimate in the eyes of the law. This is convenient but is not an insurmountable difficulty if you prefer otherwise; many famous men and women were illegitimate. Why bother to marry and create complications for yourself?

# CREATION AND PROCREATION

Human beings like to procreate, to reproduce their own kind. If they could learn to create there is no limit to what they could achieve. But you have to give up procreation before you can begin to create, and few, very few, are willing to do that.

Let me try to explain the difference between creation and procreation. It's really all in the point of view. Ordinary men and women treat Nature as something external to them. They talk about Nature procreating because they see the continuous birth and death of the samsara surrounding them. Because of ignorance they conveniently forget that they too are part of the copulating game, insignificant worms in the samsara themselves. They self-identify with their own limited bodies and personalities. This puts them under the control of Nature, and they are not even aware of it; they remain subject to the Law of Karma and to rebirth.

If they could go beyond their limitations they could actually see that Nature is really doing the creating. Nature has control over the patterns that manifest, and all the reproduction in the world is just the natural outcome of the impulse of Nature. Therefore, it is Nature who creates, and ordinary mortals who procreate.

Humans think it is the other way around, out or ignorance. They believe that through sex they are creating a child. Why should they want a child? They just want someone to reproduce their own attributes, someone who will appreciate and love them. Just as Shiva and Shakti generate universes in which beings can, by means of hard penances, come to the stage of admiring and loving the Father and Mother of the cosmos, a man and a woman produce a child in the expectation of receiving love and admiration from it. But this is really procreation because they are unaware of the rnanubandhana, the impulse which impels them to do it. Real creation becomes possible only when they become aware of that impulse and transcend it. However, if everyone realized all at once their true selves then there would be no one to fall prey to Maya and continue to ride the wheel of birth and death. Nature, therefore, keeps almost everyone in ignorance. Isn't it wonderful?

Conception is in itself a wonderful process. All the sperm have the same determination: "I must go through the cervix to the uterus, get into the tube, locate the ovum, and unite with it." The ovum is single and passive; it doesn't have to search for the sperm. The sperm have to swim hard against the current, and, of the millions ejaculated, only one is finally accepted by the egg. What can we learn from this?

First, the male should always be the active partner and the female the passive partner in the sex act. This is Nature's way, as exemplified in the physical process of sex. A man will never be able to penetrate if he cannot maintain an erection, and even after penetration he must make movements. The woman needs to do nothing but lie still and allow it to happen. She can cooperate if she pleases, but it is not at all necessary.

One of the problems with Westerners today is that some women are attempting to become the aggressive factor in the relationship. As I mentioned before, this is because they were males in their previous existences, and their present male partners were the females then. Although it is easy to give in to these past tendencies it is better to resist them and to learn the gender roles appropriate for your sex this time around. The male is meant to be dominant because Shiva must always control Shakti. This is why the male should be on top during copulation and why the woman must be beneath him. Shiva must be on top to control. If the woman is on top Shakti is in control, but Shakti knows no control. The result? The male might become a pervert, because the free-flowing Shakti will cause his perverted karmas to emanate from the causal body. The idea that the woman should actively climb on top of the man is completely against Nature. What happens during Vajroli is different, of course.

Second, only that sperm which will provide the specific heredity required by the spirit who is to take birth will be selected by the egg. The sperm having the strongest rnanubandhana with the ovum is always the winner. If the child is meant to be born

blind or deformed or mentally retarded, only that spermatozoon which fits the bill in its entirety will make it to the egg.

"Gahana karmano gatih": The ways of karma are profoundly deep. Sometimes even when there are plenty of sperm they
run into a "No Vacancy" sign when they try to meet the egg.
If there is no Jiva with sufficient rnanubandhana or if the horoscope which would result will not fit the requirements of the
Jiva or if there is some curse, you may pour in liters of semen
and still conception will not occur.

If there is enough rnanubandhana to attract some Jiva then
that disembodied spirit will impel the sperm and ovum to meet.
When they unite the two become one; duality is ended. But
this unity, like the unity of orgasm, is very temporary. Because
of the overwhelming joy of the union the sperm and ovum procreate and form billions of cells. As the zygote begins to divide,
duality begins again.

Until the heart starts to beat the Jiva is in a state of bliss, at
one with Krishna, in a state of union with the Absolute. Once
the heart starts to beat personalized existence begins, separation from the Beloved. The Jiva really begins to self-identify
with the fetus only after the heart starts to beat. The Jiva enters
the zygote at the moment of conception, to be sure; otherwise
growth and movement would never occur. We say, though, that
life really begins in the fourth month, and after the seventh
month the Jiva has a firm grip on the fetus because it is then
that the fetus becomes viable if premature labor occurs.

The Jiva in the womb has a memory of past lives. This explains
why the fetus kicks and moves about: It recalls its past freedom and resents being trapped in a cramped womb, surrounded
by hot, fetid intestines, tortured by the spicy food, intoxicants,
and other inappropriate things its mother indulges in. The subtle body completely self-identifies with the fetus and enjoys
the placental food. Despite the torments of living in its own
waste products it never wants to leave the womb, because it
remembers its past lives and comprehends the mistakes it has
made. It promises God that if it is permitted to remain in the
womb indefinitely it will worship with concerted mind.

At the moment of birth, though, the fetus is cut off from the placenta. Because it craves food it projects its mind outward — and forgets its past lives. When its head is squeezed coming through the birth canal it forgets everything and comes into the world screaming, "Koham? Koham? (Who am I? Who am I?)" Some hear in its cries "Uma! Uma!" Uma is one of the names of Shiva's wife, Parvati. By crying "Uma!" Shakti is calling, "I am here!"

The embryo or fetus is the characteristic of Maya. At the time of birth the fetus forgets all the promises it has made to God about what it will do after its birth because the mother and father were copulating only for pleasure, not to have a child. Even in those couples whose aim was to procreate, the last moments of coitus produce such great passion that they forget everything except the bliss of sex, and this is what makes the child forgetful as it is born. Out of a million cases maybe one couple will unite for the specific purpose of producing progeny and will keep that determination even through the orgasm. That child will remain fuzzily aware of his past existence: He will have a sort of ESP.

Why should a guru call the disciples who come to him "children"? Because in a very real way he is creating them, though not through the usual method of procreation. He is not interested in the body at all, only in what is within the body.

Jesus said, "You must be born again." He meant that you must be given a new birth by your guru. The guru must recreate you after first destroying you. Your ordinary physical birth pushes your face into the slush of the samsara. The guru gives you a new birth which takes you out of the world.

Doesn't it make sense then for an Aghori to die to the world? Once you are dead you can be easily reborn, and this time with full consciousness of who you are. When a guru "mates" with his Shakti to create a disciple, he does it not for pleasure but to fulfill a specific purpose. Such a "child" is bound to be clairaudient and clairvoyant, isn't he?

This is why a true guru will always be celibate. He is not interested in using his semen for mere procreation; he preserves it for something better. Today everyone pooh-poohs this idea. They say, "Semen is only a natural product. There is no harm in evicting it as much as you like." In fact, I was told that one theory making the rounds in America now is that if a man does not ejaculate at least once every forty-eight hours that he runs the risk of enlargement of the prostate! How absurd! What rubbish! The fact is, too much emission of semen is much more likely to cause prostate enlargement in old age than is too little ejaculation.

# OJAS

For creation you must use the semen in a different way than the way you use it for procreation. Semen is that substance in the male body which has the ability to create. Only procreation is possible if it is expelled from the body, ejaculated during the sex act. If it is retained within the body, stored instead of being wasted, then real creation becomes possible through ojas. Ojas is the source of the body's metabolic energy, the Jathara Agni. Loss of semen means loss of ojas and thus loss of digestive power. Ayurveda cautions that all diseases result from disturbed digestion, which explains why Ayurveda always also cautions that the wise man should preserve his semen.

It is said in Ayurveda that ojas is derived from semen, but this is not quite so. Ojas exists in association with the head and the nervous system. In fact the "aura" or "halo" which you can see around a person's head is composed of his or her ojas. When I say that loss of semen causes loss of ojas you must remember that sex is all in the mind. Before the penis surges into erection there must be a mental command for it to do so. When thoughts of sex fill the mind the Kama Agni (Fire of Lust) becomes inflamed. Heat is anathema to ojas. The Kama Agni causes a disturbance in the ojas, which alters the brain chemistry and directs the endocrine glands to begin to secrete. The effect is first felt on the prostate in men and the Bartholin's gland in women. Whenever oozing from these glands occurs you can be sure that ojas is being dissipated. During celibacy the ojas goes on and on harmonizing itself.

Women are lucky in that every month all the filth in their

blood is drained out. This is the function of menstruation, and each menstrual cycle strengthens a woman's ojas because there is less waste material in the body to disturb digestion or brain chemistry. Unfortunately, since women are nine times more passionate than men most of them will find that this increased ojas merely serves to increase their sex drive. They will be impelled to copulate more, and all the benefits will be lost. Ayurveda recognizes that the same substances which rejuvenate the body also act as aphrodisiacs and warns that when a rejuvenating effect is desired, sex must be restricted.

Ordinary sexual activity destroys ojas, but so do thoughts of sex and sexual fantasies even if you do not act on them. In fact continual brooding about anything is equally devastating to the ojas because thought causes the mind and brain to heat up and all this mental heat, no matter what the cause, causes excessive physical heat. According to Ayurveda excess heat in the body leads to constipation, the root of most diseases. Heat also causes hypersecretion of all the glands, which in turn excites the mind via the body. It's a vicious cycle. Excess coolness in the body can be readily dealt with; excess heat is dangerous. Any unnatural heat ruins the ojas just as surely as does an inflamed Kama Agni.

Likewise, harmonious thoughts increase ojas. How often have you heard someone say to a pregnant woman, "What a glow you have about your face!" That glow is the aura, composed of ojas. You might think that a pregnant woman's ojas would be low because her body tissues are being depleted to furnish nutrients for the baby. But because of the emotions of motherhood, the overwhelming love for the child being formed, ojas actually increases.

# CONSERVATION

If you want to progress from the state of being a donkey in human form, one who lives for eating and procreating, to a higher state, you must conserve your semen. If you are female you must preserve the vaginal secretions which pour out during excitement and sex. The need for celibacy is the same in both sexes. There are dozens of good reasons for *Brahmacharya* (celibacy), but we will consider just a few.

First, Newton's Law of Motion: Action and reaction are equal and opposite. When a man indulges in too much sex or masturbation he kills millions upon millions of sperm. He gets a little thrill out of it, but he must reproduce all those living beings again within his body. Celibacy is not meant to remove all pleasure from life; it is meant to avoid killing sperm, among other things. After such an overindulgent man has died isn't Nature right to make him be born as a spermatozoon for at least seven births? Then he learns what it is like to be wasted: living quietly in the body, a brief moment of joy, freedom, and — finished. And such a man will continue to be reborn as a sperm until he can locate an ovum with which he has some rnanubandhana. You see, hells are not imaginary. Some of them exist outside the earth but many exist right here. It's just that we can't see them easily. When you become aware of the real significance of, say, *Kumbhipaka*, the hell in which you are born and reborn as a spermatozoon, well, then you will say, "Oh, yes, now I realize. . . ."

Second, if you are not interested in sex then it will be impossible for any voluptuous, passionate young woman to entrap you, or if you are female for any man to sweet-talk you. Since you have nothing physical to take from anyone you will never have to subject yourself to scheming lovers and succumb to their wiles. The more you indulge in sex the more your mind becomes attached to it. This makes it far easier for someone, human or spirit, to use sex as a bait to hook you. Abstinence, Brahmacharya, is safer.

Third, Brahmacharya makes your nerves very strong. Sex is a nervous response of the body. The more you enervate your body the more mentally unstable or "infirm" do you become. You can't afford to have weak nerves if you want to perform Aghora sadhanas because the first wild shrieking spirit who comes along will reduce you to a gibbering wreck, or will give you such a rude shock that your nervous system will collapse and you'll die of heart failure. Or, if your guru wanted to give you some of his Shakti, your nervous system might not be able to take it, in which case you would run amok.

Fourth, the body's Agni controls not only the body's digestion but also that of the mind, which has to digest all the new things it learns every day. Loss of semen causes loss of ojas which dulls the mental digestion, which is especially bad for spiritual aspirants, who must develop subtle perception.

Fifth, the physical pleasure of sex arises from the stimulation of nerves in the genitals, resulting from the friction caused by the movements of the penis in the vagina or anus. Our ancient Indian scientists knew the value of the anus as an erotic center, mind you. Be it vagina, anus, or mouth, the friction produces heat, which destabilizes the mind. The more you copulate the less firm will be your mind. As I've noted, firmness of mind is especially essential in Aghora.

Sixth, years of Brahmacharya will develop great strength of ojas. Your aura or halo will develop to such an extent that whoever meets you will feel refreshed and relieved afterward. The ojas will harmonize both you and those around you. This is the hallmark of a real saint, the test you can use to separate the men from the donkeys.

Finally, copulation causes a disturbance in the Ether Element because of the friction vibrations and the queer thoughts which are engendered in you as a result. These sex vibrations are tremendously irritating to deities and other high ethereal beings. Since most sadhanas involve the attraction of an ethereal being to you, sex is contraindicated in sadhana, absolutely. I once made the mistake of teaching a Ganesh Mantra to a man who could not control himself. He remained celibate for almost three months and then just when he was about to achieve, he decided he had to have some sex. He went in to his wife, who unsuccessfully tried to prevent him from sleeping with her. After enjoying himself twice he went to sleep. In a dream he saw an enraged elephant chasing him and giving him a good slap with its trunk. The next morning his face was swollen to twice its normal size. He was removed to the hospital and died that night.

Ganesh is the lord of the Muladhara Chakra, the lowest of the energy centers, in which the Kundalini lies sleeping. Now just imagine: If you are doing penance to make the energy move upward and suddenly you reverse its flow and make it move downward in great spasms, what is going to happen? You will blow out your nervous system like this man did.

Consider two other benefits of remaining celibate. According to Ayurveda it takes thirty days for a drop of semen to form. In those who are good celibates the semen is so sticky it can be pulled out into a meter-long thread without breaking; very sticky. And its consistency is like cream. If it falls onto cloth it can be knocked off without staining or separating. Such high-quality semen is sure to produce high-quality progeny if used for that purpose.

Also, ojas is a living substance. We say it is derived from semen because all the Jivas in the unused sperm give up their individual existence and merge with the ojas. This can happen only in a true celibate and is a sort of blessing to the Jivas in the sperms because they become exempt from taking any future births. I mentioned that the ojas forms the halo or aura which attracts people to a saint. How could they be attracted unless it was a living substance? I am talking about a true attraction here, not some sensory enticement. Buddha's aura, for instance, affected everyone within a fifty-mile radius of wherever he was staying: They all became automatically calmer and more introverted.

I hope you know now some of the importance of Brahmacharya. Now it is necessary to consider the methods by which celibacy can be preserved. The most obvious method is simple avoidance of sex, but this is not perfect. The more you restrict yourself the more frequent will be your nocturnal emissions. If you go in for physical control you must be very thorough. Some asanas will deaden the sexual nerves. In certain rituals a thin wire is passed through the penis and tied tightly around it to ensure that not even a drop of prostate fluid is lost. But all this is limited because if the mind is not controlled, thoughts of sex will still emanate and ojas will be lost. Loss of ojas is far more detrimental to the body and mind than is loss of physical semen.

The mind must be controlled. Ganja (marijuana flowers) and

tobacco smoked together "burn" the semen if you don't eat any heavy food afterward. The tobacco makes you physically impotent, and the ganja makes you mentally impotent. This is quite useful, but it is still reliance on external agencies. You must "burn" the sex center in the brain, up in the thalamus, if you want to be perfectly free of sexual proclivities. Some people say that celibacy means never discharging semen, even in a dream; but I say that only that man who never even gets an erection is the true celibate. His penis should not even "rumble" when he gets some stimulus. Not only should a good female celibate not ooze from her vagina, but her clitoris should not even twitch once. Mental control is essential if you hope to achieve this state.

This is not an overnight process, you understand. It takes years, and a good guru is necessary. He will allow his "child" to try out sex as much as he or she likes for a month or so. After the month is over the "child" will know exactly what are the effects of sex on the body, mind, and sadhana, and he or she will understand why it is useless to try to do serious sadhana and simultaneously try to carry on an active sex life.

An Aghori takes a somewhat different approach to sex and celibacy, of course. One day I got wild with my penis. I told it, "You bloody thing, what do you think of yourself, always spoiling my sleep by becoming hard?" I went into the bathroom and found some acid and poured it over my penis. My God, it was terrible! Then, when the pain was troubling me I got wilder and said, "So, not enough, eh?" and I grated some green chilies and applied them as a poultice.

I can't tell you what agony I was in for three days, but it healed without a scar. In fact, it acted as a type of purification.

Ayurveda states that semen resides in the brain. The thick white semen from the testicles does not travel upward into the head, of course; this statement means that the brain is the seat of ojas, because the whole process which culminates in the ejaculation of semen begins with a disturbance in the mind which causes certain brain cells to be dilated. This dilation causes ojas to move downward and impel the seminal movement via the neurotransmitters. A firm mind means firm ojas and no emission of semen; loss of mental control means loss of both ojas and semen.

Firmness of the mind is always difficult, if only because you have so many rnanubandhanas with so many individuals of the opposite sex that you will always be running into someone with whom you once had a sexual relationship, no matter how far you try to hide from society.

Once a certain lady used to come and offer fruit and what-have-you daily to a certain celibate sadhu. The day came when she asked if she could massage his legs. He permitted her to do so. In the course of the massage her hand accidentally touched his penis. "Don't touch that!" he commanded. "That is *Mahapapa* (the Great Sinner)."

The next day, to return the favor, the sadhu started to massage the lady. Accidentally his hand touched her vulva. "Maharaj," she said, "don't touch there. That is *Naraka Kunda* (the Pit of Hell)."

The sadhu, however, had become excited by the touch of her genitals and said to her, "You know that the only place for sinners is hell. Therefore, if I now put the Great Sinner into the Pit of Hell all the sin will be extinguished." The lady, who had also become excited by his touch, was only too ready to agree. And that is how the sadhu came to lose his celibacy.

Even if you can maintain your physical celibacy you may still get yourself into trouble if you are not careful. Shankaracharya (the great preacher of Vedanta) was once made to learn a good lesson because he forgot that mental Brahmacharya is more important than physical Brahmacharya. He wanted to debate with Mandan Mishra on religious texts in the city of Mithila. Entering the city he made his way to a group of young women at a well to ask for directions to his adversary's house. The girls had a nice laugh at his expense when they heard why he had come and told him, "Maharaj, before you try to debate with Mandan Mishra first debate with his parrots, and if you can defeat them then only think of going on to him." Shankaracharya left in a huff, but once he reached Mandan Mishra's house he saw the truth of what they had said: All the parrots in the big banyan trees encircling the house were reciting texts they had memorized because of Mandan Mishra's habit of practicing out loud in his garden.

Shankaracharya was greeted warmly by his opponent, who realized what the zealous young man had in mind. Recalling the obligation a host has to his guests Mandan Mishra offered food to Shankaracharya, but it was indignantly refused: "No, I have come to debate, not to eat." Mandan Mishra's wife told him, "You will have your debate without fail, Maharaj, but first please do enjoy a meal with us." Shankaracharya was adamant, however, so the debate began.

Before long it became clear that Mandan Mishra could not win. Suddenly his wife said to Shankaracharya, "Maharaj, the texts state that the husband and the wife are two halves of the same being. You must also debate with me, the Vamangi, the left half of my husband." Shankaracharya had no choice but to agree.

She began to discuss the erotic art, the *Kamakala*. Her opponent had never had any experience of women and was therefore unable to answer her. Moreover, as he was a sworn celibate there was no way he could go out and experience sex in order to learn about it. What to do? He asked for a twenty-four-hour recess of the debate. Mandan Mishra's wife smiled at him and said, "Maharaj, nowhere in the rules of debate is a recess permitted. You are about to lose. But that's all right; you are our guest. Take your recess." Only Ma could be so generous, even at the cost of victory.

Shankaracharya went back to his disciples and told them to guard his body carefully. He then went into a trance and used his subtle body to enter the physical body of an old king who had just died. Everyone in attendance on the king was astonished, to say the least, to see the ruler jump back to life. His wives — kings always possess large harems — were especially astonished because he immediately called them in to him. Some of them noticed a change in his personality, especially during lovemaking, but they feared for their necks and dared not say anything.

Having thoroughly learned the science of love from these ladies, Shankaracharya returned to his own body. The next morning he defeated Mandan Mishra's wife in the debate. Then, feeling generous, his ego pampered by his success, he said grandly, "Now, Mandan Mishra, I am pleased to appoint you head of my monastery at Jyotirmath near Badrinath."

Mandan Mishra's wife laughed in Shankaracharya's face and said, "At one time I thought you were a true ascetic, but now I see you are a fake just like all the rest."

Shankaracharya got the shock of his lifetime and said, "What do you mean?"

She replied, "You teach that the physical universe is just an illusion and that Maya does not exist. If you are not your body but are the pure, undefiled Universal Soul as you claim to be then your vow of celibacy applies to your body and to your mind and to your entire consciousness. How could you then legitimately enjoy sex through your subtle body? Are you not guilty of breaking your vows? Is this not a stain, a stigma, on your ochre robes of renunciation?

"Moreover, if the Universal Soul is all that exists in the universe and all else is illusory then you and your debating and your success in this debate are also illusory. If you, I, and my husband are all the same Universal Soul, then with whom are you debating? Yourself? Isn't it a contradiction in terms?

"My husband is named Mandana (construction); he believes in building things up. He encourages and provides confidence to those who come to him. You believe only in destruction — all for what? To prove to the world, which you believe to be illusory, that you are unconquerable in debate. What is your value? Can you compare with my husband?"

Shankaracharya had to keep quiet. Shakti had taught him a good lesson.

Actually there is some distinction between physical and mental Brahmacharya, even though Mandan Mishra's wife was correct in her argument that a sworn Brahmachari must observe total celibacy. It is never bad to preserve bodily celibacy even if you must perform mental sex to complete some rnanubandhana. Nor is it bad to preserve mental Brahmacharya, to be completely aloof from the body, if you must perform physical coitus to fulfill some rna. This is how an Aghori works, in fact: The body does whatever it must do to complete its rnas, and the mind is a passive observer, never self-identifying with the actions of the body. It is unbelievably difficult, though.

Someone once asked me, "If Tukaram Maharaj was really a true devotee of God, concentrating on Vitthala (Vishnu) twenty-four hours a day, how could he have had two wives and fathered so many children?" This is a good question which deserves a careful answer. Tukaram Maharaj was never apart from Vitthala mentally even while his physical body continued to fulfill its rnanubandhanas. His rnas with his wives included sex, and his body performed the sex act with his wives. His mind, though, was never aware of his body or of what it was doing. His mental Brahmacharya was perfect, so he could father children and still remain pure.

But my questioner was not completely satisfied with this explanation and posed another question: "If Tukaram Maharaj was not self-identifying with his body, who was? The penis can become erect only when the ego self-identifies with it. If Tukaram Maharaj's ego had lost itself in Vitthala, what remained to self-identify with his penis?"

I love to answer such questions, because their acuteness shows me that the people who are listening to me are thinking about what I have said. Something must have been inside Tukaram's body self-identifying; this much is clear. And one other thing is clear: It wasn't Vitthala. If it had been Vitthala or some other deity, or if Tukaram Maharaj had self-identified with the Universal Soul during copulation, then the power of the deity would have been transmitted to the children, even to some tiny extent, and they would have become spiritual giants. But they didn't; they were perfectly ordinary, mundane. There must therefore have been another personality present, one with sufficient rnanubandhana with Tukaram's wives to perform sex with them through the medium of Tukaram's body. Tukaram Maharaj was not even observing it, though; he was elsewhere.

Rnanubandhana *can* be completed without physical sex. An ethereal being lacks a body with which to copulate. If that being desires sex it must locate a couple engaged in the sex act, enter one of their bodies, and enjoy. Self-identification must not be permitted, though; then there is no stain of karma.

Now, the practical application: Suppose there is a girl who loves me. Perhaps because of the social situation she is unable to marry me and must marry someone else. I am not ethereal, but my subtle body is. When I decide that the time is right to fulfill my rnanubandhana of sex with her I will wait until she and her husband are in a deep sexual embrace. Then, by entering his body, I will see to it that she gets full satisfaction.

She gets her satisfaction from me, which breaks my rnanubandhana with her. She is fully satiated, because I know how to satiate her; her husband would never be able to do it. But the husband knows that she is satiated and thinks he is responsible. He takes the credit for being a big stud bull, which is fine with me because by his self-identification he gets all the karma. I get my sexual enjoyment and remain untouched by karma. Everyone is happy, and I have preserved my physical celibacy.

# SVAPNESHVARI SIDDHI AND SHIVA LATA MUDRA

If you want to preserve even your mental celibacy you must have some siddhi. Svapneshvari will do nicely. Suppose I discover a rnanubandhana with a girl in France. I find it very inconvenient and time-consuming to travel to France and romance her. So, I send Svapneshvari to her in a male form. In a dream she finds herself enjoying sex with a man whose face is always hidden from her. She is satiated, because sex in a dream is always more satisfying than is physical sex. There are no inhibitions, no fear of discovery, no worry about inadequacy, no restraint to full pleasure in a dream. By satiating her in this way my rnanubandhana with her is broken. She never knows who has come to her and never cares to know. There is no karma and no interruption of either my mental or physical celibacy.

Absolute celibacy is too far away for most people, of course, but our Vedic religion has provided for everyone no matter what their level of achievement. If you restrict yourself to having sex with one partner, for example if you are married and engage in sex only with your spouse, this is also Brahmacharya, the Brahmacharya appropriate for married people. And as long as you observe total celibacy during specific periods of penance you too can achieve great things, if you work hard.

However, even a married man can practice absolute celibacy and still fulfill his sexual duty to his wife if he knows Shiva Lata Mudra. He must worship his wife as the cosmic Shakti, and she must worship him as Lord Shiva. Shiva is the controller, Lata the controlled. *Lata* literally means "creeper," like the ivy which twines around a column. Because Shakti has emanated from Shiva and wishes to return to Him She is impelled to come into close proximity to Him. He is the center, the Linga, the fixed, unwavering nucleus. In order to become one with Him, Shakti gives up Her own independent characteristics and makes an absolute surrender to Him. A creeper has no support of its own, which is why it must take the help of a tree or pillar. Once it has selected its support to grow on, the creeper cannot change its mind and shift to another support: It is committed. The tree is beautified by the creeper, the creeper is supported by the tree. Neither is complete without the other.

When a man and a woman come together for Shiva Lata Mudra the woman must sit on the man's left thigh and hold his penis with her right hand. He must cup her left breast with his left hand. Like a creeper she drapes herself around him, clinging tightly like a delicate vine; and he permits himself to be clung to, offering her support.

There are three types of Shiva Lata Mudra: mundane, spiritual, and one which is beyond both the mundane and the spiritual. The mundane gives maximum sexual excitement; the spiritual is for sadhana; and "beyond" is too advanced to be dealt with here. In all types the female counts japa with her left hand, the male with his right. The mantras are specific for each type. He forgets who he is, and she forgets who she is. He thinks, "I am Lord Shiva in the form of Bhairava (the Fearful Lord), and this is my Shakti, my Bhairavi." She thinks, "This is my Lord Shiva, and I am His Grand Consort, His Bhairavi (the Fearful Goddess)."

If the couple is doing it for mundane purposes they must concentrate on exciting each other. Without realizing it she will begin to breathe through her left nostril and will direct that Shakti to him. His right nostril will be working and that Shakti of his will be directed to her. Hypersecretion of all the glands will result, and at the moment of greatest excitation cessation of breathing occurs for a moment. Then the male mounts and discharges his semen convulsively. Because of hypersecretion he will now eject three teaspoonsful of semen as opposed to his normal one teaspoonful. Because the vagina and cervix have become utterly loose and dilated the sperm will go directly to the mouth of the cervix. The result is a child, if this is done at the right time of the month. This is the Brahmacharya appropriate to the ordinary householder because by such sex, satiation occurs for a month or more and ojas is not wasted by frequent orgasms.

The spiritual Shiva Lata Mudra is quite different. The Shiva must control his Shakti very carefully to ensure that she does not become sexually excited. The couple should be able to sit together for at least three hours without the least excitation, no twitching or oozing. The girl must understand that she will not get an ordinary orgasm this way. If she waits patiently she will eventually get a super orgasm which will make her forget sex forever. If this Mudra is done properly she will go into Bhava Samadhi: Her emotions will crescendo until her mind becomes totally one-pointed, directed toward Shiva, and she will partly forget her worldly existence for awhile. Even Mahabhava Samadhi, which I call emotional highlights, is possible — total immersion in Shiva but with retained awareness of the bliss. Wonderful!

The concentration must be intense and the self-identification with Bhairava and Bhairavi perfect. Usually the couple should have already enjoyed plenty of sex together, should have experimented with sex as much as they desired, so that they can drop it for several months and work for something beyond ordinary sex. Once a couple gets initiated into this practice they develop such a liking for it that they count the hours until they can practice it again; they can think of nothing else except performing it. This is good; their minds are effectively disengaged from mundane things by this sadhana and their urge for togetherness is fully satisfied. In the beginning the woman must be willing to wait. If she is patient and works hard her experience will affect her more strongly than hundreds of orgasms all at once; she will be forever satiated.

The beauty is the wonderful play of the two partners. At one point the male will feel such overwhelming love for his Shakti that he thinks, "I must give her everything." Then Shakti becomes indignant: "I am your Shakti; how can you give me anything? You are useless without me, you could not even exist." Then Shiva smiles and says, "Oh, is that so? From where did you originate if not from me?" The intoxication of this play cannot be described; you simply have to experience it yourself to know what it is.

This play can only begin when the true personalities of the man and woman surface. Where do you find nowadays a man who is strong as a tree, solid as the Rock of Gibraltar, firm enough to support his partner without a single lapse? And where do you find a woman who is sure enough of herself to surrender totally to her partner, relying totally on him for support like a creeper does on a tree? This is why people find sex so unsatisfactory today and why they go in for dolls and dildos instead. It is no wonder that today's people are maladjusted sexually. They will get a glimpse of what real sex can be only if they study and practice this technique. Otherwise they will continue to grope about, making a mess of things, copulating without satisfaction, becoming more and more neurotic.

Once the first posture is perfected the couple moves on to the second posture: face to face, the female on the male's lap the penis near but not in the vagina. Being face to face there is no holding of penis or breast. Once they can sit this way for three hours without the least excitation there are three other stages. In the final stage there is full penetration of the vagina by the erect penis with full control: not a twitch, not a rumble. Only when this is perfected can they move on to Vajroli.

The examination of a student who might like to learn Vajroli involves making two girls sit on the boy, one on each thigh, for three hours. When the boy can do that he has achieved — a little.

I know that many of the people who read this are immediately going to jump up, rush out the door, grab a partner, sit down, and try it out. I don't mind if they do; they will learn soon enough that without adequate prior preparation it is impossible to succeed at Lata Mudra. You will simply get aroused, and even if you succeed in avoiding orgasm you will still ooze. Until you reach the state where you can self-identify with Shiva or with Bhairavi, depending on your gender, for a full three hours at a time, you will be unable to succeed at this because it is not your personality which will be achieving it; it is the personality of Shiva or Shakti which you have invoked and projected into yourself which will succeed at it. Which means that without a guru to show you the way you can try this for a hundred years and you will still be unable to perfect it. It is good to know about it, though; once you learn about it you may become truly interested in it and not merely curious about it. Once you have a genuine desire to learn it Nature will see that a teacher comes your way. Nature is never cruel. She always gives you what you want, provided you want it badly enough.

Until you do locate a teacher there are things you can do to prepare yourself, if you are willing to work at them sincerely. First you must utterly efface from your consciousness the idea that you and your partner are lovers, or husband and wife. You must treat each other as mother and son. Freud was so obsessed by the Oedipus complex because he never realized that sex was not the only form of union which can occur between two individuals. He said that all girls experience penis envy. Actually they experience the desire for Shiva's linga, which is the state of oneness, and when this desire is projected out into the body it becomes penis envy in the unenlightened individual. The effect of Freud's writings has been to make whoever reads them overly conscious of the body and, therefore, of sex. Sex is no doubt important, but it is only secondary. Freud tried to make it primary.

This is why I always say that a little knowledge is a dangerous thing. Generations have now grown up studying Freud,
learning wrong or imperfect knowledge because of his errors,
and convincing themselves that there is nothing to human interaction except sex. This is why most Americans think they are
satisfied with sex alone. Sensual love is all their parents learned.
They never developed true, deep maternal love, and since only
a pervert would have sex with his or her child that parent ends
up loving the child very little. Such parents just don't know
how to love their children, since they only know sexual love.
American children grow up without any parental love and
become so love-starved that they will take any affection they
can get. Only a few are choosy. The rest just can't help themselves.

If you look at a voluptuous woman or a handsome man and
see only the skeleton beneath the flesh, many benefits will
accrue to you. You will communicate with a deeper layer of
the individual, one closer to the center than the superficial flesh
and skin which is that individual's Maya. Loving Maya always
leads to misery; loving the skeleton at least enables you to project your love onto a form that will continue to exist even after
death. It is certainly not the ultimate, but it is an improvement.

A male should look at every woman, especially his partner,
and see Ma within her. A female should see all men and boys,
and especially her partner, as her sons. This reduces the danger of falling into sex, it teaches the couple something of parental love, and it leads to fidelity in the relationship.

Another thing: All desire for personal enjoyment or self-
gratification has to be effaced from the mind. If you have even
the slightest intention to take or gain something from your partner, that tiny desire can snowball when your nervous system
is under full load, and an avalanche of energy can result, ending in sex. You must forget how to take and learn only how to
give. Does any real mother ever ask for anything from her child?
No, nothing, not even love. And a child never need ask anything from a good mother because she will provide it without
the child's asking, which allows the child to give his or her
love freely. Shiva is known as the Great Giver. He has given

up everything and sits alone in the smashan waiting for someone to love Him. You have to become like Shiva, sitting alone
in the smashan of the world, if you ever hope to achieve at
this sadhana.

These are just preliminaries, of course; but they are essential preliminaries, and worth working hard on if you want to
obtain the benefits of this sadhana: good celibacy; fidelity to
one partner because of longing, not legalities; the presence of
Shiva and Shakti in your bodies as Avishkara; and eventual
samadhi of intense emotion.

# AMRITA

One of the benefits of perfect Brahmacharya is Amrita. *Amrita,*
which literally means "undying," is a secretion of the pineal
gland. It is the true Fountain of Youth, because through Amrita
you can preserve your youth almost permanently.

There are three important *rasas* (juices) in the world: Amra
Rasa, or Kama Rasa, which is mango juice; Charma Rasa, which
is semen (literally, "skin juice"); and Bhakti Rasa or Rama Rasa,
which is Amrita. Mango juice represents the epitome of nour-
ishing food. It strengthens the body but is an aphrodisiac, making the semen move downward. Rama Rasa becomes obtainable
only when the semen (that means the ojas, remember, not the
sticky white fluid) is made to move upward, undisturbed.
Semen, or ojas, is the pivot between the mundane world, the
world of Kama, and the spiritual realm, the world of Rama. As
they say, "Where there is Kama (lust) there is no Rama, and
where there is Rama (divinity) there is no Kama."

It might seem logical that semen would be the best diet to
increase ojas, but this is not so. I did meet a forty-year-old whore
in France who looked a mere twenty-five, and she attributed it
to drinking semen. There are side-effects, though. It makes you
more prone to certain diseases, and, more importantly, it makes
your Apana Vayu move more forcefully downward, making you
more and more sexually arousable. This is because semen is
not ojas but merely the raw material from which ojas is pro-

duced. Those who drink semen and expect their ojas to increase will obtain only physical benefits, like the French whore did. It is not so easy to extract Shakti from Maya.

Celibacy gives you access to Amrita, which must then be externalized if you want to use it to obtain physical immortality. It is not necessary that the Amrita come from your body for it to be effective on you. There are other sources you can tap. The easiest is to locate a girl who is just about to have the first menses of her life. An expert will be able to spot that moment when Amrita will be available from the corners of her eyes. She will actually thank you when you remove it, because it will feel as if a tremendous weight has been removed from her body. That weight is a good part of her Shakti. By removing it you shorten her life span by up to ten years. Don't forget the Law of Karma. Of course if you didn't remove it she would probably waste it in masturbation or fornication anyway, but that doesn't exonerate you. And besides, unless you are an expert or know where to locate one this method is of no use to you.

Or, you can procure an elephant. Do you know that this was the real reason kings were supposed to keep elephants? Most kings never knew. An elephant is not just for pomp and pageantry. If it is well cared for and becomes pleased with its master it can take Amrita from its body and present it to its master. Today no one knows how to do this, save a few who tell no one.

Even if you are married you can become immortal through Amrita, though during the sadhana and forever afterward you must observe absolute Brahmacharya, because Amrita is a glandular substance. Whenever Kama Agni, the Fire of Lust, becomes enkindled in you it causes chemical changes which would consume this substance and nullify all the work you had done to obtain it. You will then ask, "Is it wise even to try to gain physical immortality?" Well, I never had that desire. I want to die out so that I can be free of all my earthly limitations. It just depends on what you want to do. These are the facts I am presenting to you, and you have to decide what to do with them. You can use your Amrita to create more ojas, you can use it to obtain immortality, you can do whatever you please with it. But first you have to obtain it.

And don't think it is not wonderful to be immortal; it is. Think of Chang Dev, the Aghori who learned that he would only be able to meet his guru after 1,400 years. Now, in 1,400 years who knows what sort of incarnations you may have to take? What if you forget all about spirituality and miss your chance? So Chang Dev deliberately remained alive for 1,400 years and then met his guru: Mukta Bai, the fourteen-year-old sister of Shri Jnaneshwar. Yogi Chang Dev used a different method than Amrita, but the idea is the same.

Amrita is actually being produced continually in everyone's body, and continuously it drips down into the gut where it is incinerated by Jathara Agni, the fire of digestion. A Yogi can trap this Amrita and prevent it from being destroyed by practicing Khechari Mudra. The guru first tests the aspirant to determine whether or not he'll be able to succeed. If you pass this test you then must practice *Shirshasana*, the "headstand," for several hours daily until you perfect it. Many people today are being misled by half-baked Yoga teachers who tell them, "Do Shirshasana, it sends plenty of blood to the brain" — bull! They prescribe the headstand to everyone without considering its uses and restrictions. For example, those who indulge in sex should never practice Shirshasana lest they weaken themselves both physically and mentally; the brain and nerves will suffer. A little knowledge is a dangerous thing.

The real asanas are not physical anyway; they are mental. Can you even imagine what mental Shirshasana must be like? If you can you can do away with the need for the physical headstand altogether. But it is not so easy.

When your Shirshasana becomes firm your guru will begin to cut your frenulum lingua with a piece of rock salt; not a blade! He cuts only a tiny distance each day, and the salt prevents the cut surfaces from healing together. This is very delicate: If he cuts too far the student may never be able to speak again. This is not the modern idea of taking a scalpel and swish! Straight through on the first go! Oh no! There is a reason for doing it gradually.

When the frenulum has been sufficiently cut, and the tongue

can be retracted to cover the back of the mouth, the guru selects an auspicious day to begin Khechari Mudra. On that day you will be told to perform Shirshasana and put your tongue completely backward into your mouth. Your guru will warn you that whenever you feel something dripping onto your tongue you should not swallow it but instead come down out of the posture and let the secretion flow from your mouth into your hand. This is Amrita, which should be taken to your guru, who will put it into a special paan and only then make you eat it. This secretion needs to be consumed only thrice. After that your mind becomes steady, firm absolutely, which will make your meditation steady, no waverings of the mind to any side. Isn't that useful?

Amrita really *can* make you "undying," to the extent you follow the conditions. There are a lot of conditions, the main one being that you must never again enjoy sex or else the Amrita will dissolve and within a short time your body will age completely.

It is the same way with those amulets which some gurus implant into their disciples' arms or legs. These amulets have two important effects: You grow younger and younger as the years roll by, and you develop *Vak Siddhi*, which means that whatever you say comes true. When a guru gives such an amulet to a disciple two promises are extracted: total celibacy from then on and complete equanimity even in the face of severe provocation, because any curse you deliver will come true and will ruin both you and whoever you curse.

In the spiritual field, if you fall down you don't just have to stay and repeat a grade like you do in school. You will have to start all over again right from nursery school, which will take a number of lifetimes. To fool about with these things without knowing their gravity is terribly dangerous.

# VAJROLI

There is another way to obtain Amrita: the practice of Vajroli. Anyone can learn Vajroli, but for householders the prior practice of Shiva Lata Mudra is essential. So long as they are unable to control themselves this much they will be unable to do Vajroli.

To learn Vajroli you must first thoroughly clean out your body: eyes, nose, mouth, stomach, and digestive tract. The upper body is cleaned by swallowing, churning, and regurgitating water. The bowel is washed by sucking water up through the anus into the colon, churning it, and expelling it. The urinary passage is cleansed by sucking water through the penis into the bladder and through the ureters into the kidneys and then releasing it. This last process is called *Gaja Karma* because elephants (Gaja) suck up water with their trunks and playfully spray themselves for a bath.

To be able to do this you must know the method of controlling *Apana Vayu*, the body force which causes the expulsion of urine, feces, flatus, semen, menses, and fetus. I can't tell you here how you can make Apana, which naturally moves downward, go up, but consider this: If you want to urinate and you start to strain, the flow won't start; you must relax to start the stream. And in Ayurveda you are taught that if you clench your teeth tightly whenever you urinate or defecate then your teeth will always be firmly fixed in your skull and will always be healthy. How are the teeth and Apana connected? Think about it.

Anyway, after you have been able to suck up water through the penis and hold a bladder full of water for three hours you proceed to use milk, to cool the genital organs. Then ghee (clarified butter), to lubricate. Honey next; it is very sticky and hard to make flow upward. Finally, you do it with mercury, which is extremely heavy. You must use mercury which has been purified and prepared in the Tantric way; otherwise it is a deadly poison. When you can hold a bladder full of mercury for three hours without spilling a drop you have reached the level of the first qualification.

A woman prepares for Vajroli in exactly the same way: She learns to suck up water, milk, and so on, up to mercury, with her vagina. She reaches the level of the first qualification when she can hold a vagina full of mercury for three hours. You must have heard of the women of the Place Pigalle in Paris who can pick up one-franc coins from tables with their vaginas; I have seen this with my own eyes. And I am told that in Laos and

Vietnam some bargirls can smoke cigarettes vaginally, so don't think that sucking mercury into the vagina is impossible. It's not; it's just hard work.

Mercury is the most important element in Tantra. It has hundreds of uses but in this context we should note that it is the best preservative available. Half a handful of it is sufficient to preserve an entire silo of grain for a very long time. No insects or rodents dare venture near it; no fungus or mold can grow there. This was a common practice in ancient India.

When mercury is sucked up into the genitourinary tract its main effects are on the prostate in men and on various glands including Bartholin's glands in women. It causes these glands to contract. A well-contracted prostate will not enlarge in old age. Also, when these glands are contracted their secretions will not flow so easily, so right there there is some control over the sexual response. The outstanding characteristic of prostatic fluid is that it propagates life; we know this because sperm need it to stay alive. The fluid from a female's glands is called *Stri Shukra* (female semen) in Ayurveda, meaning that it should be preserved by a woman as carefully as a man preserves his semen.

A man who practices Vajroli on a woman sucks up with his penis the secretions which ooze out as she gets excited. These oozings further contract the prostate; in fact, they cause to be produced a new type of cell which mediates prostate function. The woman used for this purpose loses ten years of her life span, though, since such a great amount of her Shakti is removed. Of course a woman who knows Vajroli can "milk" an unsuspecting man of his semen with her suction. She can make him eject over and over again until there is nothing left to eject, which will sap him of all his ojas. Her glands will be well benefited by this, at his expense.

If you want to practice this technique you need a body which is in good shape. For the first twenty-three years of my life I didn't know what salt was, and I had never experienced sex. Westerners eat salt excessively all their lives, and they are introduced to the opposite sex very early. Western men who waste their semen even once every three days will suffer for it; their resistance will drop and their nerves will be affected. This makes knowledge of Vajroli all the more important. A man who knows real Vajroli should be able to satisfy dozens of females in a single night, each female having at least ten orgasms, without letting even a drop of prostate fluid fall, and once he is finished he should be able to calmly wash his hands and smoke a cigarette.

Don't forget, though, that the Law of Karma is very queer. You can get yourself into trouble even if you know Vajroli. I know, it happened to me. I had been going along merrily performing a little Vajroli on so many girls. A little only, because if I had done the full thing they would have been bleeding and in bed for months because they knew nothing of the technique. Besides, it would have shortened their lives, and I wanted to avoid that karma.

One day I met a very powerful being — a Mahapurusha, actually — who said to me, "So, you've become a beef-eater, eh?"

I didn't like the way he sneered that and got wild. "I have never eaten even a mouthful of beef in my entire life. How dare you call me a beef-eater!"

He said, "When you do Vajroli with beef-eating girls, isn't that the same thing as eating it yourself?"

I had to pull my ears at that one; he was right. When you suck up vaginal secretions you take an immense amount of Shakti, and the body's Shakti is composed of the essence of the food consumed. I *had* been eating beef that way. The Mahapurusha made me purify myself. My God! It was rough. After that I paid more attention to my partners and finally quit altogether. The Law of Karma is really rough. I've made mistakes, no doubt; I'm not infallible, as many see the Pope. But I've always confessed to my mistakes, and Nature has always pardoned me. I cannot describe to you the awesome magnanimity of Nature; it is amazing!

Control is all in the mind. Physical control, like pinching the penis at the moment of orgasm, is most crude. There are other methods. If you prepare mercury in a certain way and fill your navel with it you can copulate for days on end and never spill even a drop of prostate fluid. But this is also unsatisfactory because it is an external method; once you lose your mercury you are through. Mental control is both more refined and more efficient.

Now, the applications of Vajroli: Modern scientists claim that only the head of the spermatozoon yields the progeny, but actually millions of beings can be produced from each of the millions of spermatozoa present in each drop of semen. This is how Shukracharya, the guru of the Asuras (demons), could resuscitate all the Asura troops killed in the wars with the gods. That is why he was called *Shukracharya* (Semen-Teacher).

At the other end of the pole from the Asuras are the Rishis, who believed in family planning. A Rishi would have one child in twelve years, or even less frequently, but he would enjoy vigorous intercourse with his wife regularly, thanks to Vajroli. Once he and his wife did decide to have a child they would first decide on its sex, and then on its type: grammarian, musician, mathematician, saint, or whatever. They would then construct a good horoscope for the proposed child to be born under, selecting planetary positions according to the type of child desired. Some of this information as to what sort of child will be conceived when you copulate on a certain lunar day in a certain position has been preserved on the walls of our temples, such as the Sun Temple at Konarka in Orissa.

The Rishis knew much more than this, though. They knew all about the subtle or ethereal planets which exist along with the gross planets we can see. When the time came for the Rishi and his mate to perform coitus they would first perform all eighty-four of the postures designed especially for intercourse, using Vajroli. Then at the precise moment of the lunar day and with the correct lunar asterism predominating to maximize the child's attributes the Rishi would discharge his semen, which would go directly to the cervix — no waiting in the vagina. The Rishi would be precise to the last second, because four minutes of time means a difference of one degree of celestial arc. The couple would have the best of all factors: proper mood, hypersecretion, full excitement, precise moment. The ecstasy would be so great that it would permeate the zygote thus conceived and would produce optimal samskaras. A Rishi can control his own samskaras, of course, and can juggle them to create new genes if he so desires. Let Western scientists discover the twenty-fourth chromosome and then they may understand a little more of the mystery of life — a little.

You see, by this method of knowing what the child will become even before it is conceived you know exactly what to do with the child as he or she grows up. Isn't this a better way than coupling haphazardly like animals and producing brats? This is why I say the Rishis knew about creation and today's human beings know only about procreation.

Rishis have upward-moving semen, of course, and do not need to copulate to have children. Originally they did it by force of will alone. A Rishi would look at a woman with such intense affection that she would become pregnant. Later it was done in other ways, including mantras. Rishis can also create thousands of beings just by wiping the sweat off their foreheads. As humans forgot these ways the business of having children became degraded, and humans began to breed like animals do, using coitus.

Another reason a man should know Vajroli is that women are said to be nine times more passionate than men. Only when his wife is satiated has a man fulfilled his duty to her. He must ask her ten times, or even more, "Are you finished? Have you had enough?" But a man's ego is hurt to ask because he knows his wife may not find him satisfactory. So 99.99 percent of men never ask, and their wives are never satisfied fully.

Moreover, most men have no idea of female anatomy. Women's orgasms come in waves, while a man's is only one. A man has to last as long as he can after penetration before ejaculation. The immature man goes off quickly, and the man with a little knowledge lasts a few minutes at most. This is insufficient to satisfy the female, and since almost all people are interested only in physical sex, there is misery.

Consider the Sanskrit proverb: "Bhoge na bhogata; bhogam iva bhogata." This means that the enjoyment of pleasure lies not in the act of enjoyment but in the fact of enjoyment. Human beings have become very selfish. They want to enjoy their own orgasms and can't be bothered about their partners'. This attitude will never satisfy you, though. You can only get true satisfaction from sex when you are more interested in your partner's satiation than in your own, because only then will your partner reciprocate fully, freely, and enthusiastically and do his or her best to satisfy you. That joy of having another being attempt to satisfy you is far greater than the pleasure of the orgasm itself. This is the meaning of that proverb.

The real bliss of sex occurs when the male is able to steer his mate into a condition of absolute sexual frenzy. In order to do this the male must know each erotic center in his partner's body, and he must know the relationship between the erotic centers and the moon. The moon plays a very important role in each woman's life. *Menstruation* is derived from a word meaning "moon" since it occurs at intervals of one lunar month. In the past, women's menstrual cycles were much more regular than they are now; everything was more natural.

A different erotic center in the female body is awakened on each lunar day. If the male concentrates his passion on that center the female's passion will ignite very quickly, and the resulting orgasms will be far more intense. Finger action should be sufficient to cause a female to have ten oozings, if you know which center is proper for which lunar day. The male should cooperate with the female's body so there is no need to struggle to arouse her. This way the arousal happens automatically. It should be intuitive, yes, but intuition alone is insufficient. Knowledge of the woman's body is also required.

Do you know how many erotic centers are present in the buttocks alone? Here, I'll give you a practical demonstration on this handy teenage girl. Now, when I press here do you see the result? And that is just one finger. Look, I'll add one more finger. You see, she can't stand it, she has to break away because the excitement is too much. If I continue she will start to ooze, and if I do it with concentration she should have 100 oozings from finger pressure alone, all because I am pressing the center which is more active today.

Shiva plays Shakti like an instrument; humans should follow His lead. The erotic centers are the keys of the instrument. The male must know which key to press and when. Does the instrument ever complain about being controlled by the musician and demand to be allowed to play him occasionally? No, it's absurd. But this does not devalue Shakti in any way. Without an instrument or a voice no musician can make music. Both are essential; neither can do without the other. It just so happens that the instrument must be controlled and the musician must control; this is Nature's way. If you can think of any other way please let me know about it. I will worship your lotus feet as my guru for teaching me something new.

And remember, control is possible *only* when you learn how to give and forget how to take. Today's men not only do not know how to satiate a woman sexually, they are not *interested* in doing so. They only want to emit their teaspoonful or two of semen and relax. This is why men can no longer control women.

When someone accepts a gift from you, you have successfully inserted an element of control into your relationship with that individual. Your choice of gift and time of giving can influence events. To take, you must come under someone else's influence to create the opportunity for your taking to occur. This is why Shiva is the Great Giver. He never takes anything from anyone, so He is eternally free from the influence of Maya.

Can a musician take music from his instrument? No, he must give his experience, his expertise to the instrument, and then the instrument will automatically produce the music. In fact, a musician really has only a foggy idea of how instruments make music, unless he is only an artisan and not an artist. A real musician becomes so engrossed by his music that he is amazed when it finally comes forth from within him. The musician gives his all to the instrument, and, inspired by this gift, the instrument gives its all to the musician. It is a mutual thing. Isn't it wonderful?

The human body is a much better instrument than any musical instrument which has ever been created because you can play it in so many ways. All parts of the body have erotic significance, especially the ear lobes, navel, buttocks, and lips. In the old days, you know, there was no such thing as kissing, which began only in Kali Yuga. In Kali Yuga the mouth has assumed great importance because we get much of our prana through food and we know how to communicate only in oral speech.

Originally people smelled one another. Children would come in to their elders who would embrace them by smelling their heads. Lovers would embrace each other and take in each other's body odors. Smell pertains to the Earth Element, the most gross, physical element. Sniffing inflames the passions of those who want to enjoy coitus. All the senses are important: taste for kissing; touch for caressing; hearing, verbal and nonverbal. Sight is the most important because it permits a direct telepathic communication between the two. They can go beyond words and feelings.

The senses provide different instruments to the conductor or composer to create the symphony. The asanas are musical tunes and phrases. Our texts on sex describe eighty-four important positions for copulation. Each position affects a different group of erotic centers, like a different pattern of musical notes, and each position, therefore, has a unique orgasmic effect. An expert will perform all eighty-four postures in three hours with the use of Vajroli to inflame his or her partner so thoroughly that no sex desire will arise again for months. There is no need; he or she is too full.

I know I said that the female should under no circumstances climb on top of the male. I stand by this statement as far as sex between ordinary people is concerned, but the situation is different, vastly different, when two people know Vajroli. Then it becomes a friendly competition. I start off with one posture and try to take her off guard and overwhelm her with the sensation. She will respond by changing my posture into a slightly different one, trying to get the upper hand. A rhythm of its own develops, a musical melody, and both of us begin to dance while we are still making love. There's nothing like it; you just can't imagine the feeling.

Suppose she tries to maneuver herself on top of me. If she succeeds she will gloat: "Ha, what sort of Shiva are you? Now I will be in control." I can't allow that, so as soon as she comes on top I will suddenly, effortlessly, and gracefully transform

that posture into one in which I am in command. Then I can
tell her, "You dare not try to control me; I am your controller!" And as I speak those words she will be converting that
posture into another one more favorable to her.

When both partners have full knowledge of Vajroli there is
mutual benefit. She releases a little of her secretion to him,
just enough to lubricate his prostate; he releases just enough
of his prostate fluid to rejuvenate her. Only if they want a child
does he emit semen and only then does she permit it to enter
the cervix. A fair exchange is no robbery. This is important
from the karmic point of view, because if you suck up all the
secretions from all your partners and take years off their lives,
you are to blame for their misery and will have to pay them
back someday.

Vajroli is not a joke. A man who uses full force Vajroli on an
ordinary woman will cause her to bleed. She may even lose
control over her sphincters and soil the bed. It can cause complete revulsion for sex, or it can create nymphomania. When a
woman who knows Vajroli "milks" a man of his semen he discharges and discharges until he is empty and still must discharge. The tension becomes so great he cannot bear it. So this
knowledge is not to be toyed with, lest you ruin yourself and
others with you. When both partners know Vajroli, though,
well, there is nothing like it in the world. You'll forget all about
sex except with that partner.

Vajroli is only the beginning. After Vajroli there are Rajjoli,
Sahajoli, Amaroli, and Gaupya — but no one knows about
Gaupya except Lord Shiva Himself. These techniques are very
difficult to describe in words and can be practiced only when
the two partners can leave their bodies at will. The Vedantins
talk about "Atma krida, atma ratih, atma maithunam," meaning the love play, eroticism, and sexual union of the Universal
Soul, but they don't understand the true meaning of it. What
happens is that the male must enter the female's body with
his subtle body, and vice versa. Then the man will be able to
feel the spasms his mate undergoes as each erogenous zone is
ignited, and she can do the same thing in his body. They both
thoroughly enjoy each other's play before the final coitus occurs

Vajroli is a mutual clashing, interaction, and union of two personalities into one. Shiva and Shakti merge together into Sadashiva; the proton and the electron reunite to form the neutron. Just as in physics such a union is associated with tremendous energy, the union of Vajroli is associated with awesome Shakti, which can be used for great spiritual advancements. It is the achievement of a lifetime.

Both partners must be thoroughly prepared for Vajroli, but preparation of the female is more important since females are naturally more passionate. A female can go into samadhi through this practice only when she forgets her body totally. If she retains even a slight interest in sex the intensity of Vajroli will magnify it so much that she will drag her man down and make him again conscious of his physical body. Or, if the man's will-power is strong enough to prevent this, nothing will happen to him but she will develop a ravenous appetite for sex. This is why it is essential that you perfect Shiva Lata Mudra while you are learning to suck up water and all the rest with the genitals. Both partners must forget their sexuality entirely and their physical bodies as much as possible and self-identify totally with Bhairava and His Bhairavi.

There is no comparison between Vajroli and ordinary sex. Vajroli has nothing to do with friction and irritation. It actually creates harmony, because the movements are not random; they follow a definite set pattern. Also, the male never emits semen and the female does not ooze continuously, so neither partner's aura is dissipated. In fact the two partners mutually increase each other's auras by the effort at sadhana.

You can even take your Bhairavi into the smashan if you like and perform Shiva Lata Mudra or Vajroli with her there. Certain ethereal beings will be so irritated by your audacity that they will come and try to unnerve you. But never permit yourself to fear. You can gain control of Yakshinis in this way. But — and this is a very big but — if your Bhairavi is not absolutely firm mentally her mind will be dragged down into her body, and you will be dragged down along with her. And then you are done for. But if you can do it, it is the best possible sex, even better than copulating with a Yakshini after calling her into a corpse. This is why I say over and over and over again: If you want to do this sadhana you must have a superpartner; otherwise you'll never be able to succeed and both of you will be ruined. I was very lucky that my Bhairavi was so expert; or perhaps I was just destined for it. If you cannot find a perfect partner it is better either to forget all about doing this sadhana or wait until you can locate an expert.

# BHAIRAVI

Thus the question arises: where can you locate a Bhairava or Bhairavi and, hopefully, if you are accepted as a pupil, learn these techniques? Well, nowhere except in India. Even here only a handful know Vajroli. I do not teach everyone who comes to me because I can't be sure they will not try to commercialize what they learn. I once taught a fellow to suck up water with the penis and what did he do? He went to Germany and became a big so-called swami. When I met him afterwards, he became very uneasy and said to me, "I hope you won't let on. . . ."

I replied, "Don't worry, babu, your secret is safe with me." Why expose him? Give him enough rope and he will hang himself eventually; why should I interfere? After that experience, though, I have become quite selective. In fact I have not yet found a worthy pupil.

Of course I myself was not a worthy pupil in the beginning. Once, just shortly after Smashan Tara came to me I saw a woman pass me in the street. What a beauty! I was for a moment overcome with lust. Then I heard Ma telling me, "Control yourself. Remember that she is mortal. She will get old and wrinkled one day, and then she will die and her beautiful body will decompose. Only her bones will remain. When you look at her see her not as she is now but as she will be eventually: a skeleton."

From that day forward I forgot to look at people as they presently exist, and I started to try to look at all of them as skeletons, especially the pretty women, so that I could control my lust. It took me six years to make a thorough job of it.

No, the only way to learn Vajroli is to have an experienced partner who can make up for any deficiencies you might have. I think my partner, the Bhairavi who taught me, is the most experienced Bhairavi in India, which means in the world. As far as sex is concerned there is no one to beat her. When she came to me she looked like a fifteen-year-old girl, but she is much, much older than that. Death cannot come to take her until she herself desires it. She remains naked, but covers herself with her long matted locks, and she carries a trident, Shiva's symbol.

Once I playfully asked her, "Why don't you let me see your real form?" She showed me — and my God! it was horrible! I was nauseated by the sight: All her skin was wrinkled; her eyelids drooped down onto her cheeks, and she had to pick them up with her fingers in order to see me. She has become immortal through the use of mercury. Take one of her hairs and put it into a furnace of 1,000 degrees for one month and nothing whatsoever will happen to it. *That* is the power of mercury, the power of preservation.

And the way she taught me; none to beat her. I learned all the connections between the erogenous zones and the lunar days. She would use her mouth to demonstrate how her labia would look at each point in the process. Sometimes I would laugh at the way she would make faces, and she would get wild with me: "You old man, what do you know?" Imagine, she would call me "old man" even though I was a baby compared with her age.

In the early days when I knew nothing she guided me carefully. When I would become fatigued after hours of Vajroli and postures she would make me drink hot milk which had been medicated with mercury in a special way, and then I would be back to my old self, fighting fit. If my erection began to droop all she had to do was touch a certain nerve and woop! I would again become fully erect.

When she wanted to test my progress she would tighten her vaginal muscles and then tell me to penetrate her. My God! It was absolutely impossible; she could make her vagina as hard as wood. Once I must have become somewhat frivolous, and to teach me a lesson she let me penetrate her and then clamped down with her vaginal muscles. I thought my penis would be squeezed flat! Then she actually began to lift my body, gripping me by my penis with her vagina! And mind you, I weighed 210 pounds at that time. It felt as if my entire pubic region was being ripped from my body! She's too good, that's all I can say.

I got my Bhairavi thanks to Shyamananda Aghori. It happened like this. I was on a university trip to Hardwar with some of my friends. A little away from the city was an old cemetery in which no one was able to spend a single night alone; everyone who tried died. I don't know what happened to my friends — perhaps something or someone affected their minds — but they dared me to spend a whole night there alone. I have never been able to ignore a challenge, so I agreed. I loaded up two hip flasks with whiskey, packed some snacks, and took my trusty Colt revolver. I was fond of hunting back then, and I had decided that some wild animal must be killing everyone who tried to spend the night there. My plan was to shoot it down, using myself as bait to attract it, and stop those stories once and for all.

Night had fallen by the time I reached the place. There was an immense stone image of Ma, and I could see that it would be the ideal place from which to get a bead on my adversary, whatever it might be. I settled down in between Her lotus feet and noticed one of the skulls that lay nearby. It was unusually broad, something you think of in terms of prehistoric man, and it was bleached absolutely white. I was sure it would crumble to powder when I touched it but, no, it was quite solid.

I began to eat and drink and sat fiddling with the safety catch on my revolver. As the night deepened and the hours rolled by I started to think the whole thing was just a hoax, when suddenly I heard a rustling from the vegetation near the temple. My senses had been sharpened by plenty of hunting. "Aha," I said to myself, "it is a wild animal, and I'm going to get myself a nice trophy from tonight's adventure." At that time in my life I was completely wild because of doing so much Smashan Sadhana, and I believed in only one thing: kill or be killed. The blood lust had taken hold of me that night, with a good deal of help from the whiskey, and I sat waiting for the blighter to come into view.

After a bit I heard a low growl, which gradually came closer and closer, and before long I could see two eyes like burning coals and I knew it was a tiger. I thought to myself, "It's all very clear now. This fellow has become a man-eater. A simple explanation for the whole mystery of this place." I was just waiting for him to come into range since a revolver is only useful at close quarters, and you must get a clean shot at a tiger to drop him. If you don't drop him with the first shot you may not live to regret it. I planned to shoot him right between the eyes, and the whole matter would be finished.

Closer and closer he came, and I was becoming more and more excited: When will he come into range so I can shoot him! I lifted the revolver and aimed it, and just as he came within about thirty yards of me I decided to pull the trigger — and my hand became useless. I just couldn't move it. In that instant all my confidence deserted me. I suddenly realized that I would be killed by the tiger like all the rest. It was such a shock that I passed out.

When I awoke I was most surprised to be alive. The tiger was gone and in his place was an Aghori standing over me. I looked at him rather stupidly, I suppose, because he said, "Get up! Don't worry, I'm not a tiger to eat you up! I called you here; that's why you've come." He told me to go down to the river and take a bath, and then he explained to me that I would have to come to the cemetery every night and perform a certain sadhana known as *Sahasra Munda* (Thousand Skulls). There was an immense heap of skulls nearby, of the prehistoric type I had seen earlier, which is why the place was called *Munda Durga* (Fortress of Skulls). With Shyamanandaji's help I succeeded at that sadhana. As he said, "Anyone who wants to be an Aghori must do Munda Sadhana." The only thing is, most do Munda Sadhana with five skulls: I did it with over 1,000.

After I completed that sadhana he told me, "Now I am going to give you my Bhairavi." That's how I got her, and, oh my, what she has taught me! I don't think any other woman in the universe could have taught me so much.

Once my Guru Maharaj wanted me to accompany him to a certain locality near Nasik, but I flatly refused. I told him, "My Bhairavi is there, and if I go to meet her I will never return; I will remain with her forever because she will never allow me to leave. She will feed me mercury so that I can regain my youth and then we will practice Mudras together indefinitely. I will forget about everything else in the world, including you, so please do not insist." He got wild, but I was adamant.

My relationship with my Bhairavi was such that I never wanted to leave her. I did not leave her willingly, in fact; I was forced to. I was ordered to return to the world and continue my work here. But even though we have been separated for many years now I have not forgotten her, and I will never forget her. No other female has ever been able to satisfy me even 1 percent as much as she could, and I doubt I'll ever find any woman who will. Sexual satisfaction is the least she gave me, of course; our relationship was very different. A purely physical relationship can only be temporary; a merely mental relationship lasts not much longer, perhaps an entire lifetime. A spiritual relationship, though, is permanent, eternal, and that is all I value.

When I last visited America I talked to some Americans about ojas and Vajroli. I know that Americans are obsessed with sex and I wanted to try to impress upon them how little they really know about the subject. And I wanted to test them.

In this lifetime it is unlikely that any of them will locate a Bhairava or Bhairavi, so it will be impossible for them to learn Vajroli, or even Shiva Lata Mudra. I told them as much, in fact, just to see how they would react. Some of them had the attitude, "Well, this is very nice but it is not at all practical so we really cannot spend any time on it." Some of them, I am sure, though no one admitted it to me, went directly home and tried out Lata Mudra and found out that it was indeed impossible to do without guidance. There might possibly be even one or two who would try the Mudra or Vajroli out with several partners and then convince themselves that they had achieved. They might even start to go around and hold seminars to teach others the half-baked knowledge they imagined they had learned. I know there are plenty of "Tantrics" in America doing this sort of thing, so it would not surprise me at all if someone tried to misuse this information.

I would have been happy if even one had had this attitude: "It seems unlikely that I will be able to learn this technique this time around, but compared to it ordinary sex is nothing! I am going to make a sincere effort to worship my deity in this life with the sincere intention that next time around or sometime later in the future Nature will teach me what I want to learn."

This is the correct attitude. No effort is ever wasted. What you do not complete in this lifetime you will most certainly complete later if you have a real desire to do so. The progression will be maintained, regardless of time. Time is no barrier at all. But if you are in a hurry for knowledge you will never obtain it. In my opinion, the best things in life are worth waiting for no matter how long that wait might be. This is why an Aghori loses his fear of death. He knows that even if he dies with something unfinished, Nature will be obligated to create the conditions for him to finish his sadhana in the future. Where will Nature go?

I don't mean you should sit back and relax and say to yourself, "Why do any work now since there is no hope for success in this birth? I'll wait until I am born in the appropriate situation and then I'll see about doing penance." With this attitude, which most self-proclaimed "good Hindus" suffer from, you will never succeed even after millions of births.

Besides, you don't know your destiny; who knows what you are destined to achieve in this birth? An Aghori demands success now knowing full well that if it eludes him in this lifetime he will be able to continue later. He never slackens, though. Slackening shows the presence of residual traces of Maya in the personality: "Let me have one more little enjoyment and then I will renounce." NO! If you want to enjoy, enjoy; if you are through with enjoyment, tired of the world's deceptions, then renounce. Don't try to mix enjoyment and renunciation together; it just won't work. And once you renounce, be prepared to wait.

# CHAPTER TEN

# GIRNAR

*Human beings are nothing but sheep. I used to be in the flock of sheep, but I ran away, so it's no surprise that everyone else, all the so-called normal people, thinks I'm insane or, at the least, abnormal. And I think the same about them. Only one of us can be right.*

## GIRNAR

I've always believed that when you do a thing you should forget everything else and do that one thing with heart and soul. When I was interested in mundane pursuits I was a perfect materialist. You would never in your life have imagined that I could be interested in spiritual subjects. And when I was doing sadhana, I forgot everything else and I did it. For example, for ten months in Girnar I lived in an Arka (*Calotropis gigantea*) tree in an old cemetery, eating only Arka leaves, doing a ritual to please Anjaneya. Arka leaves cause violent purging and vomiting. Do you know how "hot" Arka is? *Arka* means "sun" and after two or three days of eating those leaves my mouth and tongue had swollen to twice their normal size. But that didn't stop me; I continued with the ritual. Aghoris always overdo a thing.

To become an Aghori you must first renounce the world completely, and that is not easy, mind you. Becoming a sadhu in the real way is no joke. Before you can become a sadhu you must do rituals for yourself just as if you had died. You *have* died — to the world. Then you offer your body, your senses, and your mind into the fire. Only then are you eligible to put on the ochre robes of renunciation which a sadhu wears.

After that your teacher will initiate you into the sadhu's mantra, "Om namo Narayanaya." Whenever you see any creature, even the smallest ant, you must remember that Vishnu in the form of Narayana lives in that creature, and you must mentally bow to Him. And when you sit for meditation you must forget the world around you and remember only your deity.

When I was a naked sadhu, or *Naga*, sometimes my ego would be hurt. I had been a wrestler so I was very heavy, and people would say, "Why isn't this fellow working somewhere instead of begging?" or they would say, "He looks like this," or "His cock is like this," but I couldn't say anything. I could only repeat to myself, "Narayana." It hurt, but it worked; I learned to endure all the taunts.

The main reason for becoming a Naga is to remove once and for all every thought for the body. When you are naked you can't hide anything, and before long you don't bother to try. However, most people harbor some shameful thoughts within and would not dare to disrobe before anyone else. Why else would sadhus wear ochre robes? Once one of my "children" who has done a lot of sadhana during his life was sitting with me and suddenly I took off my clothes and told him, "You do the same thing; we must sit naked." He didn't say a word, but took off all his clothes. It was a good test, and he passed it with flying colors. Of course he still found it a little awkward mentally, but that is to be expected in the beginning.

I used to play around like that a lot. Sometimes I would wear a *lungi* (a sarong-like garment) to go out for a drive with one of my friends. When I got fed up with the lungi I would shout at my friend, "I can't take this restriction any longer," and I would up it from my body and drive naked. The fellow would try to pacify me: "What are you doing? Think of your prestige." I'd tell him, "What prestige? Does an Aghori have any prestige?" Eventually he would calm me down and I'd put it on again. I am not as wild now as I was then, but I still hate to wear clothes.

And don't forget, if Nagas are shameless, *Nagis*, their female counterparts, are equally shameless or even more so. They love to play about together. Nagas and Nagis know a few mantras and can achieve some minor Siddhis. And, as you know, whenever anyone becomes powerful there is always a tendency to let the power go to the head. Then they go around trying to show off.

Suppose a group of Nagas and Nagis are sitting in the smashan. One Naga may become intoxicated with his power and elongate his penis. A Naga can elongate his penis fifteen feet or more; it is a simple Siddhi. One Naga I knew, Mangalgiriji, in fact, used to coil his penis up like a cobra, and after sucking up water through it and filling his bladder, would spray out the water like a fountain for the amusement of the children who would follow him around.

Anyway, one Naga would look at a female Nagi and would elongate his penis and then he would say, "Ha, look at this. Can you do anything like this? Is not mine a fine Siddhi?" And she would sneer at him and say, "Wah, wah. Why should you crow over such a minor achievement? Bring that thing over here." And the moment the head of his penis would touch her vaginal lips he would get a shock, like an electrical shock but far more intense, like a thousand scorpions stinging him all at once. And you know how sensitive the tip of the penis is. So he would learn his lesson well and proper.

When they talk about being naked, or *Digambara* (Sky-clad), which is one of the epithets of Dattatreya, the first Aghori, they are not talking about external clothes; they are talking about the three sheaths — Sattva, Rajas, and Tamas — which cover the Atma. These are the clothes which have to be removed. And once they are gone it doesn't matter what you wear on the external body; you wear whatever is appropriate. Once you get used to being naked in this way you are not affected by anything.

I used to wear one article of apparel: my *jata* (matted locks)

I know a method to make hair grow ten times faster than normal, and my jata used to reach down to my ankles. A sadhu's jata is his most precious possession. Why? Each hair is an antenna, an aerial to accumulate knowledge from everywhere. No true sadhu ever cuts his jata; he breaks it or it breaks by itself. Then he takes it to the Ganges and offers it to Ma, because the Ganges always remains in the jata of Lord Shiva; that is why He is called Durjati, because His jata is so formidable.

But I did not come to this stage immediately. For the first six months I was in Girnar I cried every night. I was asking myself, "What am I doing here? Why am I not enjoying my life back in Bombay?" But I was very stubborn. I wouldn't go back because I knew what people would say. This has always been my principle; if you want to do a thing, do it right, do it thoroughly — or don't do it at all.

After that first six months, though, I forgot all about my old life and started to enjoy my new life. I developed a routine. Every morning at 3 A.M. I would take a bath in one of the small lakes in the Girnar hills. Then I would coat my body with ash from my dhuni and sit for my rituals. I made friends with all the animals there. Some people think that in the forest you are completely alone, but there is always someone watching you. The forest belongs to the animals, after all, and they are very anxious to know who has come to disturb them.

One night after I began staying at my old Shiva temple I saw a pair of eyes staring at me from beyond the fire. They didn't come any closer that night and soon disappeared. In the next few nights they came closer and closer, and pretty soon a lion appeared, and eventually he came all the way to sit beside me. We became great friends. You know, Girnar is the last place in the world where Asian lions live. We became such good friends that when I had to leave Girnar he followed me five miles, and I had the greatest difficulty in driving him away. I called him Raja (King), and I called my female monkey Rani (Queen).

She was completely devoted to me. Once she saved my life. I had a terrific fever; I was delirious, I couldn't do anything. Rani came near me to see what was wrong. She started to talk to me, in her own way, but I was so delirious I couldn't understand and brushed her away. She persisted and in my semiconscious condition I threatened her with a firebrand, which I would have never done normally. She backed off and then ran into the jungle.

Later when I was sleeping she came with some leaves that she had chewed into a paste. She put the paste into my mouth and as a reflex action I swallowed. Then I woke up because those were the most bitter leaves I had ever tasted. I spit most of the mass out, but I had swallowed some, enough to break the fever. That demonstrated to me that animals know these things.

When it was time for me to leave Girnar I told her gently, "Rani, I am going away and I am not coming back." When she understood that I meant it she immediately leapt into a well and drowned herself. Even my mother wouldn't have done that.

My animals have always loved me. The little Pekinese dog I have now will not eat or drink when I am out of town; she must be force-fed. I think my animals are better than humans. Remember, human love today is nothing but lust resulting from rnanubandhana. Human beings will always fail you, but animals have a selfless love. They don't have any sense of "I am doing this or that"; they only do what their nature tells them to do. When they want to eat they eat, when they want to sleep they sleep, and when they want to love you they will do it wholeheartedly.

There are three important ways in which animals differ from humans. First, they can't know their parents. In the mating season a male catches hold of any available female, even if she is his mother, sister, or daughter. Second, animals can do japa — my little doggie does wonderful japa — but since they have no hands they cannot perform rituals. Third, since an animal does not know its parents it can't do Pitri Tarpana to placate its ancestors so there is no progression in that respect. Humans pay attention to kinship and can perform ritual worship and Pitri Tarpana. Any human who does not do these things is no better than an animal; worse, in fact, because it is a waste of a precious human rebirth which is fantastically difficult to obtain; you don't know. And today no one bothers, which makes most humans animals. So by living with animals I've learned how to handle humans.

I have never feared the animals in the jungles. Animals can understand everything you think — telepathically. If they sense fear then they think you are going to attack them, and since attack is the best form of defense they will attack you first. But if you show them that you want to be friendly it's very easy to make them love you — if you are brave enough. Animals will never harm you unless you deliberately provoke them.

In fact sometimes even if you provoke them they will not harm you. Once in Girnar I was being troubled by a bee flying near me and buzzing in my ear. Two or three times I tried to brush it away, but it came back each time. Finally I told it, "If you don't leave me alone I'm going to have to kill you." No response. I lifted my hand to smack it as it sat on a nearby stone. Down came my hand onto the empty stone; the bee had moved to one side. Each time I tried to hit it the bee would move to one side. It didn't fly away, it didn't try to sting me.

Eventually, I remembered Guru Dattatreya and his twenty-four gurus, and it began to dawn on me that this might not be an ordinary insect. I decided to inspect it a little more closely, and when I did I saw it rubbing its two front feet together. Suddenly I thought — or the thought was introduced into my mind, I don't know which — "you have to wash your own hands of karma in the same say." Was that bee not a guru to me?

I learned quite a bit from that little bee. Once, some years later I had an argument with a lady on the subject of her insensitivity to pain and suffering in animals. About half an hour later she went to take a bath, and a cockroach began to trouble her. It ran up her leg to a certain secret place causing her to throw the soap up into the air; then it ran onto her leg again. She picked up her slipper to strike it and ended in striking several sharp blows to her foot, arm, and leg as the cockroach evaded her. Every so often it would drop off and run to one side and cock its antennae and stare up at her, and then the fun would start all over again. No, I've always gotten along well with animals. I kept a cockroach as a pet once. I called him Ramji and kept him in a matchbox. Unfortunately, he was accidentally sprayed one day and passed away.

In my own home I used to have a small menagerie, which included at various times a chimpanzee and an orangutan. I even had a crocodile there for a while. His name was Gopaldas. I had to send him to the Bombay Zoo after he chewed off the cook's leg. It was the cook's fault; he was trying to cause some trouble for me. I think Gopaldas must have sensed it. Anyway, it was too dangerous to keep him at home. I used to visit him often at the zoo. I'd walk over to the crocodile pen and call out, "Gopaldas!" and he would amble over to me and open his big mouth wide, and I'd put some food into it.

For the longest time, whenever I had a good day at the races and was flush with money I used to go down to Crawford Market in South Bombay and purchase all the doves, pigeons, and other fowl meant for the pot and release them — just let them fly away so they could enjoy their freedom. I had enjoyed that kind of freedom as a sadhu, and I knew what it was like to be caged up. After a while I realized I might be interfering too much in karma, and I quit. But I will never forget those years in the jungle when I had only animals for friends, and I will always love them more than I'll love humans.

I have become very wary of humans. When you do something nice for a spirit or an animal they will never forget it. They will love you forever afterward. But do one thing good for a human being and all you will get is a request for something more to be done. There is no end to human greed.

That is why I always like to have animals near me. There are always new things to learn from them. Have you noticed what happens when you spell the word *God* backwards? You get *dog*. I would love to become just like a dog, because of all creatures dogs are the most loving and the most devoted. Is there any animal more faithful than man's best friend? And a dog's love is pure and unselfish. Even if you don't feed him, still he will greet you with love. A cat would never do that. And a dog has only one master; it will never obey any other.

This is the way in which you should worship God. Select one form of God to worship and then worship only that form.

No matter what happens, what difficulties you may get into, be tenacious. Never lose faith. If you behave just as if you were God's dog then you are sure to achieve. Sometime back I read in the papers about a dog whose master left him at an airport in Russia seven years before. Every day that dog meets every plane that lands, waiting for his master to come back and retrieve him. He is fed by the workers at the airport but refuses to go home with any of them. If you can develop that sort of devotion for God then you will not have to wait long before He comes to you. If you crave to see Him, He has to come! Where will He go? He is not a heartless brute like the owner of that Russian dog. But you must have that perfect, selfless devotion if you want to drag God to you. That is why I always keep a dog around me, so that some of the dog's personality will rub off on me. I am devoted to my doggie Lizoo, my Pekinese. I would give up everyone else in the world but her, just like Yudhisthira, who refused to go to heaven unless his dog was allowed to accompany him.

Now, I have never worried about animals when I was in the jungle. The forests *are* full of other dangers, though. It is great to be a sadhu — lord and master of all you survey. But you must always be wary, because solitude is the father of passion.

Once the Emperor Akbar asked his favorite courtier, Birbal, "What is the father of passion?" Emperors are like that; suddenly for no reason whatsoever they ask the most unusual questions. Birbal had no ready answer and so Akbar told him, "If you don't find out for me what is the father of passion within three months, your head will be disconnected from your shoulders." Birbal bowed low; what else could he do? His boss had given him an order.

After two and a half months Birbal had come nowhere near discovering the father of passion. He began to worry for his life. His daughter noticed his despondence and asked him the reason for it. When he told her she just giggled and said, "Call the Emperor for dinner." Meanwhile, she selected one of her serving maids who bore a certain resemblance to her and made the girl into her double.

When the Emperor came for dinner, Birbal had been sent out

so that there were only two present: Akbar and his courtier's daughter. The delicious, rich food was washed down with two bottles of heavy wine, and soon the food, the low lights, and the wine went to the Emperor's head and he indicated to the young lady that he would be pleased to have her company to bed for the night. Birbal's daughter had of course anticipated this; it was part of her plan. She consented graciously and asked for a moment to ready herself. Leading Akbar to the bedchamber she sent in her double, the serving-girl. She enjoyed sex with the Emperor all night long and then returned to her own room after he slept.

When the Emperor awoke he was suddenly seized with remorse: "I have deflowered the daughter of my best friend. How will I ever face him again? How can I demonstrate my penitence for this lapse in my morality?" And he sent for Birbal's daughter.

She entered, laughing, which amazed Akbar, who was sure she would be sobbing and beating her breast. She said, "Refuge of the world, it was not I that you deflowered. It was my double," and produced the serving-maid for proof. Giggling, she continued, "I wanted to prove to you that solitude is the father of passion so that my father's head would be spared. Are you satisfied?"

Akbar was more than satisfied. In court that day he publicly congratulated Birbal for his brilliance, and for having such a brilliant daughter, and he made a gift of a large tract of land to the girl who had lost her virginity. Of course she was thrilled that the Emperor had made love to her, so the land was just an added bonus.

This is why it is so hard to be off in some cave somewhere and maintain your balance of mind. Temptations will come to you by the dozen: celestial damsels, buxom country lasses, tribal wenches. You have to be thoroughly prepared so that you are ready for anything. But even if you are prepared you can still make grave errors which might have lasting consequences. I know.

One day in Girnar while walking about in the jungles I saw a young lady near a tree. She was really beautiful, and it looked as if she was from a good family from her looks and the way she was dressed, but I couldn't understand what she would be doing out in the middle of a deep jungle. As I passed her she said, "Mai aaun?" (Shall I come?)

Now I didn't know what to think. What is she doing acting like a prostitute out here in dense forest soliciting me? I decided that the best thing to do would be to walk on. She started to follow, and she kept repeating, "Mai aaun? Mai aaun?"

I told her, "Cats say 'Meow, meow'; are you a cat?" But she said nothing at all except, "Mai aaun? Mai aaun?"

I continued to walk, and she continued to follow until I began to feel tired. I sat down and she came near me, repeating "Mai aaun? Mai aaun?"

I was tired and fed up with her, and that made me lose my temper and say, "If you are coming, come!" And immediately I was entrapped. She was a Yakshini.

You don't know what trouble I had with her. I wouldn't dare meet anyone, even other sadhus, because she would have finished them off, she was so possessive. Anyway when I was at the tether end of my rope my Mahapurusha freed me from her. That is only a minor one of the many reasons I have for saying that I owe everything to my Big Daddy, my Mahapurusha. If I am flayed alive for millions of births it would still be insufficient to repay him.

Maya spares no one, and She never spared me either. Once in Girnar when I had to urinate I laid my fire tongs down on a rock, and when I came back it had turned into gold; I couldn't believe my eyes. I picked it up and marked the stone so that I could remember exactly where it was. My idea was to use it whenever I needed gold.

I went down to Junagadh town and sold the fire tongs to a goldsmith after breaking it into pieces; a gold fire tongs is of no use to a sadhu. Then I bought a new iron fire tongs and distributed the money I realized from the sale of the gold.

When I got back to the place where the stone had been there was no mark, no sign I had ever been there, nothing. I tried several of the stones, but to no avail. I had tried to capitalize on it and had lost it as a punishment for forgetting to rely on Nature to provide for me.

How many people really rely on Nature? Once when I was in Girnar I decided to make a test. I went without food and water to see when God would come and feed me.

The first two days were awful; my head was splitting. On the third day I decided, "If God does not come before sunset I am going to eat anyway and I will believe from then on that God is a real phony."

As the day wore on I was becoming more and more desperate for sunset, the hunger was so great and my head so painful. Suddenly about fifteen minutes before sunset a young girl whom I had never seen before came up to me and said, "Why are you making yourself starve like this? I have brought milk for you."

At first I wanted to grab the milk and drink it all at once, I was so hungry. But I had my position to consider. I had to continue with my arrogance so I said, "Go, go on, get out of here." But I wondered how she knew I was hungry. When I asked her she said, "I can see it on your face." Then I felt ashamed; my facade was not as perfect as I had hoped.

She insisted I take the milk. Still I pretended to refuse it — and then she grabbed my matted locks and poured the milk down my throat. It was like nectar after not eating or drinking for three days, and then without my mentioning anything about my vow she said, "Now, has God fed you or not?" And then she disappeared. And from that day onward I know that God looks after everyone. I have been blessed by my mentor so that wherever I go I will always get my food and even cigarettes. Even if I go to the jungle the monkeys bring me fruits. Am I not fortunate? My mentors were very good, really good, excellent.

Thanks to them I was able to perform sadhana in the Cave of the Sixty-Four Yoginis which was the high point of my stay in Girnar. You might try to visit this cave without an invitation. As you approach it, suddenly a giant cobra will rear toward you, standing bolt upright on his tail. If you know the proper mantra you can immobilize him, no doubt, but then as you move on you will start to hear the sounds of wild spirits. Suppose you are successful at immobilizing all the spirits, which is highly unlikely. Then, as you proceed, suddenly you will fall for no apparent reason and break your leg. Out on a mountain with a broken leg near a cave with a well-deserved reputation for preventing the curious from visiting it, who will come to rescue you? So there is no use in trying to enter this cave unless you have a good friend to pull strings on your behalf.

I was lucky; my Mahapurusha wanted me to perform this sadhana. Even so I had to be purified first. I was given a small leaf, and I began to vomit and purge to remove all the worldly elements from my body. For the next two days I was not allowed to drink even water, and by the third day I was really almost unable to go on. Then I was invited into the cave, and a panel of beings — I can't explain what sort of beings — welcomed me as one of their own.

I am forbidden to discuss the nature of my sadhana there but I can tell you this; the Yoginis are the companions of the Great Goddesses. This is a two-fold advantage: They can introduce you to the Great Goddesses, and they can teach you what they have been taught. Actually Shakti is the same in any form; only the details of the manifestation differ. In the case of the Great Goddess the entire range of possibilities of Shakti are divided into nine or ten aspects. For the Sixty-Four Yoginis there are sixty-four aspects which when taken as a unified whole represent the totality of Shakti in the universe. To succeed at the sadhana of one or two is feasible; to succeed at all sixty-four is nigh unto impossible, but the benefits if you do succeed are unimaginable.

Eventually I was ordered to leave Girnar and return to the world. I never wanted to come back to civilization, but orders are orders. When I finally got back to Bombay after being in Girnar and then wandering about as a sadhu, I used to sit in a room where everything was black: walls, ceiling, furniture, floor, everything. I used to wear a black lungi and would smoke ganja all day long and drink imported whiskey straight from the bottle. I was in my own mood all day long and never slept; to rest I would lie down for a half hour or so. The more intoxicants I would take, the more alert and silent would I become

Visitors would bring mad persons to me — stark raving, violently insane — and I would put them in my garden, and when I felt like it I would go out and give them one slap. Immediately they would become all right.

I used to experiment with new ways of curing diseases also. Sometimes I would dispense the ashes from the pipes I had been smoking, and they would do the job. Sometimes I would blow a whistle and the disease would go away instantaneously. I enjoyed having fun like that. Everyone wondered how I did it, and no one could ever understand.

When too many people would start to come to me and I would become tired of all the rush I would say, "I'm sorry, I've made a mistake. I've slipped up in my sadhana, so now all my power is finished," and this would drive most of the people away. I have done that many times, because I love more than anything else to be alone.

# DEVOTION

If I live for anything I live for my sadhana. And I cannot emphasize too strongly that to succeed at sadhana you must do whatever you set out to do with heart and soul. Never be like a prostitute, going from guru to guru, deity to deity, never selecting one as a true lover. Be like the Cataka bird, that drinks water only when the Swati asterism is in the sky. Never be happy anywhere but where your beloved is, whatever you may choose to love. Then you can get Siddhi — not otherwise.

Even when I was engaged to my wife, I would invariably get up at 10 P.M. no matter what I was doing, and would go to the smashan. She would ask me, "What do you do when you leave here?" One day I decided to take her along with me; why keep secrets from anyone? I drove to the smashan and parked the car. "Listen, while I am doing my sadhana I will not be able to come and help you out. You'll have to wait until dawn. Think it over." She said, "I'll wait in the car until you finish." I shrugged my shoulders over her stupidity, walked over to a blazing pyre, sat down, and began my rituals.

At dawn I returned to the car to find she had fainted. Foam was coming from her mouth, and her skin was cold. A nice slap brought her to her senses, and she started mumbling deliriously, "No, no, don't come near me. Take me home." I took her home, and she was in bed for a month with high fever from the fright of it. What did she see there? No one knows. And still she married me. This is rnanubandhana.

My wife says I'm a fool. Hundreds come to me to be treated and get their work done, and she says I'm a fool. I don't cash in on my abilities! It doesn't matter. Although we can't get along together, still I refer to her and respect her as my first guru, because if it hadn't been for her nagging I would never have rushed up things like I did; a blitzkrieg, if you like. She wanted me to become completely materialistic because she married me for my money; but it was not possible. If it had happened we would not be talking together here today. Therefore I thank her for making me realize the futility of life. You see, I have an Aghori's frame of mind: challenge and response. Either I die or I succeed; either I kill you or you kill me. I picked this up in the jungle as a sadhu, and also when I was a wrestler. That competitiveness has always been there.

Once when I had gone to see my Junior Guru Maharaj after a long interval, I went to the cave I kept nearby and found some other Aghori sitting in it. I got wild. The beauty of that cave is that no one ever sits there when I am gone, but inside it is always spotless as if it were being regularly cleaned. It is full of whitened skulls, and snakes drip off the ceiling. Many of my friends have seen it, and they have all become frightened. There is a tree outside which gives a different type of fruit in each month of the year. You can obtain one fruit from it each day, and with the cool water from the spring within the cave you can live splendidly.

I told the other Aghori, whose name was Bhuta Nath, "Look, this is my cave. If you want to remain alive you had better pack up and leave immediately."

He started to bluster: "This may have been your cave but now it belongs to me. If you don't like it I don't care. Get out!"

What arrogance! This was serious. I told him, "I am warning you for the last time. I have nothing against you, but I can't be responsible for what my friends will do to you if you stay here any longer."

He just continued to blather, "Do you want to see what I can do? If you don't leave now I will kill you."

Unfortunately the moment he spoke these words he vomited blood and died. I buried his body; who will waste money for wood to cremate him? About some things it is necessary to be very strict.

But you can't punish just anyone who makes fun of you; only those who should know better like Bhuta Nath. Besides, to punish someone is also to create a new karma, even if that someone deserved it like Bhuta Nath did. Every action produces an equal and opposite reaction: Newton's Law of Motion. Eventually you will have to pay for each and every karma you create unless you find someone who is willing to take some of your karmas away from you and endure them himself, which is quite unlikely.

A sadhu has his own karmas to worry about, and rarely will he take anyone else's karmas to reduce that person's sufferings. I have tried it, and I have suffered for overstepping my limits. I took the karmas of one fellow suffering from throat cancer just to spare his children from being fatherless. For forty days I couldn't even drink water. I survived on sips of lime juice mixed in a glass of soda.

Now I know what cancer is like. You see, if the patient will have to suffer for six years, you can suffer yourself for six months or six days, depending on the strength of your penance, because the austerities make the reaction easier to bear. But suffer you must.

Usually, however, a sadhu will say, "You have performed the action and enjoyed the fruit at the time. Now you are enjoying the reaction. Please learn a good lesson from it and don't make any mistakes again." You may find fakirs to help you, because they are more emotional, but only a few sadhus are exceptions to this rule.

I know the truth of this story personally. There was once a girl who married and was happily living in Bombay when she developed leprosy. Her husband and his family threw her out of the house, and her own family refused to take her in. In despair she went to Girnar. In the jungle she found a sadhu sitting on his dhuni. When he saw her he grunted at her several times, but she still refused to move. Finally, he had to say, "Ma, please do leave here. The sun is about to go down, and it is very dangerous to be out in the jungle at night."

She replied, "I have come to Girnar to find some Baba who will cure me. Until now all the sadhus and fakirs I have met could do nothing, and if you also can't do anything I have decided to kill myself because I cannot stand it any longer."

The Baba didn't say anything after that, and he continued to sit by his dhuni, she sitting nearby. Night fell and the cold set in and she started to shiver, but she didn't move. At about 3 A.M. the Baba got up to have his bath. When he came back he smeared himself with ash from his dhuni, sat on the ground, and called the girl over to him, and motioned to her to sit on his lap. Then he embraced her — and she became free of the disease instantaneously. I can take you to her today; she is a grandmother now. Her husband and everyone else had to admit that she was cured.

And the Baba? Well, he had to suffer terribly for forty days, agony. That sort of compassion you find in only one out of thousands of sadhus and fakirs. A householder Aghori cannot afford to be so cruel. He has his own obligations, his people to protect and provide for, and he must be compassionate. To wear ochre robes is really a terrible responsibility and that is why I don't wear them. While I don't, I am a normal human being and I can play around as I like. I can enjoy my life and make mistakes. But when I put that on, I can't afford to make even a single mistake.

This is another reason why I continuously test the people who come to me to learn something of spirituality. Some of them think they are ready to go out into the jungle without any preparation whatsoever. But do they realize what it means to divorce yourself from all your comforts and live like a sadhu? Once I met a sadhu in a North Indian forest. He was an Englishman, actually, but he had spent twenty years in India already when I met him. Some of our bigoted Brahmins claim smugly that Westerners will never be able to succeed at our sadhanas perfectly; but that is all bull. Actually Westerners have some qualities which are rare in Indians nowadays. For example, they are thorough in whatever it is they do. This sadhu, named Must Ram (literally "Intoxicated with Rama"), was as perfect a sadhu as you will ever find. When I met him he had injured his leg and the wound was full of pus — and termites. Yes, termites. I felt sorry for him; I was sure he must be suffering some disturbance in his meditation on that account. So I volunteered to cure him.

"Oh, no, no, don't bother," he told me in elegant English, "why disturb them? Let them eat, let them eat." Can you imagine? Would you be able to say the same thing if it were your leg which was being devoured by insects? I doubt it; not in the beginning, at least. Which is why I tell the people who come to me, "If you cannot concentrate properly in Bombay where you have all the facilities, food whenever you want it, a comfortable bed, and so on, how could you possibly concentrate out in the jungle with mosquitoes swooping down at you at odd hours, with a rock for a bed, and whatever you can beg for your dinner?"

I never wanted to leave Girnar, but I can see now it was the right thing to do. I've learned so much about the world and the people who live in it. I can understand how they can be miserable, and I try to help them out of their misery, physical or mental, so that they can, maybe, remember God occasionally.

I love to play about with my "children," to teach them new things, and to help them overcome their bad habits. One day one of them may even develop sufficiently to be fit to become a disciple. One of my American "children" told me once, very sweetly and sincerely, "I am really proud to be able to say I know you, and I am so glad that I can love you and that you reciprocate my love, that it is mutual. I just hope my love is not a burden to you." Wasn't that a nice thing to say? But very naive.

I told him, "Your love is no burden to me because it is a very inconstant love. You love me some of the time, your wife some

of the time, your other friends part of the time, and some of
the time you are overcome by self-doubt and are not sure who
you love or even if you *do* love. If your love ever becomes real
love then it will definitely be a burden to me, because then I
will have to work hard to live up to it."

The purpose of sadhana is to develop real love. But nowadays it is so difficult to do proper sadhana because of all the
obstacles. The secret is to be sincere about whatever it is you
take as your sadhana, no matter how insignificant or unim-
portant it may seem to you. God is not interested in big sadhus
or saints; God is interested only in sincerity. That is why
Krishna cannot do without Radha. She can remember nothing
else except Krishna, and Her remembrance drags Him to Her.

When Khinaram Aghori cured that dancer of leprosy, or when
the Baba in Girnar cured that Bombay girl of leprosy, the love
that Khinaram and the Baba showed was infinitely greater than
any love you have ever experienced in your life. Why? Because
first of all, it was done knowing full well that the opposite party would never be able to repay such a gift. Normally lovers
work on the principle that "a fair exchange is no robbery." A
lover loves his or her partner only because he or she is confident that the partner will return that love. How many people
love without any expectation of return? Secondly, it was a love
which was so great that Khinaramji and the Baba were willing
to suffer for the opposite party. It is one thing to love without
any expectation of return; it is a very different thing to love
with the intention of suffering in the other's stead. Sometimes
you will find mothers who can do it, especially animal mothers protecting their young. This is why I am always desirous
of sitting in the lap of the Mother, so that I can always be learning how to love. *This* is real love, and this love is a real burden.

Where did this love come from? Did Kinaramji want to enjoy
sex with the dancer? Did the Baba look at the young lady's body
before agreeing to cure her? No. Ordinary love for the flesh can
never go so deep because of the instinct of self-preservation.
This was love directed inward to the Atma, the fragment of
the Universal Soul which dwells in everyone. Overwhelming
love for God made these things happen. That Baba, and Khin-

aramji likewise, thought, "Wah, Lord, are you suffering? Let me relieve you!" Real love changes things.

Generally, people say the aim of life is *Moksha*, or salvation, by which they mean freedom from being obliged to take birth again on Earth. But I believe in a personal God and I say to Him, "Lord, let me be born over and over again thousands of times, but don't take your face away from me. Make me a blind leper for centuries but never desert me. Always keep me in your heart and in your eyes." My Beloved loves to play about with me and I love to play about with Him, and the result is emotional highlights: Mahabhava Samadhi! Can you prevent two lovers from meeting? No, even if they have to meet in the road or in some public area where everyone can see what they are up to. Do they have any sense of time or place? No! "Kamaturanam na bhayam na lajja": Fear and shame do not exist for those afflicted with the disease of desire. And Bhakti is far more intense than physical love. Two souls merge into one another; can anyone describe it? To achieve it you must forget the external completely and go deeper and deeper within.

So go on with your sadhana, longer and longer until you can't live without your deity, and He or She can't live without you. Then go further; go so deep that you forget even the deity. The deity then will feel so miserable without your love and remembrance that He or She will run after you and demand worship. This becomes such a bondage of love that you can't escape it. You become lost, absolutely lost, useless to the world, lost within yourself playing with your Beloved.

And when that happens your perspective on life will undergo a radical change. You'll see things completely differently, because you are no longer part of the usual current of worldly events, so your priorities will be determined by your Bhakti. Here is an example.

Once in the South there was a king of the Chola dynasty who was a great devotee of Rama. One day while the court bard was reciting the *Ramayana* (the epic of Rama's life and adventures) aloud to him, the narrative reached the point where Sita was taken to Lanka. The king suddenly jumped up and said, "Immediately prepare the forces for an attack on Lanka. Why should Lord Rama worry when I am here to serve him? I will see that Sita is returned!"

No one at the court had the courage to tell him that all this had happened long before. So, he sailed at the head of his fleet and duly conquered Lanka. Then he ordered his generals, "Find Sita!" Since they were aware that to refuse a royal order meant death, they made a show of searching and reported that no Sita was present. This mystified the king, who was on the point of losing his temper, until it came out in the course of a conversation that the Ramayana had happened thousands of years ago. Then he realized, "Oh, no! What have I done? I have unnecessarily conquered Lanka!" He gave the kingdom of Lanka to one of his sons, his own kingdom to the other, and went out into the forest to live the life of an ascetic. He became a great saint. Devotion like that will always pay dividends.

When you have Bhakti your attitude becomes quite different. Once Narada (an immortal devotee of Vishnu) asked Lord Vishnu to explain to him the difference in state between a Yogi and a devotee, a follower of Bhakti. Vishnu told Narada to follow him down to Earth. On Earth as they strolled along they came upon a Yogi hanging upside down from the branch of a large tree. The Yogi asked Vishnu, "How many more births will I have to take to be free of the cycle of birth and death? My penance is so terrific that I should achieve very soon."

Vishnu said, "In spite of all your penance there is still a little left for you to do. You will have to take two more births yet."

On hearing this the Yogi got down out of the tree and walked off in disgust, saying, "In spite of all my strenuous efforts and austerities I will still have to take two more births? What sort of justice is that? Forget it; there is no use in continuing with it."

Narada and Vishnu walked silently on a little farther and saw a devotee singing and dancing by himself under a spreading banyan tree. Seeing Lord Vishnu the devotee prostrated himself fully on the ground and said, "Oh, my blessed Lord, how kind of you to come and visit me! How wonderful that I have been permitted to see you! Would you be kind enough to tell

me how many more times I will have to take birth before I can
be free of the wheel of existence?"

Vishnu replied, "I am sorry to have to tell you this but you
will have to take birth again as many times as there are leaves
on this tree."

The devotee shouted for joy, "Only so many times? And I
feared there might be no limit. The time will pass almost unno-
ticed." And he began to sing and dance again.

Vishnu smiled and said, "Oh, is that the way you feel about
it? Then come with me right now."

Then Vishnu asked Narada, "Do you see the difference between a Yogi and a devotee? The Yogis still try to hold on to
their egos, and what do they get? The devotee accomplishes
great things by offering up the ego to the Beloved."

There is a cliff in Girnar. When a sadhu has done penances
for years and years and has finally despaired of life and can no
longer stand to live without his deity, he will walk to that cliff
and throw himself off in a frenzy of anguish — and nothing
will happen to him. He will have passed his test and becomes
eligible to be taught further. False sadhus have tried it, to attract
attention to themselves, and all of them died. True devotion
is the only force which can go beyond death.

When you get close to your Beloved there comes a time when
you cannot continue to exist separately, and your own personality is lost in that of the deity. Each deity has unique characteristics which give a wonderful flavor to the play. When you
embrace Anjaneya, it is as if electricity had been given to all
parts of your body. All the cells begin to jump and sing. And
what is so marvelous is that in the blood, for instance, if the
white blood cells are too many and red blood cells too few, or
vice versa, they will automatically go back to their proper levels. In the brain every cell is dilated, every blood vessel is dilated. And that is why they call it Supreme Bliss.

Anyone who follows the path of devotion wants to get the
vision of his deity because he is dying to catch a glimpse of his
Beloved. He longs for his deity so much that the form of the
deity is actually created in the astral body, and then it projects
and plays with him. All through this process he experiences

the joys of intense emotional highlights. This is why Aghoris are always the best devotees, because they forget everything else when they remember the Beloved. Their longing is so intense that they cry, wail, tear their flesh, starve themselves, anything to lose their physical consciousness and attract the deity. An ordinary devotee can never be so intense as an Aghori.

Once an Aghori told his disciple, "Take this pot and fill it with water, but don't go near any lake or river."

The disciple thought to himself as hard as he could, and then he wandered around awhile before returning with an empty pot. The guru looked up at him and said, "There is only one way to fill this pot — with your tears. When you love your deity so much that you cannot bear to be without Him, that you cannot exist unless you have a glimpse of Him, that you are ready to kill yourself unless He shows Himself to you, and when you cry continuously until the pot is full, then only are you fit to do Aghora sadhanas; not until then."

Another day the guru told the same disciple, "Build me a fire without wood." The disciple made an effort, but to no avail. When he confessed his failure to the guru, the latter shook his head and said, "Until your heart catches fire with the intense longing for your deity; until you burn yourself to ashes and continue to burn even then; until you become flame yourself, you can never succeed at Aghora."

The scriptures describe the stages through which one passes when overcome by Shakti. First, you must forget your body. If you worry about your body how will you concentrate on your Beloved? When you can no longer remember your body you are on the way. Then you begin to sweat as the emotion builds up. Next you cry. First you cry because of the separation; and later you cry because of anticipation, out of joy when you feel the deity is really going to come to you. When the deity enters your body and embraces you, you begin to tremble and shake because of the overwhelming bliss of the embrace. And then you lose yourself in the fusion of the two personalities into one. If you are a super-Aghori you maintain this state permanently; if not, you can develop the emotion whenever you please and play with your Beloved at any time. Then you are beyond all the limitations of your physical body, and therefore of karma and fate also.

Once the great Hindi poet-saint Tulsidas, during his period as a wandering sadhu, came to a certain town, where a lady offered him food. In India we always believe in feeding sadhus, birds, animals, all living things, because you never know when God is going to come to you. God may come in any form, and we feel that if we feed everyone, eventually we will feed God and our work will be done. After eating, Tulsidas told the lady, "Please ask for anything, and I will do it for you."

She laughed in his face and said, "Maharaj, plenty of saints have come and none of them have been able to give me what I want."

"But I am Tulsidas," he said, a little offended, "and I will give you what you desire; just speak it."

The woman sighed over his stupidity and said, "I want a son."

Tulsidas went into meditation and after a few minutes came back to earthly consciousness and said, "Ma, I'm afraid that a son is not in your destiny."

The woman smiled and said, "That is what I told you in the first place, but you wouldn't listen to me. However, you are always welcome for food." Tulsidas went on his way.

After some time an Aghori came to the town, and upon learning about the lady who was unable to have a child he decided to do something about it. One day he walked down the street in front of the lady's house, shouting, "Who will feed me? I am offering a child for every *roti* (flat bread tortilla) I am fed! One roti, one child! Ten rotis, ten children!" When the lady heard this she invited the Aghori inside and told him, "But Maharaj, it's not in my destiny to have children." The Aghori replied, "I piss on destiny!" She fed him eight rotis, and in eight years she delivered eight handsome sons.

After twelve years Tulsidas again visited the town. As he walked down the same street he saw the eight boys and was immediately enamored by their beauty and intelligence. They called their mother, and she invited him inside and told him, "Do you remember that you said I had no sons in my destiny?" When Tulsidas heard that the Aghori had given them to her he went into meditation to ask Rama about it. He said, "Raghuvira, when you would not allow me to give this lady sons, how could that filthy evil-smelling Aghori do it?"

Rama smiled at him and said, "Tulsi, that Aghori is something different from you. He has gone beyond the limits of being a saint and living in Sattva." Then Rama decided to teach Tulsidas a good lesson with the help of the Aghori, and suddenly He started to shout, "Oh, I have a terrific pain in the heart. Please, Tulsi, get me a heart from someone so that I can get some relief."

Tulsidas got scared: If something were to happen to Lord Rama what would be his fate as Rama's chief devotee? So he ran out into the street shouting, "A heart! Lord Rama needs a heart! Who will give his heart for Rama?"

The Aghori, who was relaxing under a tree, heard him and said, "Tulsidas, come here." When Tulsidas came the Aghori said, "Now I know how much love you have for Lord Rama. If you really loved Him, you would have given your own heart instantaneously when He asked. Here, if Lord Rama wants a heart, let Him take mine," and so saying he ripped open his chest with his fingers, tore out his heart, and handed it to Tulsidas.

When Tulsidas went back into meditation to offer the heart to Rama, Rama smiled at him and said, "Now do you see how a real lover behaves with his Beloved?" And Tulsidas had to keep quiet and acknowledge the Aghori's greatness.

Once when I was in Girnar I was moving about with a sadhu named Ganga Das, a great devotee of Anjaneya. He had gone to a temple of Anjaneya to worship, but the priest told us, "You naked sadhus, get out of here! The wives of some important merchants from Bombay are coming here to worship. They will be embarrassed to see you!" And he refused to let us into the temple.

Tears filled the eyes of Ganga Das, and all he said was, "Wah, Anjaneya; I could never have believed You would feel embarrassed to see me. Doesn't matter; I am ready to go." And we turned to leave.

As we left the temple enclosure the image of Anjaneya ripped itself from the wall and began to follow us! We walked on and on and it followed us faithfully all the while, the priest standing thunderstruck behind. I don't know how many miles we covered but eventually Ganga Das relented and turned to worship the image. The image never returned to the original temple; the trustees arranged for a new temple to be built over it where it finally came to rest.

This is just an example of what I mean when I say that when you really get close to your deity, He or She cannot do without you and will go to any lengths not to offend you. There is a beautiful bondage of love. But only an Aghori can ever reach such heights; others are just too timid.

You can't just go out and try to develop love like this; it takes years. But everyone can make a beginning. Every morning when I wake up I do three things. First, I remember that I'm going to die. This gives urgency to the way I will live that day. Second, I spend five minutes in thanksgiving to Nature for being permitted to live, to have this chance to experience, to learn, and to achieve. And third, I resolve not to cheat my consciousness during the day. As long as I don't cheat my consciousness nothing I do during the day can stain me; but if I do something wrong I know I am likely to end up like the boy whose guru swallowed the fish and then regurgitated them back up, alive.

There are several little things like this I do during the day, just to keep my mind under control. I always make it a point to eat a green chili or two each morning, first thing. And you know how hot green chilies are! It is to remind me of the time when I had only chilies and water to eat all day long, because of my sadhana. That morning chili tells me, "Forget not, forget not."

And there is a practice which I follow every night before going to sleep. It is very simple, but it has helped me immensely and it can help anyone who uses it. It involves only three questions: Have I lived? Have I loved? Have I laughed?

*Have I lived?* Have I made the best use of the time provided me during that day to grow, to learn, to develop?

*Have I loved?* Have I reached out to everyone I met and made them aware of the love in my heart and eased their burdens of self-mistrust and self-doubt?

*Have I laughed?* Have I seen the humorous side of even the most painful incident?

If the answer to any one of these questions is no, then it is a matter for remorse. One more day has passed and I am another day closer to my death, and I have not exerted myself to my fullest potential. This is enough to make me work harder the next day and try to make amends, before Mahakala comes and catches me unawares. It is this intense desperation to live life to the fullest which is the hallmark, the stamp, of a true Aghori.

# GLOSSARY

*Adya:* Lit. "first, original." Used as a synonym for the Adishakti, the first or original Shakti which manifests from the absolute and is the Mother of all the worlds.

*Aghora/Aghori:* Lit. "non-terrifying." Aghora is the most extreme of all Indian sects, concentrating on forcible conversion of a limited human personality into a divine personality. An Aghori is a practitioner of Aghora.

*Apana Vayu:* One of the five forces in living beings which cause movements in the body and mind, the other four being Prana, Samana, Vyana and Udana. Apana is the downward-moving force, and is in charge of excretion of urine, feces, flatus, menstrual fluid, and semen, and also delivery of the fetus.

*Atma:* The soul, the indwelling spirit which animates a living being. The Jivatma is the individual spirit which imagines itself trapped in a physical form, subject to the limitations of embodied existence. The Paramatma is the Universal Soul, the totality of spirit in the cosmos. All Jivas or Jivatmas belong to the Paramatma.

*Bhairava/Bhairavi:* Lit. "the Terrifier." A name for Lord Shiva and for his consort. In sexual Tantra the Bhairava is the male, who self-identifies with Lord Shiva, and the Bhairavi is the female, who self-identifies with Parvati, Shiva's Grand Consort.

*Bhang:* A preparation of Cannabis leaf paste and milk which is mixed with spices and sugar. Even strictly abstemious Hindus often take bhang on holidays like Diwali and Mahashivaratri, in honor of deities like Lord Shiva who take bhang regularly. Shiva regards bhang as a wonderful tool for spiritual advancement if properly used, and a good way to ruin yourself if misused.

*Causal Body:* The third of the bodies possessed by an animate being; a warehouse in which all an individual's karmas are stored. Karmas are projected from the causal body into the subtle body (the mind) and then into the physical body. (See "Subtle Body.")

*Chillum:* A pipe used to smoke marijuana or hashish mixed with tobacco. It is three or four inches long and is straight, tapering from a wide bowl to a thin mouth.

*Dhuni:* The fire tended by a sadhu. A sadhu is said to sit "on" his dhuni, meaning close by it, concentrating on it.

*Ethereal Being:* A discarnate personality, the quality of whose influence is defined by his or her degree of spiritual advancement.

*Fakir:* A wandering Muslim holy man.

*Gunas:* Lit. "qualities" or "attributes." The Three Gunas are the three fundamental attributes of conditional or limited existence: Sattva (equilibrium), Rajas (activity), and Tamas (inertia). In its purest state the mind is pure Sattva, and the two chief mental disturbances are Rajas (overactivity) and Tamas (inactivity).

*Jiva:* The individual personality which undergoes rebirth, because the karmas stored in the causal body need a physical body to permit their expression. (see Atma)

*Jnana:* Transcendent wisdom. Knowledge (Vidya) is an outward projection or objectivization of this innate, living wisdom.

*Kali Yuga:* The fourth of the four ages through which the cosmos passes in cycles of 4,320,000 years. Kali Yuga is supposed to last 432,000 years, and is characterized by lack of interest in spirituality among the populace, which leads to materialism, atheism, and the perpetration of various cruelties by stronger beings onto weaker ones.

*Kilana:* Lit. "nailing." It is the process by which a spirit or other ethereal being is "nailed down" or captured with a mantra, and made to remain in a certain location for a specific purpose.

*Lunar Asterism:* "Nakshatra" in Sanskrit. One of the 27 or 28 divisions of the sky through which the moon passes in a month and the sun passes in a year. Traditional Vedic astrology uses Nakshatras instead of zodiacal signs for its calculations.

*Ma:* Vimalananda's generic term for the Mother Goddess, the cosmic potentiality for creation. All females were to him embodiments of this universal principle of motherhood and motherliness.

*Mahapurusha:* Lit. "great being." Vimalananda used this term to mean an ethereal being whose power is unlimited or almost unlimited, who can manipulate the cosmos at will if He so desires.

*Nirvikalpa Samadhi:* A state of consciousness in which all dualities are finally transcended and only awareness of the Paramatma (Ultimate Reality) remains. No consciousness of body or individuality is left.

*Paan:* A chaw composed of betel leaf smeared with slaked lime, catechu paste, and spice, into which betel nuts have been added. Paan is chewed after meals as a digestive and is said to have aphrodisiac qualities.

*Pitri Tarpana:* A ritual performed for a deceased human, usually a father or mother or other progenitor, to satisfy any lingering cravings which that individual might have had. Properly performed, this assures the individual an auspicious rebirth and enables him or her to maintain their spiritual progression.

*Prasad:* Any substance, usually food, which has been offered to a deity or saint, or to the image of a deity or saint, and which is then partaken of by a disciple or devotee. Prasad is supposed to contain a tiny amount of the deity's or saint's Shakti, which can exert a spiritualizing effect on the partaker.

*Rishi:* Lit. "Seer." Anything a Rishi sees or perceives becomes reality, because a Rishi is an ethereal being of the highest

class, one who is almost totally unlimited, who can travel
anywhere in the cosmos and do anything at all. The Rishis
"saw" the hymns of the Vedas, from which all the knowledge of ancient India was derived.

*Rnanubandhana:* The bondage of karmic debt.

*Rudra:* Lit. "the Crier," or "He Who makes others cry." Rudra
is the ancient name for Shiva, the god of death, and is so
called because he makes everyone cry who comes into contact with Him, because He separates them from their limited existence, to which they are tightly attached.

*Sadhana:* Any spiritual practice. Aghora Sadhana is designed
to replace the Aghori's personality with his deity's personality by creation of the deity's form in the Aghori's subtle
body.

*Sarvavidya:* The totality of manifested knowledge. This is a
Siddhi which involves control of all Shakti in the cosmos.

*Shakti:* Energy; the ability to perform some action. Shakti is
always female in Indian philosophy.

*Shava:* A corpse.

*Siddha:* An "accomplished one." Anyone who has obtained a
Siddhi, or supernatural accomplishment, is a Siddha. Vimalananda restricted his use of the word Siddha to indicate those
beings who have achieved immortality.

*Smashan:* A charnel ground; an area in which dead bodies are
burned or buried. This word is derived from "ashmashana,"
or "place where rocks lie," which suggests that burial was
once more common in India than it now is.

*Subtle Body:* The astral body; the sheath of existence between
the causal and subtle bodies. The mind inhabits the subtle
body. Karmas projected from the causal body must first pass
through the subtle body before reaching the physical body
for their expression.

*Tattva:* Lit. "thatness." A category of existence. For example,
the Three Gunas are Tattvas because they are attributes, and
the category of attribution is a Tattva. The Atma is also a
Tattva.

*Vajroli:* A yogic practice in which a fluid is sucked into the
penis or vagina by muscular force. During the sex act Vajroli

can be used to suck up the partner's secretions for both physical and spiritual benefit.

*Vasana:* A tendency of the individual personality which produces habitual modes of action, often inherited from one's ancestors. Vasanas make people do what they do in spite of themselves because of the power of the inherent tendency.

*Wah:* An exclamation of amazement, surprise or revelation.

*Yaksha/Yakshini:* A Hindu angel (male and female respectively); an ethereal being who was once human and because of his ability in sadhana attained to this status after death.

*Yama:* Also called Dharmaraja, or King of Righteousness. He is the judge of the dead, evaluating their activities while on Earth and determining which paradise or hell they go to while awaiting rebirth.

*Yantra:* A diagram which acts as a receptacle for the power of a mantra. Tantra is the ritual by which the Yantra is empowered by the mantra. Any substance can be used for a Yantra, but Vimalananda averred that the best of all possible Yantras is the human body.

Printed in Great Britain
by Amazon

35637002R00188